Latinos, Inc.

Latinos, Inc.

The Marketing and Making of a People

Arlene Dávila

UNIVERSITY OF CALIFORNIA PRESS
Berkeley · Los Angeles · London

University of California Press
Berkeley and Los Angeles, California

University of California Press, Ltd.
London, England

© 2001 by the Regents of the
University of California

Library of Congress Cataloging-in-Publication Data

Dávila, Arlene M., 1965–
    Latinos, Inc. : the marketing and making
of a people / Arlene Dávila.
        p.   cm.
    Includes bibliographical references and index.
    ISBN 0-520-22669-0 (cloth : alk. paper)
    ISBN 0-520-22724-7 (paper : alk. paper)
    1. Hispanic American consumers.   2. Market
segmentation—United States.   3. Hispanic
Americans—Ethnic identity.   I. Title.
HF5415.33.U6 D38   2001
658.8'34'08968073—dc21   2001016206

Manufactured in the United States of America

10   09   08   07   06   05   04   03   02   01
10   9   8   7   6   5   4   3   2   1

The paper used in this publication meets
the minimum requirements of ANSI/NISO
Z9.48-1992(R 1997) (Permanence of Paper).♾

To Laura Feliciano, in honor of her strength and ingenuity

Latinos are changing the way the country looks, feels, and thinks, eats, dances, and votes. From teeming immigrant meccas to small-town America, they are filling churches, building businesses, and celebrating this Latin heritage. . . . In America, a country that constantly redefines itself, the rise of Latinos also raises questions about race, identity, and culture—and whether the United States will ever truly be one nation.

Brook Larmer, in *Newsweek,* July 12, 1999

Contents

List of Illustrations

Acknowledgments

A lot always happens in the aftermath of researching and writing a book on popular culture and the media. Latinos have continued to gain rapid popularity in mainstream culture, sustaining the aura of momentum and of a coming of age in greater society that they were rapidly attaining when I started my research. New media initiatives have also been launched, developing, transforming, and feeding into established narratives of Latinidad. Particularly relevant to these dynamics is the rapid development of Internet marketing, a medium that more than any other traditional medium facilitates the segmentation of Latinos into particular market niches. This segmentation was highly feared by most of the marketers I spoke with when I concluded my interviews in 1999. Many of them had been in the industry long enough to recognize that differences among Latinos could be talked about, but never fully recognized if they were to protect the homogeneity of their target market. After considering the potential implications of these developments, however, I refrained from the urge to write a new chapter on the Internet or to attend one last marketing meeting. As I read the copy of the manuscript before its publication, I stood reassured that my main observations, dynamics, and conclusions would not be altered by the discovery of one more Latino pop star, the development of another Hispanic magazine, or the advent of one more Latino Internet portal. I also reminded myself that it was not an introduction to Hispanic marketing sources that I provide in this book, but an analysis of the social, political, and cultural dynamics affecting the representation of Latinos and the pitfalls of commercial Latinidad. And, regrettably, these dynamics are not so easily altered by the advent of new marketing and media developments as this work will show. The broadcast of the first Latin Grammys, held during my last reading of the manuscript, provides a relevant example. Through this marketing bonanza, audiences throughout the world were exposed to the "strength" and "vitality" of Latin culture, yet the awards' simultaneous veiling of regional musical genres and the ensuing criticisms about the dominance of SONY affiliated artists and of artists already popular in the Anglo market underscored the problems of commercial Latinidad and the need to examine the structures and dynamics behind its production, circulation, and consumption. These issues are the subject of this work.

This book benefited from the comments and good wishes of many colleagues, friends, and readers who commented, read, or discussed with me different parts of the manuscript and were central to its development and completion. First and foremost, I would like to thank the anonymous readers, as well as George Lipsitz and Elizabeth Chin, who provided valuable insights with great care and enthusiasm for the work. I thank them both for their excellent comments and support, and Elizabeth in particular for the numerous ethnic marketing clippings she sent me from Los Angeles in solidarity with the issues and concerns of this work. This project was also shaped by numerous and continuous conversations with colleagues such as Stuart Ewen who graciously read my first draft and supported the idea of this project from its very inception. Thanks are also due to my friends and colleagues Maureen O'Dougherty, Agustín Laó, Steven Gregory, Jerry Lombardi, and Kate Wilson, who contributed to the project throughout its research, development, and writing stages. I also received valuable feedback from Marco Jacammet, Bonnie Urciuoli, Martín Vega, Juan Flores, Virginia Domínguez, Jorge Duany, Victor Hugo Viesca and Tomás López-Pumarejo. In a very special way, I also thank my former advisor, mentor, and friend Delmos Jones. Unfortunately, Del passed on while I was beginning the ethnographic research for this work in New York City but his passion and thoughts about the commodification of difference were pivotal to my thinking about this project, as were his initial encouragement and help. I trust that those who knew him will see his influence and a little bit of Del in this work.

Portions of this work were presented at the American Studies Association meeting, in Montreal, Canada (November 1999); at Yale's Latin American Studies Series (February 1999); at the University of Massachusetts Speakers Series in Boston (November 1999); at Brown University's conference entitled "The Racial State" (October 1998); and at New York University (February 2000). At each event, I benefited from intelligent discussions of my work and from comments from my audience of students, faculty, and the general interested public. I also received valuable help from my former colleagues John Burdick, Karin Rosenblatt, Beverly Mullings, and Linda Alcoff, who also read and commented on one of the first incarnations of this work.

The research that became part of this book was supported in full by the Wenner Gren Foundation, the National Science Foundation, and the Ford Foundation, which allowed me a full year's leave to work toward the completion of this work and facilitated my hiring a number of students on a part-time basis from 1997 to 1999. Their help and their commitment to the goals of the research and the issues discussed in this work are deeply appreciated. The researchers included Jenny Rodríguez and Alejandra Torres, who helped me collect advertisements and monitor industry developments; Frank Nuñez, who also helped me recruit for and conduct one of the focus groups with Latino media viewers; and Tyrone Savage and Kalpana Fernandes, who assisted me with the organization and editing of this work. Research assistance was also provided by the Center for Media Culture and History at New York University, which served as host site during part of the research, and by the Center for Puerto Rican Studies at Hunter College, which provided office space when I most needed a break from my crowded apartment in the city, as well as the location for the focus group discussions. At the Center for Media Culture and History, I benefited from the help and feedback of Faye Ginsburg, Barbara Abrash, and Toby Miller, and at the Center for Puerto Rican Studies, from the help, comments, and the many conversations with my friends and colleagues Gabriel Haslip-Viera, John Nieto-Phillips, and Miriam Jiménez. I also thank the Advertising Educational Foundation for helping to arrange the internship at Batten, Barton, Durstine & Osborne (BBDO) and Doug Alligood for serving as a mentor during this internship. At the University of California Press, I had the privilege of working with Naomi Schneider and Jan Spauschus Johnson, and I thank them both for their unrelenting assistance and professionalism. Lastly, my deepest appreciation goes to the numerous informants who were so generous with their time and so enthusiastic about my research. I will not mention any of them by name, as I am aware that my book may be considered controversial to the larger marketing community, but I am especially thankful to Jorge Reynardus, Christian Dobles, and Ellen Gutiérrez, who offered initial and continuous help throughout the duration of this research.

Introduction

"Latinos are hot, and we are not the only ones to think so. Everyone wants to jump on the bandwagon, and why not? We have the greatest art, music, and literature. It's time we tell our stories." With these words, actor Antonio Banderas welcomed all to the first advertising "Up-Front" presentation by the Spanish TV network Telemundo. Summoning advertisers to "jump on the bandwagon," he echoed a promise that is repeatedly heard in corporate headquarters and at advertising conventions alike: that Latinos are the hottest new market and that those who target them will not regret it. That Latinos are hot is not at all surprising. It is becoming increasingly common to see aspects of Latino culture popularized in mainstream culture, with salsa outselling ketchup and taking over dance floors, and a growing number of corporate sponsors interested in Latinos as a target market. That a famous Spaniard like Antonio Banderas should become the spokesman of U.S. Latino culture, which is overwhelmingly Mexican, Puerto Rican, Hispanic Caribbean, and Central American, is also not surprising. Although Latino social movements in the 1960s defined themselves against anything Spanish, such distinctions have since been countered by the growing consolidation of a common Latino/Hispanic identity that encompasses anyone from a Spanish/Latin American background in the United States.

Central to this development is Hispanic marketing and advertising. Long before the current popularization of Latin culture, this industry first advanced the idea of a common "Hispanic market" by selling and promoting generalized ideas about "Hispanics" to be readily marketed by corporate America. Thirty years later, the existence and profitability of this culture-specific market feeds one of the fastest growing sectors of the marketing industry in the United States. Over eighty Hispanic advertising agencies and branches of transnational advertising conglomerates spread across cities with sizable Hispanic populations now sell consumer products by shaping and projecting images of and for Latinos.

This book examines the Hispanic marketing industry and its role in the making and marketing of contemporary definitions of Latinidad. I explore Hispanic marketing as a self-identified arena of Latino self-representation which, dominated by corporate intellectuals of Latin American background in the United States and directly tied to the structures of the U.S. economy, serves as a fruitful entry point into an analysis of the complex interests that are currently involved in the public representation of this emerging identity. I start from the premise that the reconstitution of individuals into consumers and populations into markets are central fields of cultural production that reverberate within public understanding of people's place, and hence of their rights and entitlements, in a given society. Looking at Hispanic marketing is therefore particularly revealing of the relationship between culture, corporate sponsorship, and politics, and moreover can illuminate how commercial representations may shape people's cultural identities as well as affect notions of belonging and cultural citizenship in public life. In particular, I point to the greater importance of these processes among Latinos and other U.S. minorities. Although these populations have historically lacked access to public venues of self-representation, it is in the market and through marketing discourse that they are increasingly debating their social identities and public standing. These issues are consequently reduced and correlated with their "advertising worthiness and marketability," cautioning us against the facile celebration of Latinos' commercial popularity as an infallible sign of their "coming of age" and political standing.

The growth and popularization of a single ethnic category for peoples of Latin American background in the United States, such as "Hispanic" or "Latino," is a relatively new development.[1] First generalized by federal agencies in the 1970s, a common identity for the diversity of "Latino" populations has since been nourished through census categories, state policies, and the media, prompting questions about the political implications of this development and the ways in which people reject or embrace the identification of "Latino" or "Hispanic" in everyday life.[2] One of the most influential forces behind this identity, however, the Hispanic marketing and advertising industry, remains largely unexamined.[3] On and on, Latinos' marketing popularity is uncritically treated as a sign of their "coming of age" in U.S. society or else, equally uncritically, condemned as a sign of their commodification; but seldom have studies looked at marketing as constitutive of U.S. Latinidad. Similarly, most studies on Latinos and the media have tended to focus on the mainstream media, such as Hollywood films and network TV, repeatedly reminding us that Latinos/Hispanics are too often excluded, and that when they are portrayed, narrow and simplistic stereotypes are inevitably employed. What research has seldom noted is marketing's influence on the public projection of U.S. Latinos and the complex processes and multiple contradictions behind the production of these representations, such as the involvement of "natives"—that is, of "Hispanics"—in their very production.

As part of their struggle for political enfranchisement since the 1960s, Latino populations have become increasingly concerned with their own representation and involvement in all types of media (Rodríguez 1997; Noriega 2000). In this context, the development of culturally specific marketing has been generally regarded as a viable means to correct the former stereotypical commercial portrayal of Latinos. We need only to contrast Latinos' earlier commercial representation as thieves, as in Frito Lay's controversial Frito Bandido character, or as stinky bandidos, as in the Arrid deodorant ads in the 1960s and 1970s, with contemporary Hispanic-generated ads to note their pride-worthy images of beautiful, upscale, affluent, and successful Latinos.[4] Hispanic marketers have even gained praise from media scholars for providing corrective and valuable alternatives to Anglo-generated images (Peñaloza 1997),[5] and they themselves have adopted this "politically correct" outlook by marketing themselves and their productions as more aware, informed, and sensitive than those generated by their mainstream counterparts.

However, behind such lavish portrayal of Latinos lies a complex industry that stands at the forefront of contemporary Latino cultural politics and that points to the complex dynamics affecting both their public recognition and continued invisibility in U.S. society. Throughout, I suggest that this industry's political economy, history, and composition are directly implicated in the global processes and transnational bases that sustain commonplace understandings of Latinos as a "people" and a "culture." The production of Latinos as easily digestible and marketable within the larger structures of corporate America is therefore revealing of the global bases of contemporary processes of identity formation and

of how notions of place, nation, and race that are at play in the United
States and in Latin America come to bear on these representations.

These processes are evidenced in the discourses of authenticity engendered by this industry to defend the existence and profitability of Hispanics as an authentic and thus commercially valuable market. Primary
among such discourses is the promotion of Latinos as a "nation within
a nation," with a uniquely distinct culture, ethos, and language. Such
ideas, as I will show, are fed and maintained by sources as varied as the
precepts of contemporary U.S. multiculturalism, nineteenth-century
ideas of Latinidad developed by Latin American nationalist ideologies,
and Anglo-held beliefs about "Hispanics" evidencing the varied sources
that are strategically put into service in the commercial representation
of Latinidad as forever needy of culturally specific marketing. In these
constructions the Spanish language is built as the paramount basis of U.S.
Latinidad, as is evident in the industry's common designation of "Hispanic marketing" and "Hispanic-driven media." Its premise and rationale
for existence are not only that there are basic differences between Latinos and other consumers that need to be addressed through culture- and
language-specific marketing, but also that there is a continuous influx to
the United States of Spanish-speaking populations that would not be
reached by advertising were it not for this type of marketing. Latinos are
also repackaged into images that render them pleasing to corporate clients,
such as in the garb of the traditional and extremely family-oriented and
stubbornly brand-loyal consumer, which I suggest responds more to
mainstream society's management of ethnic others than to any intrinsic
cultural attribute of the Latino consumer. Through such strategies, I show
that Latinos are continually recast as authentic and marketable, but ultimately as a foreign rather than intrinsic component of U.S. society, culture, and history, suggesting that the growing visibility of Latino populations parallels an expansion of the technologies that render them exotic
and invisible.

At the same time, my analysis recognizes the importance of Hispanic
marketing in the development of U.S. Hispanic media as an ethnic- and
culture-specific nexus for the creation and sustenance of alternative "public spheres," or modes of representations, as well as for "desegregating
the dollar" by promoting more equitable commercial investments in minority populations (Weems 1998). These issues are actively debated by
contemporary scholars in relation to the increasing commercialization
and privatization of public life, which require us to examine advertising
and marketing as central to the constitution and imagining of contem-

porary identities. As the following discussion will make apparent, however, I reject the simple categories of ethnic and culturally specific media, and advance instead the need for more nuanced analysis that un-
covers the power structures in which such media are also embedded.
Categories such as ethnic or Hispanic media have tended to exempt any
other medium with "Hispanic" or "Latin" as part of its appellation from
critical scrutiny, thereby reproducing simplistic oppressor/oppressed
dichotomies that veil complicity and alliances, as well as differences in
backgrounds, political stances, and subject positions, among and across
members of what is supposedly "the same group." Accordingly, Latino
stereotypes are seen as the product of some faceless "corporate America," with more appropriate images of Hispanics resulting from the involvement of Hispanics themselves at all levels of production.[6] In contrast, my goal is to analyze Hispanic marketing in relation to rather than
in isolation from wider dynamics in order to suggest that such representations are in fact produced in conversation and often in complicity
with—rather than as a response or challenge to—dominant hierarchies
of race, culture, and nationality.

To this end, my examination is an ethnographic one: a momentary
look upward to the circles where these images are shaped. I thus place
little emphasis on the finished images and texts generated to represent
"Hispanics" and focus instead on the political-economic interests and
processes involved in their production, along with their consumption by
the people to whom they are geared. It is these active processes of production and consumption that I consider most revealing of the dilemmas
affecting the conceptualization of Latinos as a distinct group and the
wider social and political implications of such representations, since they
elucidate the role that commercial representations play in the social imagining of populations.

MEDIATING IDENTITIES

The media's role in the construction of identities is currently at the forefront of contemporary cultural studies as part of a growing interest in
the new vectors through which people assert and communicate national
and social identities in an increasingly mass mediated and transnational
world (Ginsburg et al. 2001). Recent research turns our attention to the
historical specificity of the media in cross-cultural settings, their involvement in local politics, and the multiple ways in which publics interpret and negotiate media messages (Abu-Lughod 1993, 1999; Foster

1999; Mankekar 1999). This research has similarly pointed us to the multiple ways in which media texts communicate categories of identity and serve to incorporate or mediate people's relationships within any given group or society, such as by establishing public spheres of debate or facilitating the maintenance of alternative identities. Anthropological research on the media, in particular, has addressed these issues through ethnographic examinations that underscore the complexities involved in the production, circulation, and consumption not only of media texts, but of audiences, messages, and meanings.[7]

This work intersects with recent ethnographic work on the media, albeit my focus is primarily on U.S. commercial media, an area generally neglected by anthropologists and seldom examined ethnographically in the cultural studies literature. Studies of commercial media and advertising in the United States, as well as its impact on U.S. minorities, are abundant (Cashmore 1997; Frank 1997; Gray 1995; Salem Manganaro 1996), yet anthropologists have largely overlooked the U.S. media, even when it constitutes the largest advertising and media market worldwide, and hence a determinant influence in the global rendering of marketable identities.[8] Such an emphasis is of course not surprising, considering that it is the dominance of Western media that fueled the widespread use of the media as a tool for asserting cultural and national identities, as well as the very growth of the anthropology of the media and of anthropologists' growing interest in its use as a tool of social activism and cultural assertion (Ginsburg 1991; Ginsburg et al. 2001; Turner 1992). At the same time, however, the contradictory processes of globalization and the local repercussions of the commodification and commercialization of culture in contemporary U.S. society have received considerably less attention than have similar processes in "foreign" contexts (Howes 1996; Marcus and Myers 1996). A growing ethnographic interest in global cultural industries, such as advertising, has pointed to the central place of culture and ethnicity in the workings and operations of these industries and to patterns in the commodification of culture for mass consumption (Foster 1999; Moeran 1996; Miller 1995; Mazzarella 2000). Nonetheless, we lack detailed ethnographic examinations of how these processes operate in the context of U.S. daily life, affecting the commodification of U.S. racial and ethnic minorities.

We know, however, that the increasing specialization of the U.S. media—part and parcel of a global advertising trend to tap into the culture-specific characteristics of a given market, be it along gender, race, lifestyle, ethnic, or national lines—is helping to feed and maintain particularized social and cultural identities (Chin 2001; O'Barr 1994; Halter 2000). In this vein, some have argued that target marketing is contributing to the "breakdown of America" by fragmenting its constituent segments and limiting the spaces for mutual recognition and debate (Turow 1997), while others, including media activists, have conversely seen in this trend the creation of incipient "public spheres" that can become vehicles for alternative interests or lead to more just forms of participatory democracy.[9] In this way, Hispanic marketers' interest in creating a self-contained market can help us apprehend some of the localized repercussions of global trends in advertising, particularly what Miller (1997) has called the "revolt of the local," involving the appeal to the supposed intrinsic differences of particular populations, as individuals are turned into consumers and populations into markets. Such appeals to authenticity corroborate the ubiquity of particular racial and nationalist ideologies and even of global hierarchies of culture and place in the commercial imagining of populations, prompting us to analyze how they come to bear on or are purposefully deployed by the many interests that coalesce in the marketing of difference. Anthropologists have long noted how particular nationalist ideologies are necessarily implicated in the production of a range of media texts (Mankekar 1999; Abu-Lughod 1993; Naficy 1993; Rofel 1994), yet advertising additionally reveals how dominant discourses of identity, race, or nationality come to bear on these representations, given the advertisers' dual and direct attachments and obligations to different interests and constituencies. These dual engagements, we shall see, turn Hispanic creatives and advertising professionals into brokers and mediators of preexisting hierarchies of representation as they seek to shape definitions of "Hispanics" that meet both the expectations of their corporate clients and those of their prospective audience of consumers. By focusing on one segment of the U.S. advertising industry—a division of ethnic and targeted marketing—I intend first to provide a more complex basis for theorizing the political and social potential of the advertising industry for members of the growing "Latino" community, as well as for other ethnic populations in the United States. Second, I mean to assess the local ramifications of global trends in the advertising industry, which increasingly affect not only the growing U.S. Latino community, but also other segments of U.S. society, as well as global markets worldwide. Following these global trends in segmented and targeted marketing, one finds that they too are increasingly subject to similar strategies of containment and representation, leading to analogous processes to those described in the following pages.

What is uniquely interesting about Hispanic marketing is its present status as one of the few unified marketing segments in relation to the so-called U.S. general market and the pivotal role played by "culture" in its construction. In fact, the same trends that are fragmenting the so-called general market in the United States along the lines of lifestyles, gender, or race—over and above the actual increase of Hispanic populations—are fueling the importance of Hispanics as a unified marketing segment. This fragmentation has dwindled the size of other U.S. demographic and marketing segments, rendering "Hispanics" one of the last identifiable and sizable market niches. For, in contrast to "women" or "teenagers," who are simultaneously segmented according to lifestyles, age, tastes, or race, "Hispanics" remain a protected segment by their mere definition as a homogeneously bounded, "culturally defined" niche. It is this definition, which makes all "Latinos" part of the same undifferentiated "market"—whether they live in El Barrio or in an upscale New York high-rise, or whether they watch Fraser or only Mexican *novelas*, or love Ricky Martin or consider him a sellout—that is foremost behind the apparently greater representation of "Hispanics" within the spheres of corporate America.

The equation of marketing with Latino representation or, as stated by Banderas, the idea that Latinos' marketing popularity marks the time "to tell our stories," is another primary concern of this study. Analysts of consumer society have long noted the relationship between consumption and identity and the use of this relationship to sell products by presenting them as ways to achieve self-fulfillment or lay claim to particular statuses or social identities (Friedman 1994; Ewen 1988; Halter 2000). The same has been documented for ethnic and racial identities, which advertising has associated with or embodied in a number of products and commodities as a means of interpellating people as ethnic, raced, or national consumers (Chin 2001; Kondo 1997; Wilk 1993, 1994). However, as the current context of U.S. multiculturalism continues to heighten the political importance of the idiom of culture and of cultural identities for contemporary cultural politics, the cooptation and promotion of identities by marketers demand consideration, especially regarding their implications for wider issues of representativity and social rights (Gordon and Newfield 1996; Fusco 1995; Hall 1991a, 1991b). The homogenization of a heterogeneous population into a single "Latino" market, for instance, while increasing the visibility of Latino populations, coincides with larger processes of partial containment and recognition of ethnic differences that are at play in other spheres of contemporary

U.S. society, such as at the level of politics and social and cultural policies; in fact, it is an intrinsic component of such processes. In analyzing the social implications of culturally specific marketing, we therefore need to begin by looking at the multipurpose and dual nature of these initiatives, at the level of both production and reception. That is, we must examine culturally specific marketing as a site that simultaneously serves the multiple interests of those who profit from difference as well as the interests of those subordinate populations whose attainment of representation is essential to contemporary politics. As such, these initiatives can be experienced in contradictory ways as a medium of marginalization or, alternatively, as a repository of language, culture, and traditions by its target publics. Exposing these nuanced dynamics is a primary goal of this work.

ADVERTISING: THE PRIVILEGE OF
COMMERCIAL DISCOURSE

Before examining the contemporary significance of Hispanic marketing, we need to consider advertising as a relatively privileged discourse of communication in light of consumption's present role for conveying identities and aspirations in a world fully implicated within the politics of signification (Leiss et al. 1997). The contemporary situation is one fully embedded in a "promotional culture," where we are told that the discourse of advertising and promotion has permeated every aspect of symbolic expression (Wernick 1991) and where what Sharon Zukin has termed "the symbolic economy" increasingly dominates the wider economy, prompting questions about the political importance of this commercial sector and the extent to which it shapes people's subjectivities and the terms of political debate.[10] Among other issues, research now ponders the political implications of the commercial imagination of particular populations and the significance of the individuation of tastes, issues, debates, and desires for contemporary processes of identity creation. Has the market reconfigured the meaning and value of contemporary citizenship? Is it solely as "consumers," some ponder, that people are subjects of representation or their needs worthy of consideration? (Firat and Dholakia 1998; García-Canclini 1995).

These questions signal important developments in the way we conceive of politics and citizenship, as well as a reassessment of how our notions of belonging are communicated. This type of inquiry marks a shift from the formerly strict division in media studies between the rational sphere of politics and the commercial sphere of entertainment, which must be carefully kept apart if some idea of an informed and "enlightened" participatory democracy is to exist. These precepts underlie most analyses of contemporary culture, from Habermas's well-known denunciation of the commercial media as responsible for the demise of the bourgeois public sphere and rational debate, to most contemporary studies of popular and mass-mediated culture, which have also had to confront this legacy in order to vindicate commercial media as a realm worthy of study in relation to the norms of public debate and hence of politics. Guiding these concerns is the ongoing privatization of everyday life as a result of globalization, which, in its challenge to the centrality of production and the state as guarantor of services and social rights, is more than ever positioning consumption and all the mechanisms through which people are being addressed as consumers as central bastions of contemporary politics. In this new context, we are challenged to redefine what we mean by publics and political projects, as well as the relationship between citizenship and consumption, as a step toward exposing inequalities and injustice in the realms of consumption, such as in people's access to the media and to other mechanisms of cultural interpellation and identity formation (Yúdice 2001; García-Canclini 1995). The challenge is thus not only to recognize the blurred nature of mass-mediated culture's genres and messages and to point to their variable and unintended modes of public consumption, but to recognize that in a context where nothing escapes commodification, commercial culture cannot be easily reduced to sheer pleasure or commercial manipulation, but must be considered as constitutive of contemporary identities and notions of belonging and entitlement.[11] In fact, historians of mass culture have pointed to the equation of American citizenship with consumption and the illusions and promises of commercial culture since the outset of modern merchandising. As Stuart and Elizabeth Ewen (1992) note, merchandising played a key role in the integration and "Americanization" of new immigrants at the turn of the century through its linkage of democracy with the consumption of goods. Marketing was therefore always involved in the making of public identities, although this role is far more pervasive today, given its preeminence as a sector of communication, itself evidenced in the heightened growth of specialized ethnic and target marketing.

In this way, marketing strategies can help illuminate the ways in which public identities and cultural citizenship are constructed in the current transnational context in which individuals are vested not only with ju-

ridical competences, obligations, and entitlements (or the lack thereof)
endowed by the state, but also with particular modes of belonging based
on their "culture." As the growing literature on transnationalism clearly
illustrates, the new diversities ensuing from transnationalism and the flow
of populations and cultural goods have not only opened possibilities for
new pluralities and hybrid identities, but, most significantly, created new
demands for establishing "belonging." And two variables seem to be constant in these processes: culture, involving the existence of particular and
lingering hierarchies of race/ethnicity/language/nationality that mediate people's position within any given society; and consumption, insofar as—whether as exiles, citizens, permanent residents, or immigrants—
individuals are consumers first and foremost.

Studying the production of commercial mass-mediated culture can
therefore help us uncover some of the ways in which notions of belonging and citizenship as well as the hierarchies of culture, race, and nation
in which they are based, are produced and negotiated in the demanding
new context of transnationalism and displacement. For citizenship, far
from the universal juridical category it is still often thought to be, is
implicated in inequities of culture, race, and gender, which ultimately
determine who is or is not part of a given nation and on what grounds
(Alejandro 1993; Lowe 1996; Ong 1999; Williams 1989). It conveys normative ideals of culture, language, gender, and race, denoting lesser or
greater degrees of belonging according to how closely individuals ap-
proximate such ideals within a given nation-state and its particular dominant conflations of these "identity" variables. These dynamics have been
amply attested to by U.S. minorities' contradictory experiences with the
canons and promises of universal citizenship. Even as legal citizens, members of these groups have not reaped the benefits supposedly afforded by
"citizenship," while their cultural, racial, and linguistic difference renders them forever suspects and potential threats, bringing up the abiding concern of this book's opening epigraph: "whether the United States
will ever truly be one nation." It is in this tenor that writers have advanced the concept of "cultural citizenship" to emphasize the intricate
connections between cultural visibility, as the assertion of cultural difference from normative ideals, and political enfranchisement. According to Rosaldo and Flores (1997), for instance, cultural assertions are a
medium through which Latinos and other subordinated groups in the
United States may attain cultural citizenship and thus "claim space in
society and eventually claim rights," which may serve as a means of ex-

panding claims for political entitlements in the future. Yet cultural citizenship can be seen alternatively as an intrinsic component of how states organize and manage difference, a medium for normalization through the accommodation of difference (Dávila 1999a; Ong 1999). This leads us to consider claims of cultural citizenship not solely as a means to expand "entitlements," but also as they may serve to reformulate the frameworks of recognition and debate. To what extent do ethnic commercial media affect normative citizenship ideals when establishing assertions of belonging on the basis of a different culture or language than those informing a particular nationalist ideology? Can such assertions have an impact on dominant structures of subordination, or do they simultaneously render such visibility into a venue of containment and subordination? And what can we learn from the making of the "Hispanic consumer" about Latinos/Hispanics and their status and sense of belonging in contemporary U.S. society?

Particularly relevant for probing these issues is the range of technologies for quantifying and measuring the attitudes and cultural competences of particular populations in order to codify and establish "truths" about people as consumers (Miller 1998). Advertising is particularly relevant here, given its dependence on market research methods aimed at demarcating consumers and at packaging culture for mass consumption. To the extent that these involve generalizing conventions about people's "culture," we are summoned to inquire into how these concepts are produced and disseminated and into whether and how they converge with other discourses circulated in greater society to affect not only individuals' ranking as potential consumers but also their cultural identities and their social and political standing in public life.

In particular, we need to analyze commercial media in conversation with other venues of signification, neither in opposition nor in collusion, but rather in relation to state-produced ideologies and other existing frameworks that may affect people's belonging on the basis of race, culture, or nationality. Also important to consider is the relative "privilege" vested in these different domains of signification by the particular historical and structural specificities in which they operate within a given society.[12] Thus, I posit that the importance of marketing to Latinos and other minorities needs to be assessed in direct relationship to their peripheral status in U.S. society and, consequently, to their constrained access to mass-mediated forums that shape their public representation. For Hispanic marketing is certainly not the only sector that promotes definitions of Latinidad in public life. Since the 1980s, a number of social advocacy, political, artistic, and scholarly organizations have either adopted or shifted to a pan-Latino position aiming to advocate for or be representative of, as the case may be, the totality of the U.S. Latino or Hispanic population.[13] However, despite calls for Latin unity, the goal of pan-Latino political unity remains tenuous at best. Documented instances of inter-Latino political unity at the neighborhood level (Padilla 1985; Jones-Correa 1998) have not been paralleled by nationwide "Latino agendas" within the Hispanic advocacy and not-for-profit sectors, which not only suffer from budgetary constraints,[14] but also lack the type of nationwide projection enjoyed by commercial media. Simply put, Latinos' marketing power may be amply discussed in mainstream society, but their political power is yet to parallel the exuberant excitement they currently trigger among marketers. Consider for instance Flores and Yúdice's (1993) discussion of the contradictory stances toward Spanish of marketing strategists and U.S. state and social institutions: the former embrace language difference, and the latter treat it as a threat to the U.S. national community, as evidenced by the passage of Proposition 227 ending bilingual education. Similar contradictions will be evident throughout this work. I would thus argue that no other field of cultural production matches Hispanic marketing in its historical role of promoting unified, uncomplicated, depoliticized, and hence readily marketable definitions of Hispanidad, leading to the influential status it currently enjoys in its public dissemination relative to other sectors. It is therefore not surprising that the recent front-cover article in *Newsweek* featuring the growth of U.S. Latinos interviewed not politicians, labor leaders, or scholars, but important Hispanic marketing personalities such as Chrissy Haubegger, editor of *Latina* magazine, or Nelly Galán, Telemundo's programming director, or that it called young Latinos Generation Ñ, a term coined by Hispanic marketers, or that it drew its statistical information from Strategy Research and Arbitron, recognized marketing sources. The importance of Hispanic marketing as a site of Latino signification is also evident when we consider that Latinos are becoming increasingly invisible from the mainstream media as advertisers target Latinos through "Hispanic" media, furthering their exclusion from media airwaves. Of the twenty-six new TV shows premiering on the major broadcast networks for the fall 1999 season, not one included a minority person in a leading role, while minorities on secondary shows were also sparse. The TV landscape is still a "white, white world" (Braxton 1999). The results of these trends have been recently documented by Noriega's study of Chicano cinema and Latino media activism: Latino employment and representation at all levels of the media remain at persistently low rates and have, in fact, decreased relative to the growth of Latino populations, while U.S. Latino productions are persistently shunned by traditional venues of production and distribution (Noriega 2000). Meanwhile, the Hispanic networks have been largely closed to U.S.-based Latino producers and productions, having historically operated as "transnational" rather than ethnic media by importing cheaper Latin American programming into the U.S. market rather than producing new programs.[15]

This makes advertising images, as far-fetched as they may be—after all, advertising is about the world of aspiration and desires—uniquely interesting as products that are produced and shaped with the U.S. Hispanic market in mind, contrary to most of the images produced by the "Hispanic" TV network whose interest spans transcontinentally toward Latin America and beyond.[16] In fact, Hispanic marketing stands in a parallel yet contradictory relation to most of Hispanic TV: rather than in direct alliance, it competes with Latin American advertising agencies, with its profitability more directly predicated on its ability to project itself as a representative venue for U.S. Hispanics rather than Latin American consumers.[17]

Finally, the U.S. Hispanic marketing industry is also uniquely revealing of contemporary definitions and representations of Latinidad, given the structural and communicative demands of advertising. Their condensed format, and their need to empathize, charm, appeal, or shock a potential consumer in thirty to sixty seconds entail a great deal of simplification and typification (Leiss et al. 1997), which bring to the surface the tropes, images, and discourses that have become widespread as generalized representations of Hispanidad. Advertising thus exemplifies the processes through which, by addressing Latinos in culture-specific ways, marketers break new ground and disseminate old and new material for the conceptualization of a trans-Latino identity that spans class, race, and nationality. Of course, the outcomes of these processes are never reducible to mere impositions or fabrications. Advertising does not invent meaning for a commodity, but works by transferring to it meaning from the social world (Williamson 1978); and while its generic "mass-appeal" construction may make it a likely mirror for dominant values, it simultaneously depends on its partial incorporation of and engagement with popular interests (Hall 1981; Fiske 1996). Advertisements are thus complex texts that, as stereotypical or outlandish as they may be, are always entangled with the interests, desires, or imaginations of those whom they seek to entice as consumers, and are always the result of negotiations in the process of depicting the consumer. As we shall see, in the case of Hispanic marketing these processes involve attempts to incorporate an audience spanning different nationalities, classes, and ethnicities, among other variables, as well as the always lingering expectations of Anglo corporate staff and their own preconceptions of Latinos, among other interests present in the making of generic commercial representations of Latinidad.

HISPANIC/LATINO

So far I have been using Hispanic/Latino interchangeably, as most people in the advertising/marketing industry do, and as I will, for the most part, continue to do throughout this book. Yet it is by the name "Hispanic marketing" that this industry is most commonly known, and this indicates its nature and scope. First, this terminology is undoubtedly due to the business preference for the officially census-sanctioned category of "Hispanic," over "Latino," a term of self-designation more connected to social struggles and activism (Noriega and López 1996). "Hispano" and its English translation "Hispanic" had been used as terms of self-designation by Spanish-origin populations in both the West and the East since the nineteenth century.[18] In the West, in places like New Mexico, Mexican-origin elites self-identified as "Hispano" to mark their Spanish legacy and hence their class and racial superiority over most Mexicans, while in New York, which had a more diverse population of mostly Spaniards and Hispanic Caribbean people, "Hispanic" had been generalized as a pan-ethnic term (Laó 2001; Haslip-Viera and Baver 1996). By the 1960s and 1970s, however, the terms "Hispano" and "Hispanic" were seen to be contrary to the cultural nationalism that accompanied larger struggles for civil empowerment by both Chicanos and Puerto Ricans and thus as a denial of their identity and a rejection of their indigenous and colonized roots.[19] Ironically, it was shortly after these cultural struggles that the U.S. government coined the official designation of "Hispanic" to designate anyone of Spanish background in the United States. This explains why Latino activists generally regard "Hispanic" as a more politically "sanitized" terminology than "Latino/a," even though both terms are equally guilty of erasing differences while encompassing highly heterogeneous populations and can be as equally appropriated for a range of politics.

The industry's official designation as "Hispanic," however is not solely due to the term's official status but is also meant to mark the importance given in this industry to the Spanish language as the key marker of Hispanic/Latino identity. Unlike "Latino," which could be potentially applied to any person of Latin American origin, "Hispanic" evokes Latin American populations' common origins in Spain. The exception is of course Brazil and Brazilians, whom Hispanic marketers generally exclude from their definition on the basis of their language.

At the same time, the dominant use of "Hispanic" in this industry does not imply its wholehearted acceptance by everyone involved. As a general rule, people in the industry use "Latino" and "Hispanic" interchangeably to refer to the target population, leaving "Hispanic" as the preferred appellation for the industry. "Latino" is also more common among the younger generation of marketers as opposed to "Hispanic" which is most commonly used by its founders and most established practitioners. "Latino" also enjoys more widespread acceptance as a politically correct term in contrast to "Hispanic," which is more evocative of Spanish conquest and colonization. Thus, while few of my informants were overtly critical of these terms, when they were, they were more likely to qualify their use of—and hence to be more critical of—"Hispanic" than "Latino." Overall, however, while both terms are used equally to sell, commodify, and market populations of Latin American background in the United States, all agencies used the official name "Hispanic" most frequently to present their work, themselves, and their target audience in their marketing presentations, printed materials, and brochures, suggesting the widespread adoption of dominant frameworks of representation within the industry at large.

Having said this, while I will be using these terms throughout this book, my intention is not to reify or take for granted this category but to go beyond contemporary studies on the growth and development of this seemingly common identity, which have tended to analyze it as a given, unitary, and unproblematized construct, whether it is called "Hispanic" or "Latino/a." By analyzing and documenting the inclusions or exclusions generated by the processes of Latinization, and the way in which discourses of pan-ethnicity intersect with dominant hierarchies of race, class, and gender, my purpose is to transcend the issue of terminology which has certainly not thwarted the commodification of peoples of Latin American backgrounds in this country.

From this perspective, I treat Latinization as the "out-of-many, one-people" process through which "Latinos" or "Hispanics" are conceived and represented as sharing one common identity. These processes are not properly seen as a top-down development, resulting from the commodification and appropriation of Latino culture or from self-agency; rather, they stem from the contrary involvement of and negotiations between dominant, imposed, and self-generated interests, as will be evident in the discussion of Hispanic marketing. The ensuing enactments, definitions, and representations of Hispanic or Latino culture from such continuing processes are what I define as "Latinidad."[20] Finally, though I am aware that "Anglo" is no less problematic than either "Hispanic" or "Latino" for erasing differences into a common category, I will nonetheless use "Anglo" as a general designation for the staff and representatives of "mainstream" and "general market" agencies as well as those at advertising corporations. Hispanic marketers use "gringos," "Americanos," and "Anglos" almost interchangeably to define those in the general market industry, but always as a function of the general assumption and awareness that this larger industry and its staff are white and that "general" and "mainstream" agencies serve largely as pseudonyms for "white non-ethnics."[21] By using "Anglo," I thus seek to emphasize this white "Anglo-Protestant" ideal, devoid of blacks, Latinos, or any other "ethnics," that provides the dominant reference against which Hispanic marketers produce their creations.

FOLLOWING THE CORPORATE INTELLECTUAL:
DOING FIELDWORK ON A FIELDLESS SITE

I have already established that my goals are simultaneously broad and minute in terms of my dual interest in the larger political and economic contexts affecting this industry and in the everyday processes by which Hispanic images are constructed. Hence readers may be wondering how a study of a nationwide industry can be conducted by one person and mostly within New York City, where I resided during my research. Such questions now typically arise with regard to any ethnographic study in the demanding, mass-mediated, and global context where the feasibility of ethnography as traditionally conceived (in terms of a long-term stay and actual observation in a specific location) is increasingly called into question (Gupta and Ferguson 1997). Anthropologists have even called for multisited ethnographies (Marcus 1998; Bright 1995) or for collaborative research with which to meet the ethnographic challenges presented by global phenomena such as the mass media and global marketing (Foster 1999). Certainly, the concept of "ethnographic fieldwork" was always contentious—"the field" was always a social construction and never as bounded as once thought.[22] Current concerns about ethnography in an age of "globalization" are therefore primarily a call to rethink methodological possibilities, arising from the unavoidable reality of global cultural flows, in which phenomena like the mass media are always implicated. Because these processes are not always easily observable nor amenable to participant observation, ethnography as traditionally conceived can no longer be seen as the single and "royal road to holistic knowledge" (Gupta and Ferguson 1997: 37): we must consider it now in conjunction with the range of other knowledges concurrently produced by sources as varied as the media or an international convention. Hence my study draws primarily from research among New York Hispanic ad agencies, but it includes information gained from travel to national marketing conventions and from interviews with ad executives in San Antonio and Chicago. Easing my task is the fact that Hispanic marketing, though a complex industry that spans the United States and has important transnational origins and connections, has particular, localized dimensions. For example, it revolves around a small network of key players, people who not only know but have worked and competed with one another, and who largely attend the same conferences, meetings, conventions, and social events. Many pioneers of the industry even live in the same neighborhood in Miami, have forged fictive kinship relationships, and keep apartments in the same upscale buildings in New York City. They thus constitute a circle of corporate intellectuals, not solely according to the most fundamental definition of intellectuals as those involved in the creation and circulation of knowledge, but also in the sense of their belonging to common networks and occupying similar positions within corporate America.[23] After all, while they are successful entrepreneurs sharing a business and profit orientation, Hispanic marketers are in an ancillary position within the structures of corporate America, assisting in but never dominating the commodification and marketing of Latinos in this country, insofar as they ultimately lack direct control over their ad agencies, which are entirely or partly owned by global advertising chains, and their ads are always subject to the approval of their corporate clients.

The existence of a nationwide network among Hispanic marketers afforded me relatively easy access to different areas of the industry that put me in contact with several of its founders and allowed me to trace major changes in this industry as well as continuities in the representation of Latinos. The fact that I could present myself as a university professor who would be writing a book on this industry and am an educated, Spanish-speaking, light-skinned Latina, close to the ideal "Latin look" (discussed later), also facilitated my entry into their circles. This, along with a concerted effort to dress fashionably during interviews with my contacts, meant that I presented no threat to their normative ideal of Latinidad, while most of them thought that whatever I might write would help validate their industry—that any writing is publicity. Access to Hispanic marketing professionals was also facilitated by my location in New York City, the U.S. advertising capital and, as we shall learn later, the birthplace of the Hispanic advertising industry. While Los Angeles is the largest market in terms of the number of Latinos, and San Antonio and Miami are currently key sites for some of the largest and most important Hispanic agencies, I chose New York as the focus of my study because it is home not only to many of the largest Hispanic advertising agencies, but also to the Hispanic marketing industry's original founders and to the headquarters of several nationwide advertising-related establishments. New York is also the second largest Hispanic/Latino market in the United States, as well as one of the most heterogeneous, thereby functioning as an important "homogenizing pot" of Latinidad. In contrast to Los Angeles and Miami, the first and third largest Hispanic markets, where Mexicans and Cubans are still more numerous than other Latino groups (Strategy Research Corporation 1998), New York has seen a growing diversification of its Latino population: Puerto Ricans, who made up 80 percent of the city's Latino population in the 1960s, are now only 43 percent of all Latinos; whereas the number of Dominicans and Central Americans has been increasing rapidly.[24] Focusing on New York thus allowed me to identify regional and national trends in the marketing of Latinos in the United States, as evidenced in the development of nationwide advertising strategies by New York–based agencies, while maintaining contact with both advertisers and consumers in a local setting, in keeping with my goal of following their daily operations.

Among the obstacles that I encountered to my intended plan of research was the characteristically competitive and secretive nature of advertising, which deterred me from becoming a direct observer of many decision-making sessions and business pitches to clients. I had originally intended to carry out an internship in one of these agencies, but feeling that such a strict association with one agency would disqualify me as an objective outsider among other agencies and informants, I discontinued my internship and shifted instead to periodic visits to different advertising agencies and to being a participant-observer in meetings, national conventions, and other important industry events. I did, however, spend three weeks at BBDO's Special Markets Division in New York City as part of an Advertising Educational Foundation–sponsored internship, an experience that serves as the backdrop for the final chapter. The book is thus based on interviews with different advertising staff at sixteen agencies, most of them in New York City, as well as on participant observations at industry events, meetings, and conventions carried out from the summer of 1997 to that of 1999.[25] This information was supplemented by content analysis of their advertising disseminated in both the print and broadcast media, and by monitoring major developments in the Hispanic/Latino-oriented and general market industry in trade magazines and ethnic-specific media. Except for chapter 1, which provides the bulk of the historical analysis, pseudonyms have been used for informants where necessary in order to protect their identity and abide by their clients' demands for confidentiality.

Finally, aware that media analysis is incomplete without an analysis of the reception and consumption of these advertising strategies by the people to whom they are addressed, I kept close contact with media activists in New York City, such as members of the local chapter of the National Hispanic Media Coalition, and conducted a series of focus group discussions and one-to-one interviews with self-identified Latino consumers. These discussions were aimed at documenting the nuanced processes by which people negotiate commercial messages and, in particular, at exploring what the public reception of images of Latino identity may reveal about the consolidation or rejection of dominant definitions of Latino identity that are disseminated in the media.

The outcome of this research is organized into six chapters. In chapter 1 I provide an overview of some of the general political and economic trends that have affected this industry from the outset, paying particular attention to the people and interests involved in marketing to Latinos, their background and motivations, and the greater social and economic context leading to the growth and development of culturally specific advertising. This chapter probes the political economy of cultural flows (Abu-Lughod 1993), that is, the larger political and economic processes and Latin American bases that sustain this industry's development and current scope. Here, I suggest that the commercial representation of U.S. Latinos has sustained particular hierarchies of representation that are indicative of wider dynamics affecting contemporary Latino cultural politics. These include disjunctions in class, race, and national background among, first, the mostly Latin American intellectuals who have dominated this industry from its onset; second, the Anglo-dominated structures of corporate capitalism that hold ultimate power in the commercial representation of Latinos; and, third, the prospective audience of "Hispanic" consumers. As a direct outcome of these distinctions, the expertise of "Hispanic" creatives and of workers in the industry at large has been based less on their commonality with the average U.S. Hispanic consumer than on generalized conventions that are circulated in the industry as "knowledge" of this imagined consumer. Chapters 2 and 3 analyze the conglomerate of distinct nationalities, and the materials, images, and themes used to transform these dissimilar and intersecting identities into generic representations of Latinidad. Chapter 2 reviews the dominant ideas about the Hispanic consumer disseminated in the media by analyzing marketing reports and the publications on "how to market" to Latinos produced by the research marketing industry, a key agent in creating knowledge about this market through the identification of general cultural values that are supposedly characteristic of the "Hispanic" consumer. I examine the ideas used to present Hispanics as a "nation within a nation," distinct and disparate from the wider U.S. society, and explore their origins in nineteenth-century Latin American nationalist discourse. Chapter 3 turns to the constituent components of the "Latin look" (Rodríguez 1997), by examining advertising texts and the elements that are emphasized or excluded in the public representation of a population whose members differ in class, race, nationality, time of arrival, and citizenship status, among other variables. This chapter also includes an examination of how dominant representations of Latinos may reflect and reproduce existing social hierarchies and power relations within contemporary U.S. society. I also trace how popular interests and materials generated by a diversity of Latino populations are inserted in media texts in ways that provide for their partial representation but also for the containment and accommodation of ethnic and cultural differences into normative notions of Latinidad. Chapter 4 documents some of the micropolitics and negotiations between corporate clients and agency directors involved in the production of commercial representation of Latinos, and analyzes what they suggest about the pervasive hierarchies of race, culture, and nationality in these representations. I then turn in chapter 5 to the changing media context in which Hispanic promotions are ultimately placed, by analyzing programmatic changes at the principal Spanish TV networks, Univision and Telemundo, during the length of my research. This analysis is particularly relevant today, given the rapid and dramatic changes in media forms, formats, and programming in recent years that are likely to affect current definitions of who is Hispanic/Latino and what are the best venues to target this constituency. I will argue that despite a lack of real innovation, debates over programming and over the nature of its target constituency speak to the place of language in the construction of Latinidad, as well as to the specific realms, be it the U.S. or the greater Latin American context, against which this identity is and will continue to be defined in the future. Finally, chapter 6 analyzes the reception and consumption of these advertising strategies by the people who are their targets. Drawing on focus group discussions with self-identified Latino consumers, I document the nuanced processes of negotiating commercial messages through the appropriation and transformation of their meaning. I also look at what people communicate about themselves and their social realities through their consumption of the media and explore its impact on the public consolidation of U.S. Latinidad. As will be apparent from these discussions, for many U.S. Latinos, a common identity is far from based on a Spanish-centered notion of "Hispanidad," or media-generated notions of Hispanic authenticity.

The conclusion probes the dominant portrayals of the Asian American and African American in relation to the Hispanic consumer to emphasize continuities and differences in the way they are rendered as culturally specific "markets." I argue that it is to U.S. society's fears about its "others" that ethnic marketing, not solely Hispanic marketing, responds and that in presenting such unrelenting images, ethnic marketing ends up responding to and reflecting the fears and anxiety of mainstream society, reiterating in this manner the demands for an idealized, good, all-American citizenship in the image of the "ethnic consumer." Ethnic marketing hence becomes the interlocutor for these populations vis-à-vis mainstream America, the site that regulates and mediates its ethnics—the immigrant, the alien, the raced, and the underclass—into their respective places within U.S. racial and ethnic hierarchies, creating in the process myths of peoplehood for these populations where docility, family, and spirituality run triumphant.

CHAPTER I

"Don't Panic, I'm Hispanic"

The Trends and Economy of Cultural Flows

Today 50% of all bookings at Radio City Music Hall
are Hispanic artists. Salsa outsells ketchup in the Midwest.
Nachos beat hot-dogs at movies. What's happening? Simple:
A cultural and marketing phenomenon known as the U.S.
Hispanic market.

Bromley Aguilar Associates, media kit, 1999

Hispanic marketing is now a multibillion dollar industry, spread throughout Los Angeles, Miami, Chicago, New York, and every other center with
a large concentration of Latina populations. Some thirty-five years ago,
however, what is now considered one of the fastest growing segments of
the marketing industry was primarily fueled by a handful of recently arrived immigrants of mostly Cuban origin who struggled to promote the
profitability and even existence of this language- and culture-specific market. This first generation has since attained an almost mythic status in the
Hispanic advertising industry. They are considered its founding figures
and credited both with the industry's gains, including its current profitability, as well as its evils, such as the stereotypes bequeathed to younger
generations, making them a natural starting point for delving into the
industry's origins and present scope.[1]

This chapter provides an overview of some recurring issues affecting
the growth and current operations of the Hispanic marketing industry.
It is informed by interviews and conversations with some of these founding figures, who, when recalling their experiences, brought up many continuities with the present. Recurring issues in their discussions suggest
that the industry faced similar dilemmas from the outset. Among these
issues are the continued marginality of the Hispanic advertising indus-

try vis-à-vis the general market and its structural vulnerability stemming from its long-time dependence on a static and marketable vision of what is, in fact, a fluid and heterogeneous population. As I argue below, this dependence, directly informed by U.S. paradigms of racial and ethnic organization, sustains ongoing disjunctures between a coveted Hispanic public and those seeking to speak for and about it. These discussions also revealed that the Hispanic marketing industry, like any culture industry, does not simply manufacture cultural symbols and ideas, but simultaneously reflects dominant hierarchies of representation and the greater political economy structures affecting the commodification of Hispanics in this country.

To emphasize these issues, I forego a strictly chronological account of the industry's origins and instead draw from these narratives some introductory segments on trends that were repeatedly mentioned as having had the greatest effect on the industry's establishment and ensuing development. These include the Latin American foundations of the U.S. Spanish TV networks and of the marketing industry and its organization along ethnic and linguistic lines, the growth and consolidation of the category of "Hispanic" for peoples of Latin American background in this country, and global trends affecting the advertising industry at large.

SHAPING HISPANIDAD FROM LATIN AMERICA

Latin America has always figured prominently in the imagery of Latinas in this country and, as will become evident later, a great part of the Hispanic media's mission and function has been to serve as the venue in which U.S.-based Hispanics can consume and experience Latin America from within the U.S. context. One of the great contradictions of the U.S. Hispanic media, however, has been that while supposedly geared to the United States and not Latin America, it has nonetheless been highly dependent on transnational Latin American media conglomerates and developments, dynamics which the United States has been very much involved in fostering. This is evident in the evolution of the Spanish TV networks, the most important force behind the growth of a culturally specific U.S. Hispanic market.

While advertising for U.S. Hispanic populations dates back to the very origins of Spanish-language media at the turn of the twentieth century,[2] commercial broadcasting and national television networks provided the greatest impetus to the growth of Hispanic advertising as a specialized industry, as they did for the advertising industry in general.[3] This began in the 1960s, when independent brokers began buying intermittent time from English stations for Spanish TV and culminated in the creation of the Spanish International Network (SIN), later renamed Univision, and of Telemundo, national networks that now have subsidiaries and affiliated stations throughout the continental United States.

To understand the impact of these national networks, we need to consider that prior to their development, marketing to Hispanics was mostly a local endeavor. Former staff of the few New York City Hispanic advertising agencies that existed in the 1960s recalled that their business was centered on local radio stations and was highly dependent on direct promotions through bodegas, Puerto Rican–owned markets that proliferated in New York's Puerto Rican neighborhoods during the 1950s. Network television, however, quickly transformed advertising into a national endeavor. Not only did it create a dependable and steady base for placing advertising by providing continuous programming for Spanish-speaking populations,[4] but it also formed the basis for the conceptualization of Hispanics as a nationwide community, linked and imagined by the networks.

This development dates to 1961 when Emilio Azcárraga, a Mexican television entrepreneur and the main figure behind Televisa's Mexican TV empire, purchased TV stations in San Antonio and Los Angeles, establishing SIN/SICC (Spanish International Network and Spanish International Communications Corporations). Azcárraga had long tried to import Televisa's programming into the United States, yet, faced with the undoubtedly racially motivated institutional opposition to any type of Spanish TV, he decided that buying entire stations, rather than intermittent time from American stations, would enable him to secure the importation of his programs. The purchase had to take place in association with a group of employees and business partners in order to circumvent FCC rules preventing noncitizens from owning more than 20 percent of any U.S. TV station.[5] Despite this, Azcárraga and Televisa retained operational control of the stations, assuring the Latin American basis that has shaped the industry's subsequent growth. SIN/SICC quickly expanded to sixteen stations by the mid-1970s, and after becoming the first U.S. network connected by satellite in 1976, it became pivotal in the conceptualization of a nationwide U.S. Hispanic market.

Prior to the satellite connections, each SIN station operated independently, negotiating its own advertising contracts and programming schedule. Programs sent by SIN's network to its stations would travel from one station to another, leading each station to operate in its own time frame with respect to serials, advertising, and shows. Connection via satellite brought about a growing standardization in the programming and lowered risks in its projection, which in turn facilitated the distribution and transmission of advertising. Advertising agencies could finally negotiate with a network rather than with individual stations, and thus assure clients that their ads would reach a nationwide audience. By 1982, SIN could claim to reach 90 percent of Latina households through its sixteen-station network, its one hundred repeater stations, and more than two hundred cable systems (Rodríguez 1999: 38). Later renamed Univision, SIN attained its present reach of twenty owned and operated stations and twenty-seven affiliates throughout the United States, encompassing almost every center with a sizable Latina/Hispanic population. Thus, more than any previous medium, the networks helped forge and maintain an ethnic niche for the Hispanic market, with regard not only to the general market, but also to other minority markets, such as the African American and Asian markets, both of which lacked a national television network through which to constitute and renew a nationwide market. As one agency owner put it, "The networks meant that we existed and were here to stay."

The U.S. Spanish networks now dominate advertising budgets and thus have been most influential in the development of the Hispanic marketing industry.[6] In particular, they have been a major force in sustaining the historically close ties between the Hispanic advertising and media industry and Latin America, thus helping to preserve the dominance of Latin American producers and productions. Univision, the highest rated Hispanic network, is a perfect example of this. Until the late 1980s, its precursor SIN/SICC served more as a receptacle for Mexican programming, with over 90 percent of its network hours devoted to programs directly aired or imported from Mexico (Avila 1997; Gutiérrez 1979). This dominance led to accusations of excessive and unlawful foreign control and even to the court-ordered sale of the network in 1986 and its acquisition by Hallmark/First Capital, which renamed it Univision. In reality, however, this change in ownership and control was just temporary: in 1992 it was bought by Jerry Perenchio, in partnership with Azcárraga's Televisa International of Mexico, which thus reacquired partial ownership of the network, and with yet another media empire in Latin America, Cisnero's Venevision Media Group of Venezuela, which also owns a sizable portion of other Latin American network stations. The Latin American transnational connections that characterized the U.S. Hispanic media market from the outset were thus quickly reestablished.[7]

Telemundo, for its part, although always in the hands of U.S. corporations, having been launched by Reliance Capital in 1986, and recently bought by Sony, Liberty Media, Apollo Investment Fund, and Bastion Capital in 1998, has also maintained direct links with the Latin American media market. However, it was not Mexico but Puerto Rico that figured prominently in the development of what would later become Telemundo. Behind its development were media personalities like Carlos Barba, a soap opera actor in his native Cuba, who had previously worked in the development of Venezuelan and Puerto Rican television. Brought to New York by Columbia Pictures, which owned the Puerto Rican channel where he worked at the time of their purchase of New York's channel 47, Barba was soon made director of programming, consolidating the New York–Puerto Rican connection through the importation of island-made Puerto Rican programming that he thought was more relevant to the mostly Puerto Rican Latina population in the city. In contrast to SIN's mostly Mexican programming, channel 47 emphasized New York–filmed shows of Puerto Rican personalities like Mirta Silva, Boby Capó, and Polito Vega, and later the importation of Puerto Rican–produced shows like "La Taverna India," "El Show de Chucho Avellanet," and "El Show del Medio Dia," all of which kept channel 47 directly tied to Puerto Rican television. This programming synergy would continue until the channel's purchase by Telemundo Group, not surprisingly named after the Puerto Rican channel 2, whose American owners at the time were behind the establishment of the U.S. Telemundo network in 1986. After its foundation, Telemundo continued to rely mostly on Latin American programming until its acquisition by its present owners, who are discussed in a later chapter. Although aimed at the U.S. Hispanic population as a whole, its programming shifted from Puerto Rican fare to mostly Mexican and Venezuelan imports, dubbed American movies that are still key to its programming, and a few U.S.-produced shows.

The continued involvement of particular Latin American countries in the U.S. Hispanic market through Televisa or Venevision, however, could not be described as a reversal of cultural imperialism. Hollywood's exports to Mexico far exceed Mexico's involvement in the Spanish market, and U.S. investments in Mexico's cultural industries have continued to escalate after NAFTA (McAnany and Wilkinson 1996). What is undeniable is the continued merger of the U.S. Hispanic market with that of Latin America and the dominance of the Latin American media mar-

ket, particularly of the countries with the strongest media empires, such
as Mexico and Venezuela, in these arrangements. This undoubtedly has
also led to one of the many disjunctions at play in the Latina-oriented
advertising industry, consisting of the enduring gaps between the producers and consumers of these images fueled by the structural demands
of an industry claiming to represent U.S. Latinas even though its very
structure has historically been more directly tied to a Latin American
rather than a Latina infrastructure. Among other issues, these transcontinental connections have traditionally made the Spanish language central to the market, and looked to Latin America as the source of talent
and programming. Consider for instance that Univision's profitability
has traditionally been predicated on its ability to show the same programming as in Latin America—also benefiting from producing in pe-
sos and selling in dollars—instead of investing in new programming and
productions. Moreover, while there has been a greater emphasis on U.S.-
based productions for the U.S. market since the mid-1980s, these programs have, as I discuss later, generally been developed as potential exports with the Latin American market, not solely the U.S. Hispanic
market, in mind. Univision already licenses and distributes the talk show
Cristina to over eighteen countries and the four-hour game, contest, and
entertainment show *Sábado Gigante* to twenty, while Telemundo sells
its current affairs magazine *Ocurrió Así* to twelve foreign markets
(Aponte 1998; Tobekin 1997). Similarly, the stations' all-Spanish policy has led to a heavy reliance on the artistic pool of specific Latin American countries, where "authentic" Spanish speakers are often recruited
to work in the United States. Even the guests for *Cristina, Sezvec,* and
Sábado Gigante are often brought in from Latin America to assure their
acceptability for the Latin American media market. These processes
will be more closely examined later. The issue here is the strong Latin
American connections that have attended the growth of the U.S. Spanish network, making their development far from a U.S. self-generating
process.

The development of the Hispanic advertising industry evidences similar although unique transnational trends of its own. First the industry's
growth was tied to the migration of Cubans and Puerto Ricans to New
York City throughout the 1950s. By the 1960s, a steady influx of mostly
working-class Puerto Rican migrants fleeing massive unemployment generated by the island's development and modernization project of Operation Bootstrap had produced a sizable Spanish-speaking presence in
New York, a strong incentive for entrepreneurs to develop programming

and marketing for this population. Cuban immigration after the Cuban Revolution, meanwhile, brought key figures of the well-developed Cuban publicity, entertainment, and marketing industries who were ready to tap the marketing opportunities arising from the changing demographics in the city. Indeed, Cuban executives who had previously been involved in advertising and marketing in Cuba were behind the development of the first and largest advertising agencies that targeted populations of Latin American background, not only in New York City but also throughout the United States.[8] For example, SAMS (Spanish Advertising and Marketing Services), the first and largest full-service Hispanic advertising agency in the United States, was founded in 1962 by Luis Díaz Albertini, who had worked for McCann Erickson and for J. Walter Thompson's Cuban affiliate in Havana, and later in the local Godoy and Godoy, where he handled U.S. brands such as Del Monte, Kellogg's, and Scott paper. Similarly, the founders of Conill Advertising, headed by a husband-and-wife team, had owned a successful agency in Cuba, where they marketed a variety of U.S. products for the local market as well as for other Latin American countries. Some accounts even traveled with particular advertising personalities from Cuba, as in the case of Colgate, which had previously been represented in his native Cuba by José Luis Cubas, founder of Siboney U.S.A. Thus, the dominance of Cubans in the development of the contemporary Hispanic advertising industry arose from previous attempts at globalization by the international advertising industry, whose early extension into places like Cuba and Mexico was fundamental to the subsequent development of the advertising agencies targeting U.S. Hispanic populations.[9] Cuban publicists who would later become leading figures in the U.S. Hispanic market were not new entrants to the structures of American advertising and of its publicity industry, but had long functioned as marketing and modernizing agents at home.[10] As such, they had previous knowledge of American corporate clients, products, and, most important, contacts in corporate America who would provide a pivotal advantage in obtaining clients and in networking for their clients. Rafael Conill, founder of Conill Advertising in 1968, which would become one of the largest Hispanic agencies by the early 1980s, was greeted at the airport upon arrival by an old American business friend from Cuba. As I was told by his wife, Alicia, this is the same friend who later helped his pitch to Campbell's Soup for the U.S. Hispanic market account. And while it took them over three years to get some business from Campbell, it was such contacts that enabled them to secure contracts with national clients.[11]

Many of these Cuban advertising executives also had extensive contacts throughout Latin America, since they had represented U.S. products in these markets, which provided them with additional knowledge about and exposure to different Latin American countries and supported their eventual role as brokers of a pan-Latina identity in the United States. In this light, the work of the Conills and of other Latin American advertising entrepreneurs to create and reinforce the idea of a nationwide Hispanic market surfaces as the extension and transposition of an already existing vision to the U.S. context—the idea of "Latin America" as a common market for the United States, although Latin America was now not external, but within the very confines of the United States.[12] Indeed SAMS' early accounts, such as Lorillard cigarettes (makers of Kent and Newport), were initially commissioned for the Latin American, not the U.S. Latina, market, and key leaders of the industry such as Alicia Conill herself worked for Latin American accounts during their early years in the United States prior to working exclusively for the U.S. Hispanic market.[13] Thus, although Hispanic advertising agencies had been operating since the 1960s, the idea of a U.S. Hispanic market would only become important in the late 1970s and early 1980s. Prior to that, Hispanic agencies advertised mostly for the local New York market or else represented clients in Latin America. Alicia Conill, for instance, recalled turning down Latin American accounts in order to convince clients to focus on the U.S. Hispanic market as an exclusive and profitable market totally independent of Latin America.

Neither the industry's Latin American antecedents nor its founders' previous contacts with U.S. corporate clients, however, would have sustained its development had they not been supported by a nascent ethnic economy based on close connections among the first generation of Cuban advertising entrepreneurs. As has already been documented for Cubans in Miami and Puerto Rico (Cobas and Duany 1997; Portes and Stepick 1993), the entrepreneurial success of the first generation of New York's Cuban advertising executives who arrived after Castro's revolution was predicated on their shared class background—most were educated and of upper- or middle-class extraction—and on the establishment of an ethnic economy where ethnic ties were central in dispensing credits, employment, and economic opportunities. As the founder of one of the most important independent New York Hispanic shops explained in response to my inquiries about the involvement of Cubans in this industry, most were the sons of *"pequeños comerciantes"* of Spanish background who had been steeped in the ideology of business ownership. Those with no direct involvement in Cuba's advertising industry had nonetheless been exposed to U.S. brands and to their commercialization, which, my informant argued, provided the "perfect transition" for their involvement in advertising and marketing. As he explained when recalling his early years in the United States, "I remember talking at dinner with my family about the marketing opportunities here, of what was available here and there. Because there was a long tradition of marketing in Cuba, and we had long been exposed to the brands." Like other successful Cubans in this industry, this executive emphasized that the relative economic advantages enjoyed by Cubans back home did not guarantee their eventual success in the United States. They came as exiles and refugees, he noted, "with five dollars in their pockets" and—echoing what I was told by others—with only a "psychological disposition" to succeed and aspiration and ambition in their blood. Clearly, however, such "predispositions" were connected to the cultural, if not economic, capital that most of them shared as members of a privileged entrepreneurial class that was already successful in Cuba and had prior connections to marketing and sales. Also central to their success were the ongoing personal relationships among them, some of which originated back in Cuba and carried over to the United States, and some of which were forged in the United States. Castor Fernández and Jorge Reynardus, for instance, were two central advertising figures in New York and owners of their own advertising shops, who were neighbors in Cuba and lived together in New York, where they studied together at Baruch College. The founding directors of agencies that were in greatest competition for national advertising accounts throughout the late 1970s, Conill Advertising and Castor Advertising, were such close friends that Rafael Conill became godfather to Castor's sons, and they were once neighbors in Miami. Such relationships were central in assuring the Cuban presence at the outset, transforming these early agencies into training grounds for some of the most important figures in the industry. Rafael Turaño, who later became director of Univision, worked at SAMS as did Sarah Sunshine, an advertising veteran now with Bravo, which in turn was founded by Daisy Exposito, who used to work with Alicia Conill at Conill Advertising. From Castor Advertising emerged Jorge Moya, and Vidal and Jorge Reynardus, who now have two of the last independently owned shops in New York City.

Other agencies founded and led by Cubans during the 1970s include Font and Vaamonte, founded in 1977, and Siboney, first established in Cuba in 1954, later moved to Puerto Rico, and finally opened in the

United States in 1983. The Cuban presence in the advertising and marketing industry, particularly in the eastern United States, though much less dominant today, is still noticeable in the likes of Eduardo Caballero, Tere Zubizarreta, Daisy Exposito, and other recognized pioneers.

Beyond the eastern United States, Noble and Associates and La Agencia de Orci in Los Angeles had similar origins in Latin America, although their founders/creators were mostly advertising executives from Mexico. Noble and Associates, for instance, was the product of Ed Noble, a Mexican advertiser and one of Azcárraga's business partners in his acquisition of SIN, and Richard Dillon, an American who had worked in Mexico for General Foods for ten years and whose multiple contacts with Fortune 500 companies, as he himself noted, allowed this agency to rapidly become one of the largest in the business. Richard Dillon later went on to found Mendoza Dillon with a Mexican creative from Young and Rubicam in Mexico who was trying to open his own agency in Los Angeles, without Dillon's contacts and hence without success. Similarly, La Agencia de Orci was founded by Hector and Norma Orci, who moved to Los Angeles from Mexico to start a Hispanic ad division for McCann Erickson Worldwide, and from that division, created La Agencia.[14] Only a handful of advertising agencies in the West, such as Sosa and Associates, founded by Texas-born Lionel Sosa, were the product of U.S.-born Hispanics. Following the dominant pattern of the market, however, these too wound up importing most of their creatives from Latin America or from among the Latin American creatives working for their New York competitors.

However, the Latin American origins of the U.S. Hispanic market are not solely the result of prior connections between Latin American and Anglo-American entrepreneurs. The trend evokes the highly racialized context in which this industry developed. Numerous times I heard members of the first Hispanic marketing generation assert that they had created the market because they were not *acomplejados* (shamed and embarrassed by their identity), as were most Latinas they encountered in the United States. Comments such as this testify to the different subject positions, class and racial backgrounds, and levels of awareness relative to U.S. racism and discrimination among the U.S.-based Latina and the recent arrival, which need to be acknowledged as major factors affecting the initial involvement and ensuing success of the recent arrival in this industry's development. As explained by Eduardo Caballero, founder and director of Caballero Spanish Media and a widely recognized founding figure in the industry,[15]

What happened is that we Cubans got here with no fear of being discriminated against. We did not think of discrimination. And perhaps they were discriminating against us, but we were not aware of it. We just thought that we should speak Spanish because that's what we spoke. We had not passed through the process that many Puerto Ricans and Mexican Americans had gone [through] where you could not present yourself as Hispanic. You had to hide that you spoke Spanish because you would otherwise be looked down upon. I have Mexican American friends whose mothers packed Mexican food for lunch and who threw it away before arriving at school, just because they knew that if they were caught eating a tortilla or a taco, they'd be hit. And they spent the whole day without food. I remember traveling in the subway here in New York, back when I used the subway before I had made it in my business, and I saw all of these Puerto Ricans—because most people here were Puerto Ricans back then—and you saw people reading *El Diario* but covering it up with the *Daily News*, hiding the fact that they were reading Spanish in public. . . . So the problem was a lack of identity, or more exactly people's shame about their identity. I know this may sound harsh, but it was a reality that as a general rule people were afraid of their identity and that this was what hurt the market's development the most. It was only with the growth of the media that most Mexican Americans realized that it was OK to speak Spanish; that it was no crime. So the media did contribute extraordinarily to solving the identity problem, which was the greatest problem there. Because the Hispanic market always existed, but the Spanish-speaking Hispanic market had to be created.

Not all Cubans I spoke with were as willing as Caballero to talk about racism or to acknowledge the different degrees of discrimination faced by Latinas in the United States. What most of them did share with Caballero, however, was a tacit agreement to assess the relative pride of Latinas in their culture by imposed standards—mostly by a single variable, their use of Spanish in public life—and hence by the same standards of the recently arrived Latin American entrepreneurs intent on creating "Hispanics" as a Spanish-speaking market. Still, the lack of experience with U.S. racism by Cuban immigrants in the 1960s was undoubtedly crucial to their success in furthering Hispanidad. They, unlike their U.S.-based Latina counterparts, had not yet fully internalized its subordinate status and could adopt more freely the attitude expressed by Caballero: "We should speak Spanish because that's what we spoke." This, of course, does not mean that they were exempt from discrimination. As will be evident later, they are indeed aware of racism and see Hispanic marketing as a tool for promoting pride in all things Latin. Our discussions, however, were characterized by a distancing on their part that allowed them to position themselves as the primary examples of Hispanidad and the "uplifters" of all things Hispanic, while distinguishing

themselves from most Hispanics. The following statement by Carlos
Barba is evocative of this type of positioning:

> This is a business, but at the same time, this has also been my life's mission
> involving defending human values, those of the Hispanic community, so that
> we get the respect that we deserve and we have equal opportunities with the
> rest of U.S. citizens. Simply put, our mission is to make sure that the Hispanic
> community gets more respect by helping Hispanics grow professionally and
> spiritually. To motivate Hispanics so that they register and vote, and to en-
> courage people to preserve our language and our tradition so that we con-
> tinue being what we are, a humble race but one with a big heart and great
> ambition.

Comments such as these are common among advertising entrepreneurs,
who referred to their role as one of uplifting and enlightening Hispanics regarding the "right" way of being Hispanic in this country. In the
process they would position themselves strategically as Hispanic while
maintaining an ambiguous relationship to the bulk of the Hispanic/Latina
community. After all, as different as they may in fact be from most U.S.
Hispanics, it is in their self-presentation as Hispanics that their success
and legitimacy would reside.

THE ETHNIC DIVISION OF CULTURAL LABOR

A direct result of the Spanish-language-centered infrastructure of the U.S.
Hispanic marketing industry is an ethnic division of labor whereby the
Latin American corporate intellectuals from middle- and upper-class
backgrounds rather than U.S.-born Latinas generally dominate the creation and dissemination of "Hispanic" images in this country. Obviously,
divisions and hierarchies based on structural or departmental distinctions
at different levels and stages of production in various culture industries
are common features of the media production process (Lutz and Collins
1993). Yet beyond these characteristic distinctions, the Hispanic marketing industry's Latin American connections have led to the dominance
in the U.S. media market of what the industry calls "Spanish-dominant"
Latinas, who have relocated to the United States as adults, often to pur-
sue advanced studies, or who have had previous experience in the advertising and marketing industries in some of the major Latin American
markets for U.S. brands, such as Mexico and Venezuela, and who have
kept their so-called grammatically correct Spanish-language skills. Accordingly, highly privileged and educated Latin American recent arrivals
are more likely to be found in creative departments, where demands for

"perfect language skills" bar most U.S. Latinas. The latter are more common in production or in client services departments, which require what was described to me as "their more Americanized" skills to handle corporate clients or negotiate with other segments of the industry. The industry craves highly educated, bilingual Hispanics whose ethnicity does not present a problem to Anglo clients and who can accurately represent and translate Spanish creative concepts for Anglo clients. These are what America Rodríguez, after Ruben Rumbaut, has called the "one-and-one-half generation," which they define as "those who were born in Latin America, but were educated and came of age in the United States" (Rodríguez 1999: 5), providing them a simultaneous insider and outsider perspective into U.S. Hispanics and corporate America. However, for creative jobs, a "pure Latin American" import coming from one of the major transnational advertising conglomerates in Latin America is the most favored due to his or her "fresh" and untainted language skills. Indeed, during my research, several agencies had just hired someone directly from South America to run their creative departments, following a common pattern in the industry, which still complains of not being able to find creative talent in the United States.

This lack of talent is not about lack of education or training. Many of my Latina students graduating with majors in communications, for instance, would be barred from entry into Hispanic marketing, or pushed to behind-the-scenes operations, solely on the basis of their language skills. The inequalities of this ethnic division are evident when we consider that in the advertising industry at large a position as a "creative" on the staff that conceives of an ad's creative strategy is far more visible and prestigious than any other position dealing with research, accounts, or clients. It is the creative who wins prizes and name recognition, what Dornfeld (1998) has called "career capital," based on Bourdieu's (1993) discussion of the anti-economic logic that predominates, to various degrees, different fields of cultural production. Beyond financial compensation, such capital provides the creative with prestige and connections in the industry that may allow him to found his own agency at a later time. I say "him" purposefully, because gender disparity accompanies this ethnic division of labor. While women have attained positions of power within the industry, the most renowned, or at least many of the most frequently mentioned creatives during the course of my research (such as Tony Dieste, Roberto Alcazar, Luis Miguel Messiano, Sergio Alcocer, Jorge Moya) were all Latin American–born men, as were most agency directors. Except for the few fully independent agencies, however, ultimate power is held by the American investors who have bought many of these agencies. Yet, whether Spanish or English is dominant, most Hispanic marketers are at odds with the average Hispanic consumer in terms of class, race, and background. After all, many Hispanic marketers and creatives are highly educated and have even come to the United States with secure jobs in the industry after having worked in transnational advertising companies in their home countries.

A representative example of this trend is Maruchi Gómez, who was hired by New York–based Vidal Reynardus and Moya (VRM; now the Vidal Partnership) to work on the Heineken account on the recommendation of a corporate client who had worked with her in De la Cruz, Miller's agency of record in Puerto Rico.[16] She in turn brought in a friend from Lopito and Howie, another Puerto Rican agency, to work at VRM. At VRM there were six Mexican women who had all worked at Noble and Associates in Mexico and had found employment in the agency through each other's contact. The three Mexican creatives, Sergio Torres, José Hernández, and Mariano Andrade, who at one point worked at New York City's Castor Advertising, are another relevant example. José Hernández, who joined Castor after working at Ferrer Publicidad in Mexico, was hired at Castor Advertising only because his résumé landed in the hands of his friend who, in turn, got his job in New York through another friend he met in the Dominican Republic, where he was sent on assignment by Mexico's Leo Burnett. When that friend migrated to the United States, Sergio came, and through him, José. In between, Sergio had worked in production in Venezuela, where he met Mariano Andrade, who, through his assistance, eventually also found employment at Castor. José, a former anthropology major in Mexico, even drew me a kinship chart to explain the multiple connections that make this industry, in the words of another agency director, a "private club where everyone knows each other," but one easily joined by people with advertising backgrounds in places like Mexico, Venezuela, and Puerto Rico.

This ethnic division of labor is also apparent in the Hispanic entertainment industry. Whereas Univision's programming department has traditionally been dominated by Latin Americans, mostly Cubans, its sales staff at the management level is no longer "Hispanic" but Anglo, recently recruited from major networks like ABC and Fox. This "vanillization" of the network, as critics have dubbed it, reminds us that while a Hispanic's authenticity may be profitable for creative purposes, it is a hindrance for entering and successfully operating within the inner circles of corporate America. In this realm, Anglos have the contacts and command the greatest authority, as reflected in the record increases in advertising revenues at Univision as a result of their hiring Ronald Furman, Dennis McCauley, and Tom McGarrity, all recruited from major general market stations, to lead its sales team (Zbar 1998c: 28). Conversations with some of the station's sales team revealed that it is not their knowledge of the Hispanic market that has made them so successful but their contacts and the legitimacy that is vested in them on the basis of their "whiteness." One Anglo salesperson who admitted that his previous experience in this market consisted of a trip to Mexico or a crash Berlitz course explained, "We are not seen as just one more interest group, be it black, gay, or Hispanic, knocking on their doors [corporate clients] to get money for their own niche." Additionally, because most corporate clients are Anglo, the new team has the advantage of being seen as their potential allies. As another explained, "Clients are culturally ignorant, and the sales go better if they don't have to worry about saying the wrong or insensitive thing." Specifically, he noted, their strength lay in their common understanding that for corporate clients, Spanish TV is "tacky" or "cheesy," making their job one of speaking their clients' language and presenting it as "hot, sexy, and cool," a comment that underscored the type of overt stereotypes upon which the selling of Latinidad is ultimately based.

This infrastructure is guided not solely by the networks' concern with language purity, but also by economic considerations. Just as it is cheaper to produce and export programming to the United States, it is cheaper to film commercials in Mexico and other parts of Latin America. For evidence of the intricate links between Latin American production companies and the U.S. Hispanic market, one need only peruse trade publications like *Publicidad y Comerciales* to see the number of advertisements placed by the latter to attract filming, production, and post-production in Latin American countries. Among other advantages, filming in Latin America frees companies from paying union fees, although I have heard that informal arrangements to waive union fees were a feature of the Miami and Los Angeles production scenes. I was also told that it is easier to avoid paying residual wages (whereby actors/actresses receive a percentage of pay whenever commercials are shown) through buyouts or one-time fees in Latin America. However, the advertising staffs' insistence on the supposedly easy access to authentic-looking Latin scenes or the abundance of actors in Latin America were, in my opinion, most revealing of the Latin American biases of this industry. Are there not enough "authentic" Latinas/Hispanics in this country?

I will return to this issue when discussing the creation of the generic, pan-Hispanic look, but first, it is worth noting that the international connections that characterize the growth and development of the U.S. Hispanic marketing industry are far from unique. Increasingly, global culture industries are characterized by an attendant "new international division of cultural labor," whereby, just as has long happened with manufacturing, companies relocate or allocate portions of the production process internationally according to the logic of increased profitability (Miller 1998: 171). What the Latin American basis of the U.S. Hispanic marketing industry suggests, however, is that such international arrangements have long been a feature of many so-called local or national culture industries. Additionally, the Latin American basis of the U.S. Hispanic market brings to the forefront the ubiquitous issues of authenticity and representativity that accompany such global arrangements. For the historical connections with the Latin American media market have not gone unquestioned by the public, by critics, and by media activists who see them as responsible for perpetuating a Hispano- and Latin American–centered definition of Latinidad that excludes English-dominant U.S.-based Latinas and provides few opportunities for U.S.-generated Latina producers and productions. The Hispanic networks and media structures have therefore been criticized for erasing Hispanics and turning them into "second-class audiences" not only in the Anglo media but also within the media that are supposed to represent Hispanics in this country (Avila 1997). Also controversial is the central place of the Spanish language in the industry. While obviously guided by economic considerations, the use of Spanish is at the center of current debates on Hispanic identity and has numerous political implications. Some critics see the networks as agents in the decentering of monolingual nationalism in the United States, while others regard them as promulgating essentialist definitions of identity based on language, definitions which bar second and third generations of Latinas in this country (Esparza 1998). Before considering these issues, which certainly merit more attention and will continue to surface in different guises throughout this work, I turn first to a key factor that has helped veil this and other disjunctions in the Hispanic advertising industry: the structural identity of the Hispanic media as representative of the totality of the Hispanic population, and the role that "Hispanic" as a category has had in legitimating and veiling contradictions in the process of representation.

THE CATEGORY THAT MADE US THE SAME

When you miss *Latina,* you miss you. Subscribe today.

> *Latina* magazine, 1999

Decir Hostos y Clemente y Hector Lavoe, estás orgulloso de
lo que eres Hispano Americano, esta es tu estación. Caliente
es tu idioma, es tu música, es tu sangre, eres tú . . . ahora
New York es Caliente.

> Summer radio promotion for the new 105.9
> FM Latin Hispanic radio station

It was about time. We are no longer an obscure force, we are
finally being recognized. We are moving forward, and no one
can stop us.

> Lily Santana, listener, upon learning that
> La Mega 97.9 had become the first Hispanic
> station to attain the No. 1 spot in the
> New York ratings

It is not at all surprising that the listener in the last epigraph above would
feel ethnic pride as a result of New York City's Spanish radio station "La
Mega" attaining number one status in the 1998 Arbitron ratings.[17] Even
critics of the station felt that its number one position signaled Latinas'
growing, though unrecognized, presence and power in the city. This out-
pouring of identification with the success of a radio station that consistently presents itself as "tu estación" and "la estación de los Latinos" is
part and parcel of a second development that was repeatedly identified
as an important influence on the industry's growth: the consolidation of
a common category of identification for "Latinas," or Hispanics, and its
appropriation and continued promotion by the media and advertising
industry.

Common categories to encompass peoples of Latin American background in the United States have existed since the nineteenth century. In
New York City, which served as a center for nationalists, revolutionaries,
intellectuals, and exiles from Spain, Cuba, and Puerto Rico, "Hispanic"
had already become a generalized designation for a number of clubs,
churches, and magazines, as well as for the "colonias Hispanas" that have
developed in Brooklyn and East Harlem since the turn of the century.[18]
Yet it was only in the 1970s, when the U.S. census institutionalized a category for all populations from any Spanish-speaking country of the
Caribbean, Central or South America, or even Spain, that a common cat-

egory became standardized and widespread on a national basis. This development peaked in the 1980s, when changes in the census categorization of Hispanics that allowed people to identify themselves as of Spanish-Hispanic origin or descent, or as one of the specific Latin American nationalities that were later added to this category, revealed a 53 percent growth in the number of people who categorized themselves as Hispanic (Fox 1996: 25–26).[19]

The category of "Hispanic" is one that scholars and activists have contested and challenged. Grouping both Latin American and U.S.-born populations as well as Europeans into a single category veils the variable social statuses of the constituent groups, some of whom—like Puerto Ricans and Chicanos—are historical and colonial minorities in this country. Critics have thus rightfully argued that the homogenization of all Latina subgroups into a common category, be it Hispanic or Latina, involves the depoliticization of the history of conquest and colonization that has affected particular Latina nationalities. This is why Juan Flores insists on the need to distinguish the processes and circumstances that have led to the continuing relegation of some Latina subgroups, such as Mexicans and Puerto Ricans, to the status of racial or colonial minorities in the United States, despite their U.S. citizenship and historical trajectory in this country (Flores 2000). For others, the problem is not so much the idea of a common category but a problem of nomenclature. Without challenging the need for a common identity term to encompass these diverse populations, some have criticized "Hispanic" for its elitist evocations of Spain, its business connotations, and its imposed status, proposing instead "Latina," a name that is less evocative of ties to Spain, as the rightful political term for this population. Without engaging in a broader discussion of this category, I will note that, while controversial at the level of politics and scholarship, the official use of a single category for people of Latin American origin or descent has proven to be the most significant force in the marketing industry's development.[20] Advertisers had been lobbying for the acknowledgment of a common Hispanic culture or identity since the 1960s, and this category became the legitimization of their claims and the springboard for the industry's rapid growth after the mid-1970s.[21] As Eduardo Caballero stated, "If the census had not drafted those categories, nothing else would have worked. Based on the census, you can tell an advertiser that in Los Angeles 60 percent of the people are Hispanic and that if they only devoted 1 percent to this market, they'd be losing their money. It's a matter of logic." Moreover, while complex and contradictory, this category met precisely the needs of the advertising industry which, following the trend of the commercial networks, had seen in "Spanish" the core of a common identity for the diversity of populations of Latin American background in the United States. Most important, the official recognition of "Hispanics" as a distinct population assisted the industry's growth by promoting the view that there are indeed some essential and intrinsic characteristics that all "Hispanics" share.

As Castor Fernández, founder/director of one of New York's oldest Hispanic agencies stated, "Don't Panic, I'm Hispanic" could well have been the slogan behind the rapid growth of the Hispanic advertising industry after the 1970s. In light of the growing numbers of Hispanics, its advertisers could now reassure clients that they "knew the market; that they too were Hispanic." Indeed, through these and similar assertions, both the founders of these agencies, our Cuban-born, "authentic," Spanish-speaking Hispanics, and others involved in the industry have since established and validated their knowledge and the legitimacy of the market. Through these claims they have been able to gain an exclusive hold over a growing target market and to turn this industry into a thriving one. Specifically, this category facilitated their appeal for more profitable nationwide campaigns aimed at the totality of the Hispanic market through unique advertising—altogether new campaigns specifically designed to reach the "distinct" Hispanic consumer.

Yet, far from mere fabrications of shrewd business people, these strategies of self-representation point us to yet another recurrent issue affecting this industry from its outset: the fact that these strategies are directly implicated in U.S. racial categories which have since guided the strategies by which most Hispanic corporate intellectuals represent themselves and their market. Such claims would be of little value if they were not predicated on the dominant view that there are indeed some essential and intrinsic commonalities that are shared by all "Hispanics." They are successful only because, as I was often told, their mainstream clients always considered Hispanic advertising executives to be as "Hispanic" as residents of the barrio, whether in the Bronx or Los Angeles, and therefore able to speak for the totality of the Hispanic population.[22]

Thus, when seeking to understand the growth and current operations of the Hispanic marketing industry, we cannot ignore the influence of dominant discourses and categories of identity in the United States, and their appropriation and manipulation by advertisers as a way to extract profit from the market's intrinsic differences and particularities. This has traditionally involved emphasizing their Hispanic identity, asserting that "they too are Hispanic," and thus rightful advocates for "Hispanics" vis-à-vis the "average American consumer," veiling differences of class, race, and other exclusionary principles that are mobilized in the process of representation, as will become evident throughout this work. As one agency director stated, echoing similar statements on the cultural commonality between agencies and their audiences, "What we still have to convey to our clients is that only a Hispanic can really understand our culture, our way of being and feeling, to produce a truly compelling and relevant campaign. It is not a professional that a client gets when they hire us, but a *Hispanic* advertising professional" (his emphasis). Hispanic ad professionals thus become both victims of U.S. "othering" practices, homogenized into the marginal category of Hispanic regardless of their class or educational background and their lack of identification with most Hispanics, as well as key "tropicalizers." That is, as in the view of Aparicio and Chávez-Silverman, advertisers have simultaneously become agents "trop[ing], imbu[ing] a particular space, geography, group, or nation with a set of traits, images, and values" (1997: 8), mostly by circulating dominant representations of Latinidad that draw on the exotic and the essential characteristics of the "other."

The construction of Hispanics and things Hispanic as homogeneous entities is also involved with the industry's positioning as a democratic and equalizing medium for the totality of the Hispanic population. Specifically, just as Hispanic creatives and agency owners have construed themselves as representative of all Hispanics, the industry itself has been similarly constituted as a key arena of advocacy and support for the totality of the Hispanic population. A promotion for Zubi Advertising (figure 1), published in *Advertising Age* and other marketing trade publications, provides a good example of this position. While the copy compels readers to "Erase Stereotypes" by hiring Zubi, the specialist agency which truly understands the Hispanic market, the image underscores that only a Hispanic advertising agency can uncover the upscale, white, and modern woman who lies beneath the stereotype and the Carmen Miranda sombrero. Similarly, during my interviews, most of the industry's staff repeatedly presented and credited themselves with playing a key role in challenging stereotypes and promoting a more sophisticated view of Hispanics, and with contributing to the increased representation to which, as 11 percent of the population, Hispanics are "entitled."

Such claims were as common among early founders as among young practitioners, although they were mediated by the particularities of the historical context framing their work. Undoubtedly, the first generation

Figure 1.   "Erase Stereotypes," an agency self-promotion ad by Zubi Advertising in Coral Gables, Florida, exemplifies the industry's self-presentation as a site of positive images for all Latinos.

of Hispanic agencies in the mid 1960s and early 1970s encountered a
more hostile context, a less developed media infrastructure, and even less
recognition in mainstream society. All founding figures told tales of racism
and rejection by corporate clients who were not only unaware of the existence of Latinas, but alarmed at and even afraid about the size of this
market, resisting the idea of advertising to what they considered an inferior and impoverished ghetto population. A former staff member at
Univision's sales department now working at Telemundo recalled,

> I remember being in the middle of a presentation. I was saying that there were
> nine million Latinas, which of course, I did not know for certain, but I knew
> he knew even less than I, when all of the sudden, I noticed his face full of fear.
> He wanted to know where were all of these Latinas, where they lived, in which
> locations. He had never realized there were so many Latinas and so close to
> him, in New York. And I knew that he was not interested in our sales pitch.
> He just wanted to flee.

In light of such experiences, it is not at all surprising that when recalling the strong resistance of corporate clients as well as the larger context of racism that discouraged the teaching of Spanish and its public
use, most Hispanic marketers were confident that their industry had
helped to promote pride and reverse racism with regard to the Spanish
language and Hispanic cultures. Indeed, the fact that this industry's inception coincided with civil rights struggles of the 1960s and 1970s is
not without important consequences. The larger social and political context of those times became a selling point for these agencies; many agents
recalled presenting their work as a venue of representation for the entire
Latina population, implying in their sales pitches that they advertised to
Latinas in their own "culture" and language with greater claims over
identity and representation. Later generations of Hispanic advertisers encountered a well-developed nexus of TV stations, advertising agencies,
and census data with which to prove the existence of this market. In this
context, not only the "political correctness" of selling to Hispanics but
its profitability as well have been central in their business presentations.
Never mind here that pitching around profits or tokenism is an imaginary distinction: in the world of marketing, political correctness is only
acceptable if profitable, and ethnic marketing is precisely political correctness turned profitable. Still, despite making a distinction between politically correct appeals (that is, tokenism) and appeals to sheer business
profitability, these younger professionals also saw themselves as advocates, and the industry as a forum to valorize the populations they sought
to represent.[23] Some even claimed to have joined the industry as a state-

ment of their Latina identity or to discover their roots. This was the case with Rose Vega, a young woman of Cuban background raised in New Jersey, who described herself as a *"Cubanita arrepentida,"* living most of her adult life passing for white (Anglo-American), which was facilitated by her fluency in English, lack of accent, and her whiteness. Having married an Anglo and changed her name, she said she lived as a gringa until joining Hispanic marketing, which she felt was the first step toward her own rediscovery as a Latina. Similar stories of ethnic self-discovery were recounted by other ad professionals. In contrast to the founders, however, newer generations are skeptical of overtly political pitches, which they believe make them look "less professional," and prefer instead to emphasize the market value of the Hispanic consumer. As one emphatically stated, "Back then it was an issue of politics and tokenism, but now it is their pockets [corporate pockets] that are speaking" and hence to their pockets that we should pitch.

This type of purely economic marketing pitch, however, is hindered by the industry's peripheral position vis-à-vis the general market, which necessarily implies issues of equality and representativity. Even today, when Hispanic marketing is supposedly fashionable, advertising expenditures in the Hispanic market lag well behind advertising in the so-called general market. The Association of Hispanic Advertising Agencies estimates that Hispanic marketing receives only 1 percent of all ad spending in the United States, even though Latinas are believed to constitute about 11 percent of the U.S. population (Riley 2000). The permanent resident card (figure 2) printed on the cover of *P & C*, an industry trade magazine, plays out the ironies of such disparities, expressing uncertainty about the future of Hispanic marketing. Under "Card expires" it reads, "We hope it doesn't," and at the bottom it asks, "¿No sera hora de ir tramitando la ciudadania?" or "Isn't it time to get full citizenship?" Moreover, not only are companies spending less to reach ethnic and Hispanic consumers relative to what they spend to reach non-ethnic consumers, but reaching them is worth much less than reaching the "mainstream" consumer. According to a 1999 study by the Federal Communications Commission, advertisers that regularly pay $1 per listener for general market stations pay only 78 cents per listener for minority-formatted stations and 71 cents for stations that are both minority-owned and minority-formatted (Teinowitz and Cardona 1999), as if paralleling the two-thirds value that black populations were once given relative to whites. Such inequalities in reaching the ethnic consumer have numerous repercussions, ranging from the excessive billboarding common in the "cheaper" urban and ethnic residential areas compared to the more restrained advertising seen in white residential areas, to the lower revenues of Hispanic media, even when the latter's audience share may surpass that of the general market, as in the case of New York City's "La Mega" (Schwirtz 1998). These trends also point to the multiple manifestations of racism, whereby advertising for Hispanics is seen as tarnishing the image of goods among white buyers, while Hispanic consumers are stereotyped as destitute and thus as unlikely consumers. Advertising in the Hispanic market is therefore always associated with politics and raised as a gauge of Latina representativity, inevitably forcing the industry to sell itself not solely on marketing but also on political grounds.

Evidence of these dynamics was not hard to find during my research. Within weeks of my having settled in the city, a memo by Katz Radio Group containing derogatory remarks against blacks and Latinas and implying that advertising for these audiences was appealing to "suspects, not prospects" came to light, and became the subject of great controversy in the industry and among the public at large (*Hispanic Market Weekly*, May 18, 1998). This memo, followed shortly by an episode in one of the last *Seinfeld* shows, in which Kramer stomps over a flaming Puerto Rican flag during the Puerto Rican–day parade, triggered demonstrations in front of Young and Rubicam's headquarters over the issue of equity in advertising budgets for blacks and Latinas during the summer of 1998, and turned the disparity in advertising budget into a contentious political issue throughout the year. New Yorkers saw Senator Efraín González, president of the National Hispanic Caucus of State Legislators, team up with black activist Al Sharpton to demand that corporations advertise more in the Hispanic market, and to organize the Invitational Summit on Multicultural Markets and Media in New York City in 1999 (figure 3). Aimed at exposing inequalities in corporate advertising spending in general and ethnic markets, the summit was symbolically scheduled on Martin Luther King's birthday to emphasize the political basis of their claim for equal advertising as a right and for the need of increased corporate spending in these markets.

The political implications of this industry are also evident in the appointment of Henry Cisneros, four-term mayor of San Antonio and former secretary of the Department of Housing and Urban Development for the Clinton administration, as the first president and chief officer of Univision in 1997. In hiring him, Univision was not only recruiting a highly connected politician to appeal to the intrinsic growth, political

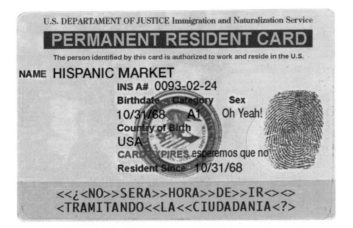

Figure 2.   An image from the cover of *Publicidad y Comerciales,* an industry trade magazine, provides a more skeptical view of the industry's gains. Photo courtesy of *Publicidad y Comerciales.*

power, and monetary worth of the Hispanic population in the quest for advertising equity, but was also reinforcing the mutuality of politics and marketing in the very person of Cisneros. This appointment is one example of a trend in the Hispanic advertising and media industry: its self-presentation as a venue for corporate America to prove its support for the totality of the Hispanic population. Attracting advertising monies from corporations relative to the percentage of Latinas, the argument goes, entails increasing the power and representativity of the Hispanic population, and constitutes a public statement of their "worth."

Clearly, these views are not restricted to the Hispanic market, but are part and parcel of the long association of consumer choice with democracy that is part of contemporary consumer society. As Stuart Ewen (1988) and others have observed, this development is part of the so-called democratizing of wealth, whereby the politics of images and style becomes a central site for reversing social inequalities, at least at the symbolic level, so central to the expression of class distinctions and power. Some argue that this trend has increased the importance of the market beyond that of the state as a central arena for mediating needs or claiming entitlements, as people become relatively more important as consumers than as citizens (García-Canclini 1995; Firat and Dholakia 1998). For Latinas and other U.S. minorities, these trends are of even greater consequence. Given the discontinuation of FCC regulations that

Figure 3.   Al Sharpton and Efraín González, co-organizers
of the Invitational Summit on Multicultural Markets, held in
1999 at the Marriott Hotel in New York City. The summit was
part of a political coalition to urge corporations to increase ad
spending in minority markets. Photo by author.

promoted minority media ownership and the current context of media
deregulation, it is as consumers or through appeals to their "growing
buying power" that Hispanics and other minority consumers must try
to influence the commercial forces that more and more affect every aspect of their lives.

   This equation of advertising revenues with participatory democracy
is, however, highly problematic. By taking advertising budgets as a measure of Latina power, the equation reduces the meaning of political enfranchisement to consumer representation—yet it is not in the market
that Hispanics are most ignored and disenfranchised. The growth of Hispanic marketing at the same time that anti-immigration and English-only
laws are gaining currency is a clear indication of such a disparity. While
still a minimal sector within the general market, Hispanic marketing currently constitutes the sector where Hispanics' opinions are most sought
after and quantified in research and focus group situations, and where
Hispanic culture is not questioned but promoted, even if only to be packaged and sold back to them. Yet another problem is that in emphasizing
the "growing buying power of Hispanics," the industry helps cloak the

poverty and inequality that afflicts a great number of Hispanics. For now, however, we should remember that neither the Hispanic media and marketing industry nor the definitions and categories generated to represent this market are reducible to mere fabrications of shrewd creatives. Neither are they devoid of political significance. Seen against the ongoing ethnic hierarchies that "make all of us the same," such constructions are at once the medium through which advertisers commodify, stereotype, and profit from what is in fact a heterogeneous population, as well as the medium through which Hispanics attain representation in a context where Hispanic images are often few or altogether absent and where the market stands at the center of struggles over representation, if not power.

GLOBAL TRENDS: SEGMENTING AND CONTAINING THE MARKET

A final issue behind the growth and development of the Hispanic marketing industry that I will consider in this chapter involves the greater advertising industry and some of the larger trends affecting its development. Most Hispanic agencies in New York City and beyond were first founded as independent entities to market products to what was until the 1980s seen as an untapped and ignored population. Yet the Hispanic advertising industry was never free from linkages with corporate structures nor from the influence of mainstream advertising agencies and trends. Recall the previous involvement of Cuban and later Mexican founders of U.S. agencies with transnational advertising agencies in their home countries. Similarly, the founder of SAMS, which is commonly regarded by advertisers as the first specialized, independent advertising agency for Hispanics in this country, originally worked with Goya products, thus evidencing the corporate and external links that affected the history of the industry. Moreover, the decentralization and expansion of many of the New York City agencies in the United States often occurred in response to the needs of specific clients who wanted to expand to these markets. Siboney, for example, prior to opening its offices in New York and focusing on the U.S. Hispanic market, had operated in Puerto Rico and moved American brands throughout Latin America.

However, since the mid-1970s, global trends in advertising affecting the general advertising and marketing industry have had an increasing impact on the Hispanic marketing industry in particular. Specifically, a renewed emphasis on segmented and targeted marketing along the lines of age, gender, race, or ethnicity (Turow 1997), as well as on integrated, or "one-stop," marketing, has directly impinged on Hispanic marketing and on the operations of Hispanic agencies. On the one hand, interest in segmented and targeted marketing facilitated the relatively rapid success of this industry, whose interest in the development of a specialized market coincided with the general trend toward market segmentation of the times (Leiss et al. 1997).[24] The flip side of this trend, however, is that by generating interest in Hispanics as a specialized market, the Hispanic advertising industry became a particularly attractive target for mergers and buyouts by major transnational agencies. Concurrent with the general interest in one-stop marketing, the acquisition of Hispanic and other culture-specific agencies targeting Asian Americans and African Americans would become a common strategy through which transnational advertising networks sought to consolidate a variety of services and markets within their own firms and attain instant expertise and credibility in ethnic marketing. The acquisition of Hispanic agencies allowed advertising conglomerates to assure their corporate clients of the standardization of strategy and message for products across different audience segments— an increasingly common demand in the industry at large. Furthermore, by incorporating them as minority-owned entities within the greater conglomerate, corporate clients could shield their efforts with a veil of "political correctness" when appealing to the minority consumer (Mendosa 1989).

Additional interest in the Hispanic market by global advertising conglomerates was triggered by a sudden public recognition of Hispanics in mainstream society throughout the 1980s. Spurred by a series of developments, including the sharp rise in the number of Hispanics revealed in the 1980 census, a 1978 *Time* magazine special report declaring that Hispanics would soon become the nation's largest minority, and the establishment of Hispanic Heritage Month in 1988,[25] the 1980s were touted as the "Hispanic Decade," arousing interest in Hispanics as consumers. This was also the time when multiculturalism was being popularized as a political discourse, which further contributed to corporate America's interest in Hispanics as a culturally specific marketing niche. This was evident both in the rise of advertising budgets for Hispanic advertising throughout the 1980s and the launching of "ethnic" and Hispanic marketing departments by major corporations such as Anheuser-Busch, Miller, Procter & Gamble, and Coca-Cola.[26] Signs of this development were obvious among Hispanic advertising agencies in New York, as most of the early Cuban-owned ad agencies were either bought by or merged with transnational advertising agencies seeking to stake a claim in a booming market.[27] The result is that today, although there are still a number of independent agencies in the city and new ones are always emerging, the industry has increasingly become dominated by transnational advertising and publicity conglomerates.

Widespread interest in the Hispanic market is similarly evident in the general media and marketing industry at large, which has seen an explosion of new magazines, publications, and media initiatives geared to Latinas (Brody 1998; Wilke 1998). Thus we see Time Warner publishing *People en Español,* Essence Communication's endorsement of *Latina,* the launching of Hispanic consumer lists by Telemarketing and List/Database companies, all part of a boom in media initiatives for Hispanics. Since the 1970s, the number of publications for Hispanics has increased by 219 percent, and since 1990 Hispanic-oriented radio stations have doubled to 594 (Whisler and Nuiry 1998). At the same time, minority media ownership continued to decrease to its current low of 3 percent (Broadcasting and Cable 1998), and is likely to further decrease as a result of the 1996 Telecommunications Act, which was devised to increase competition by reducing ownership restrictions and hence increase media buyouts.[28]

A direct result of these developments is that Hispanic advertising is increasingly a transnational issue, where global and localized marketing forces intersect in the creation and sustenance of a Latina/Hispanic identity in this country. This situation has increasingly immersed Hispanic advertising agencies within the same structures that many sought either to change or provide an alternative for, and it has added pressures, restrictions, and layers to their production of Hispanic images in advertising. It is, of course, difficult to describe accurately the range of relationships between main agencies and their subsidiary Hispanic shops. In some cases, representatives of the Hispanic shops I spoke with asserted that they were able to maintain a measure of independence from their owners, that they were able to obtain independent accounts, and that this has even allowed for more diversity of clients or greater professional legitimacy vis-à-vis the advertising community at large. One account executive explained that "it makes a huge difference when we tell our clients that we enjoy the resources of the larger agency. We may end up having to fight to have access to those larger structures, but the name association helps our pitch." Most often, however, this situation has directly eroded the turf of the specialized Hispanic agencies, placing them in direct competition with the contacts and resources of the general market agencies as well as other Hispanic agencies. As an account executive who had resigned from a Hispanic agency after its merger with a transnational entity succinctly explained, "These big agencies are acquiring Hispanic agencies because it looks good politically, but what they really want to do is control the market. They are not going to let go of corporate monies; they want to keep it for themselves, and this is how they do it." This same informant complained about the peripheral position of the acquired Hispanic agencies within the larger entity, which, she claimed, never included them in their pitches to new clients, and often tried to develop an ad requested by a client for the Hispanic market without consulting the Hispanic agency, or else reduced its role to translating ads done by the main branch. She concluded that these mergers have added another layer of people that Hispanic advertisers have to "educate" about the Hispanic market: "We are constantly giving people lessons in Hispanic 101."

Most agencies, however, are not complaining about the buyouts. At the annual meeting of the Association of Advertising agencies held in New York City in 1998, I even overheard discussions about how to make one's agency more attractive for potential buyouts, although in the late 1990s advertising conglomerates apparently prefer not to buy Hispanic shops, as they did in the 1980s, but to hire staff to lead Hispanic campaigns within their agencies, directly challenging the turf of the independent Hispanic advertising agency.

This changing context has also triggered transformations in the Hispanic advertising industry. Until the 1970s, Hispanic advertisers recalled, they worked in a relatively informal environment. Lack of research was customary, and an almost "family-like" environment existed among all Hispanic advertisers, who knew each other and worked in a competitive but nonetheless closely knit context. As Daisy Exposito, founder and still director of Bravo, one of the largest U.S. Hispanic agencies, recalled nostalgically, "When the people from Univision would come in to sell programs, it was not a sale but a reunion. They were all Latinas and *muchachones* [endearment for young men]. We would sit in an office to brainstorm about which advertiser could fund a new program. If my clients were not a good fit for a promotion, we would think of Castor (owner of Castor Advertising) or another agency. We were buddies, not competitors. These were certainly the most fun-filled years this industry has seen," she concluded, remembering the sense of camaraderie that was strengthened by ties of ethnicity and friendship among the first generation of mostly Cuban Hispanic advertisers.

Today, the environment is more competitive, and agencies find themselves increasingly pressed to define their boundaries and differentiate themselves to assure not only their own survival, but that of ethnic and Hispanic marketing itself. In this context, advertising agencies are selling not only a market but also each other, against each other. Following the general tendency towards segmentation and specialization, Hispanic advertising agencies are now positioning themselves as experts in different regional markets or else distinguishing their strategies, tactics, methods, or expertise in different product categories or promotional strategies.

In reality, however, the industry is becoming more and more uniform. Its nationwide growth has been accompanied by the downplaying of regional, geographical, and even cultural differences as criteria for the design of nationwide Hispanic campaigns. Additionally, a constant shift of staff from one Hispanic agency to another within and across regional markets has drawn the industry closer together. As stated by Al Aguilar, head of San Antonio–based Bromley Aguilar and 1998 president-elect of the Association of Hispanic Advertising Agencies, irrespective of the background of their creative staff, their geographic location, or their particularities, the main "talent" of Hispanic agencies is to bridge different backgrounds and nationalities. As he noted, Hispanic creatives are the first globalizers, long accustomed to generating representations of multiple nationalities; whether in New York, Los Angeles, or Miami, the reference for any Hispanic agency is always the abstract ideal of "Hispanics" as an undifferentiated totality.

The industry's growing consolidation is also evident in the formation of the Association of Hispanic Advertising Agencies in 1997, the first trade organization for Hispanic advertising agencies. With a mission to help "grow, strengthen, and protect the Hispanic marketing and advertising industry by providing leadership in raising awareness of the value of the Hispanic market opportunities and enhancing the professionalism of the industry," this organization has gathered some of the most important Hispanic agencies nationwide with the common goal of expanding revenues within a larger and more competitive environment. In particular, the organization advocates the use of "specialists," such as the association's own member agencies, in light of the growing number of agencies and consultant companies that are now also seeking to target this market. And to make sure that it comprises only Hispanic agencies, full membership is open only to advertising agencies devoted solely to the Hispanic market. While some criticized the inclusion of Hispanic advertising divisions of general market agencies, these too were accepted as full members as long as they had 75 percent of total billing in the Hispanic market, employed a significant percentage (65 percent and over) of Hispanic staff, and offered full services in the Hispanic market. The importance of this exclusive emphasis on Hispanic agencies becomes clear when we consider that AHAA's inception has been accompanied by the growth of multicultural marketing groups, such as Vanguard in New York and Cultural Access Group (multicultural marketing research), which are targeting Hispanics alongside Asian Americans and African Americans and thus providing an alternative to Hispanic-centered initiatives.

However, several trends in the general market are unlikely to be affected by formal organizations of Hispanic agencies. Though at a minimal rate when compared to the so-called general market, advertising expenditures in Hispanic marketing continue to rise—*Hispanic Business* reports that major advertisers are increasing their budgets to Hispanics (some at a rate of 400–700 percent), and that expenditures will reach $1.7 billion in 1998—but this money is being chased by a larger number of players and affected by larger advertising trends (Zate 1998a, 1998b). In addition, the ongoing segmentation of the mainstream market is increasingly encroaching on the traditional boundaries of the ethnic-based category of Hispanic. An example is the popular appeal of urban youth styles and the rise of the categories of "urban markets" and "urban lifestyles" and their effects on the urban-centered yet ethnic core of Hispanic marketing. This trend has led to the cancellation of ethnic marketing departments by major advertisers such as Coca-Cola and Miller Brewing, who now see in an "urban youth style" an important commonality that bridges different ethnic and racial segments in the city (Minority Markets Alert 1997). Globalization also requires greater synergy between general market and ethnic efforts, which favors the hiring of shops that are part of larger transnational advertising conglomerates rather than independent Hispanic agencies.[29] For their part, Hispanic marketers are responding by positioning themselves as experts in both worlds, able to produce ads for Hispanics as well as the mainstream market, compared to mainstream agencies whose own closed-mindedness and prejudices, they argue, have made them irrelevant. Adapting ads from Hispanic shops for the mainstream market is still more of an exception than a rule, although the fact that Hispanic-made ads are generally 60 percent cheaper than mainstream ads is likely to facilitate the crossover between markets.

Meanwhile, the Latinization of mainstream America, evident in the popularization of Hispanic culture, language, and cultural icons as marketing tools and icons for mainstream audiences—the "salsa is beating ketchup" phenomenon—is also challenging the assumption that Hispanic culture is to be used exclusively to market to Hispanics. In the mainstream channels one can now hear rumba rhythms in Burger King ads, see soccer scenes and Salma Hayek advertising Pepsi and Revlon, and recoil at the infamous Chihuahua appealing to the Argentinean revolutionary Che Guevara in order to sell Taco Bell, along with other crossover ads that, with or without subtitles, are using Latinidad and things distinctively Hispanic to sell to both Hispanic and non-Hispanic audiences. These developments involve a variety of old and new media, clients, and interests profiting from Hispanics and elaborating images of and for this market that are likely to challenge the traditional boundaries of Hispanic marketing. All these developments, however, are predicated on some definite ideas about the identity of the Hispanics who are being sold to or sought as targets, and to these ideas I now turn.

CHAPTER 2

Knowledges

Facts and Fictions of a People as a Market

> Generally they have a strong regard for the family and
> maintain close kinship ties across the generations. . . . Most
> intangibly, Latinos offer the U.S. an amalgam of buoyancy,
> sensuousness, and flair that many northern peoples find
> tantalizing or mysterious—and sometimes irritating or
> threatening.
>
> *Time* magazine (1978)

> The factor that stands out as one reads through these cases is
> that the U.S. Hispanic market is DIFFERENT from the general
> market.
>
> Roslow and Therrein Decker (1997)

Having reviewed some recurring issues affecting the Hispanic marketing industry, let us now turn to the issue of definition and attempt to address who is a Latino/Hispanic and what constitutes the so-called Hispanic market. To do so, we need to investigate the particular knowledges
and understandings of the market that inform the work of Hispanic agencies and advertisers in the industry at large. I refer to the stereotypes,
clichés, and dominant ideas about Hispanics that are circulated in the
industry, which give form to the "truth" about Hispanic consumers, informing their representation and the ways they are sold to prospective
clients. As the director of a New York shop stated, "These are the ideas
that we have been hearing for a long time and that we've ended up be-
lieving out of truth, custom, or repetition." As we shall see, these ideas
have limited the range of innovation within the industry, shaping an un-

complicated but highly marketable picture of the Hispanic consumer that leaves stereotypes virtually unchallenged.

Of course, by focusing on the popular perceptions about Hispanics that are generated in the Hispanic advertising industry, I am not suggesting that Hispanics are reducible to mere ideas. While my discussion will attempt a general critique of research, statistics, and other forms of sanctioned knowledge generated in this industry to construct the "Hispanic consumer," I do not intend to argue that, once conceived as an essentialized construct, general socioeconomic or demographic conclusions cannot be drawn about any particular population. As Foucault would put it, part and parcel of constructing individuals as subjects involves the acquisition of knowledges that ease the operations of power to effect, describe, mold, and constitute through statistics, surveys, and/or reports. Hence, I will be concerned not with the empirical accuracy of such categories but with their use and with the ways in which knowledges about Hispanics as consumers are continually abstracted from context and manipulated into conventions about "Hispanic customs and attitudes" as part of the process of selling the market to prospective clients. It is precisely through such statistics and market reviews—attesting that Hispanics are highly informed shoppers, or else gullible and extremely loyal to particular brands, or traditional, or hip and urban, according to the needs of the corporate client—that this population is continually stereotyped and constituted into an undifferentiated Hispanic consumer.[1]

The importance of such characterizations emerges when we consider that, as a result of the growing interest by advertisers in the Hispanic market, such ideas are increasingly circulated within corporate America and the public at large. We could even argue that knowledges and characterizations of the market promoted by experts on Hispanic marketing and supported by the variety of publications and reports on "how to market" to this population are even more influential than the actual advertising images aimed at Hispanics. These ideas permeate trade publications for the advertising, marketing, and media industry and, in contrast to social science and scholarly studies about Latinos or their contributions and/or subordination in this country, they are underwritten by corporate and private interests and so find their way into publications with widespread distribution and impact. Hispanic advertising and media professionals are also constantly surpassing the boundaries of their profession to become Hispanic or multicultural "experts" in corporate and nonprofit conventions and seminars, as well as in popular magazines like

Newsweek or *Time,* thereby directly affecting the public discourse and debate about Hispanics.[2] Thus, while it is obviously profit rather than politics that underlies marketing definitions of Hispanics, my interest in these categorizations stems from a recognition of the potential of "advertising discourse," embodied in research reports and in the opinions of Hispanic experts and corporate intellectuals, to shape attitudes toward and dominant definitions of Hispanics, not only among prospective clients but also within the context of U.S. society at large.

As discussed in chapter 1, cultural characterizations of the Hispanic market and of Hispanics as consumers are not new. After all, this is a market whose survival and growth always depended on some putative cultural characteristics shared among so-called Hispanics. During the early days of Hispanic advertising, most of these characterizations were drawn by Hispanic advertisers on the basis of their own instincts and experiences, and were rarely supported by research. Lack of both statistical data and public recognition of Hispanics' presence made advertising for this population an issue of "faith," as there was no way to demonstrate either the numbers or the cultural and social characteristics of the Hispanic consumer. Generalizations were also partly a function of the scarcity of advertising budgets for Hispanics. The first generation of ad executives I talked to recalled corporate clients expecting them to just know about the market—after all they too were Hispanics—rarely investing for research, as would be customary for the general market. Additionally, lack of research at this time was due to a general shift away from research within the advertising industry. As part of what Thomas Frank has described as a "cultural revolution," the 1960s saw the ad industry transform itself by co-opting "hipness" and youth culture, and by celebrating creativity over research, considered the symbol of "scientific authoritarianism" and an impediment to artistic creativity (Frank 1997: 92–96).

This situation facilitated the dissemination of very marketable generalizations about the Hispanic consumer during the industry's early years in the mid 1960s. One account manager, active for over twenty-five years, recalled how one of her supervisors successfully obtained a feminine napkin account with the argument that "Hispanic women bleed more because they are hot-blooded," convincing the Anglo corporate client to launch a special campaign for this market. Another admitted to having convinced a client to reconceive a campaign on the basis that "Hispanics don't like humor" and therefore would not appreciate the humorous strategy developed for a soap campaign for the general market. What convinced clients was the single most valuable selling tactic of the time: the "Latinness" of the founding figures of the industry, embodied in their charisma, behavior, and personality, which helped mark their authenticity and expertise in this nascent market. Staff who had worked with the likes of Pedro Font, founder of Font and Vaamont Advertising (FOVA), and Alicia Conill, of Conill Advertising, recalled how charmed their clients were when Alicia Conill greeted them with kisses—a transportation of Latin American greeting practices, not an overt practice of "tropicalization," which seemed to be the practice of the day. I was told that many would do "whatever it took," be it dance on a table or personify the Latino consumer, just to get corporate America to advertise to Hispanics as a differentiated market. As a former research associate at Univision recalled, the trend was that "if you want colorful and exotic, I'll give you colorful and exotic." I was never able to corroborate any story of dancing on a client's table, although these rumors certainly suggest the speculative context in which the first contemporary portrayals of the Hispanic consumer were born.

The performance of "Latinness" by Hispanic executives was also the order of the day at SIN. As a former staff member at Univision recalled, before the station signed up for national ratings through Nielsen, the station's only pitch to clients was that "Latinos were a heck of a lot of fun," and the way to prove this was by "wining and dining" clients based on what he described as the old rule that "the less quantifiable your value is, the better the wine you need to buy at dinner." As he noted,

> What the early pioneers did was to look for somebody inside the company who would just have a great time doing this Hispanic thing and make sure that they had as much fun as possible. Hispanic marketing is the only industry in the world with a spring break, with Calle Ocho, which became a very important part of the whole maturation process of this industry. There people saw a whole coherent marketing community, and a street of vendors, and a million people that would come down to attend the three days of parties at Miami Beach. All you needed to do was to take the brand manager to Miami, get him drunk, keep him drunk dancing salsa with beautiful women, stuff like that. And then you'd take them to the event on Sunday where you'd see a million people waiting for product samples in lines that went on for hours, and they all came back saying, "Hey, this Hispanic market thing is pretty amazing."

One result of this lack of market research was the dissemination of generalized assessments about the Hispanic consumer that were ultimately based on the self-image, class background, and experiences of Hispanic marketers. As generated by the Cuban advertisers that dominated the industry's growth, this was a view that revolved largely around the Hispanic Caribbean and the Spanish-dominant immigrant in the Northeast—a relatively recent immigrant population in contrast to Latinos in the West—as the prototype of the Hispanic. Lionel Sosa, Texas-born founder in the late 1970s of Bromley, Aguilar, and Associates, one of the first and largest agencies founded in the western United States, noted how this view hindered the industry's growth there, where there was a large population of mostly Mexican and English-speaking, not Spanish-dominant Latinos:

> They had convinced everyone that everybody is Cuban, Puerto Rican, or speaks Spanish, to the point that I had major difficulty in convincing clients that there were other types of Latinos. All jingles had a Caribbean beat or Cuban or Puerto Rican accent, and it's not that we did not like that music but that there was no room for other types of Latinos.

One of the first New York advertisers recalled that this image became so convincing that during nationwide advertising pitches, they had difficulty convincing clients, most of whom were located on the East Coast, that there were Latinos west of the Hudson River. Of course, this image was soon challenged by the advent of Hispanic marketing agencies in places like San Antonio and Los Angeles. There, another vision of the Hispanic consumer developed that was no less based on the personal experiences of those behind its production. For instance, Lionel Sosa's agency, the first and still one of the few agencies founded and led by a U.S.-born Mexican American, struggled to convince clients that there were also English-speaking Latinos who, like himself, had grown up bilingual in this country—although this alternative definition of the market never came close to eclipsing the dominant picture forged by the New York advertisers. What remained unchallenged, however, were the behavioral stereotypes that accompanied this early image of the Hispanic as a family-oriented, Catholic, traditional, conservative, and immigrant Spanish-speaking individual or, put in a harsher guise, the stereotype of the "tradition-bound, Spanish-speaking recent arrival who eats a lot, is suicidally brand-loyal, prefers audio-visual media, has a large family, does not venture beyond his ghetto-like environment, and really gets turned on by 'his culture' " (Balkan 1982: 25). As will become evident in this chapter, these ideas have constituted a convincing and nearly insurmountable definition of Hispanic identity up to the present, and continue to be as dominant in contemporary advertising today as when it first began.

The persistence of these ideas has no simple explanation. As noted by Nederveen Pieterse (1992), images of "otherness" in the media function to render less threatening that which could otherwise represent a threat or alternative to the dominant social order. Accordingly, this unthreatening definition of Hispanics who remain in their place and with their culture, and who are conservative, traditional, and brand-loyal, is one that would be as attractive to corporate America as to mainstream U.S. society, and thus one that a variety of interests beyond Hispanic advertising professionals would be likely to support. After all, the Hispanic market would only "jibe" if Hispanics were packaged as "prospects, not suspects."

Nonetheless, I would like to suggest that the saliency of these definitions rests not on their profitability but rather on their history and on the way in which U.S.-generated images of the Hispanic consumer invoked dominant ideas held by both U.S. and Latin American corporate intellectuals. Specifically, the value-laden Hispanic individual and family were not new creations but the reformulation of motifs through which Latin American intellectuals imagined themselves and projected ideas of Latin American commonality from the early 1900s onwards. In light of the growing ascendancy of the United States in the Americas, Latin American intellectuals had long developed theories of the greater worth of the Latin American civilization compared to U.S. materialism, lack of culture, and greater technological advancement, establishing in this manner "culture" as Latinos primary "domain of sovereignty" (Chatterjee 1986).[3] By emphasizing Hispanic identity's moral component, as embodied in the respect for family, religion, and tradition, advertisers simply followed the same dichotomous frameworks around which Latin American middle- and upper-class intellectuals had defined what is Latin American: more moral, spiritual, and "whole" than the materialistic American culture (Fernández Retamar 1979). These ideas were congruent with the ways in which Americans had constructed Latin American populations from the nineteenth century on, although, seen from the standpoint of the United States, these were the very traits that made these populations appear ripe for and in need of U.S. colonization, modernization, or incorporation (Johnson 1980).

The dominant picture of the Hispanic consumer was therefore not an altogether original development. Instead, it is better regarded as an archetype, constituted by motifs that, while adaptable, persist across generations (Cashmore 1997: 28). In particular, the view of Hispanics as moral and traditional represents the modern equivalent of the "balance of superiorities" between Anglos and Hispanics that characterized dominant representations of Hispanidad. As succinctly put in a marketing presentation for Colgate toothpaste drafted by SAMS in the 1970s, "Hispanics have created a balance of superiorities within the society [United States]; we are superior in culture, emotional sensitivity, delicacies of life. They are superior in technology, modernization, functionality." Accordingly, marketing to Hispanics was an issue of communicating the superiority of American goods without "insulting Hispanic superiority," that is, by showing deference to Hispanic values and culture.

Not surprisingly, these culturalist generalizations would prove extremely successful and convincing among Anglo corporate clients. They would also prove pivotal in linking heterogeneous populations in imagining and constructing a nationwide Hispanic market. Beginning in the mid-1970s, this development quickly became the order of the day. Until 1976, Spanish network television was quite decentralized. Although owned by SIN, each SIN affiliate operated independently in terms of advertising; this meant that advertisers had to sell ads to each station, hindering the elaboration of nationwide campaigns for the whole market. In 1976, however, Univision (then SIN) became the first major broadcaster to distribute programming to its affiliates via domestic satellite (Subervi-Vélez 1994). This development contributed to the networking of SIN stations and affiliates throughout the country and, as previously stated, lent strong support to the idea of nationwide campaigns for the totality of the Hispanic market.

This task, however, was teeming with complications. Marketing insights drawn mostly by Cubans in relation to the populations of the East—in its majority a Caribbean Hispanic population of Puerto Ricans, Cubans, and later Dominicans—would often fail miserably when applied to the totality of the Hispanic market. The industry is full of such stories, some of which have attained almost folktale status. A telling example was related by a Cuban advertiser who, drawing on her immigrant experience, produced an ad in which a grandmother instructs her granddaughter about the wonders of a soap she had discovered when she first moved to this country. To her dismay, this ad was found to be offensive on the West Coast, where Latino heritage predates the very foundation of the United States. As she recalled, "This was a wake-up call. It showed how little we knew back then. This woman [a focus group participant] got up and after seeing the ad insisted that this was her country, the one that had been taken from her and that it was me who was the immigrant." Fox's examination of the development of Hispanic marketing provides another example of these misunderstandings, this one involving a marketing plan developed by a Cuban radio personality for the Phoenix, Arizona, market. The audience, mostly Mexican and Mexican American, found a marketing event revolving around a giant paella, popular among Cubans, offensive for its connotations of Spain (Fox 1996: 35–36). In this context, research became necessary not only to reveal and to manage differences among Hispanics, such as those involving food and musical tastes or politics, but also, as we shall see, to reinforce early myths of generalizable Hispanic values and culture. These would continue to linger and even prosper with research.

THE TURN TO RESEARCH

Today, knowledges about the Hispanic market are still produced by Hispanic advertising professionals and legitimated in relation to their generalizable knowledge. However, since the 1980s these generalizations increasingly have been corroborated and justified by research. Prior to this, there had been publications defining the different regional markets, and advertisers had conducted some local research. Alicia Conill, discussing the development of her New York agency from her New York City Eastside apartment, could still recall the 525 taped interviews she did by herself, dressed in "humble clothing with a dark-haired wig," which she used to pass unnoticed while visiting high-density Latino communities for research, reminding us again of the always-present disparity between Hispanic marketers and consumers. As she told me, this research was pivotal in convincing national brand advertisers like Campbell's Soup to advertise in the Hispanic market, allowing her to prove to her clients that Hispanics did use their products, although often in ways not intended by the manufacturer. She could still recall the bits of information she deployed in order to win the account, namely, information that emphasized the uniqueness of this market, in this case, the uncommon ways Hispanic used their products—that they cooked the soup without water, used it as *sofrito,* or a seasoned food base. However, while Conill's 525 interviews constituted an exception in an industry dominated by the attitude described to me by an executive as "I'm a Pérez; I have a mustache; I know about the Hispanic consumer," after the 1980s, research would become a central legitimating component of the industry. Behind this development, once more, were the Spanish TV networks (Univision, then SIN), which commissioned the first nationwide Hispanic market studies, such as Spanish USA, 1981 and 1984, conducted by the research company Yankelovich, Inc., to verify their national reach. They also helped promote and fund other research, such as the first national study of the Hispanic market by Miami-based Strategy Research Corporation and Guernica's (1982) *Reaching the Hispanic Market Effectively*, which, among other publications, provided a comprehensive view of Hispanic media, marketing, and research methods. Although not exempt from methodological problems, these studies began to imagine the Hispanic market as an essentially unified entity, marking a new trend toward legitimating the market through research.[4]

Feeding this trend was the standardization of research within the advertising industry at large, which was even more essential for the Hispanic advertising industry because of its peripheral position. Hispanic marketers were aware that they had to prove themselves, their strategies, and the existence of their market to their general market counterparts. A research analyst explained, "In our market people are just waiting for the first opportunity to discontinue their Hispanic efforts or find fault in your campaign. Doing research allowed us to speak in their language." Hispanic research has since become the staple of a variety of research consultation firms as well as of the advertising agencies themselves, which have developed their own research divisions since the late 1980s, and—increasingly and most influentially—of general market research companies, which have also opened their own Hispanic divisions. Yankelovich has been publishing its *Hispanic Monitor*, detailing Hispanic demographics, values, and attitudes, since 1988; Nielsen inaugurated its Hispanic Television Index, tracing their TV habits, in 1992; and Simmons introduced its studies of their purchasing patterns in 1995. Other important sources of research include the *Ethnic Market Report*, published since 1993, and Isabel Valdes and Marta Seoane's *Hispanic Market Handbook* (1995; and Valdes's 2000 version) which I commonly heard referred to as the "bible of Hispanic marketing"; both could be found in all the advertising agencies I visited. Of course, these research sources are minimal compared with what is available for the general market and, most important, they have also not been exempt from criticism. This industry still relies largely on secondary research, particularly what Roberta Astroff (1997) has called "popular para-ethnography," that is, marketing research that does not present itself as science and therefore provides more room for the reification of cultural characteristics through stereotypes and for their legitimization by the "authenticity" of its authors.[5]

The relative abundance of such para-ethnography as well as of facts and findings ensuing from research reports have conferred an unprecedented level of legitimacy on the Hispanic market among prospective clients. Research has finally lent Hispanic agencies the credibility of numbers provided by nationally recognized firms, such as Nielsen. Advertisers are now fully versed in the numbers game, which has made Hispanics a coveted target population for prospective marketers. Thus, almost everyone I talked to and every market report I read or conference I attended repeatedly informed me that Hispanics have grown by almost 50 percent since the 1980s, and that because of immigration and higher birthrates than in the general market, they are expected to double in the next twenty years; that they constitute nearly 11 percent of the U.S. population; and that if their growth continues as projected, they will constitute the largest minority group by the year 2020. Like any Latino studies scholar in the social sciences, or perhaps with even greater facility, marketers easily handled population numbers and projections for different U.S. cities, adjusted according to census post-enumeration surveys to account for the illegal and the undercounted. By selling the idea of a sizable Hispanic population, this industry has served as a voice against the ongoing omission of the undercounted and the illegal from public discourse, although, as we shall see, and notwithstanding their claims of all-inclusive Hispanic representation, it is only a particular type of Latino that this industry has been most keen on advancing. Numbers are also constantly tossed around to show that, imagined as yet another Latin American country, U.S. Hispanics would be the fifth largest and the richest. They are also described as younger than general market consumers, which makes them more flexible and more susceptible to advertising, and research shows that 75 percent of the Hispanic population is concentrated in the top five Hispanic Designated Market Areas (DMA's) of California, Texas, New York, Florida, and Illinois, making Hispanics a population that is geographically concentrated and thus easily targeted by advertising.[6] Research has also helped support dominant clichés about Hispanics that have been upheld in the industry from the outset. In comparison to the general market, Latinos are described as having strong traditional family values, with religion underpinning those values, and having high aspirational values common to recently arrived immigrants in this country. Research has thus not presented a more complicated picture than that of Guernica's 1982 study on the Hispanic market, in which the Hispanic world view was ultimately "shaped by three determining cultural characteristics: prevalent use of the Spanish language, close family ties, and strong adherence to Roman Catholicism," so that advertising to Hispanics simply involves utilizing these three encompassing concepts (124).

Still, research has complicated many of the simplistic views of the Hispanic consumer that had long been promoted. The same report validating the importance of family among Hispanics also documents that home and family values are "markedly higher" among foreign-born Hispanics, females, older Hispanics, and Cubans, but that the importance of family fell slightly below what had been reported in previous reports, pointing to the process of acculturation that is so feared by the industry at large (MDI / Yankelovich 1994). Research has also confirmed the growing number of English-speaking Hispanics, a revelation at odds with the Spanish-centered definition of the market, along with the fact that, contrary to the long-held myths of the traditional family, growing numbers of Hispanic households are headed by working women. Such contradictory pictures are obviously not limited to "Hispanic research" but are endemic to marketing research as an industry and to the technology of knowledge. We know, after all, that marketing research serves more to legitimize its practitioners in the eyes of their corporate clients than to make consumers any less imaginary (Lury 1994; Lury and Warde 1997).

Nonetheless, the contradictory nature of research represents an additional challenge to the Hispanic industry at large, as was evident to me every time I encountered marketing staff in complete denial of the changing market, and whenever I saw the range of strategies marketers used to interpret research to best fit their preconceived notions of the market.[7] As a director of research in one of the largest New York agencies explained, "People are just afraid. Now that research is beginning to challenge common understandings of the market, some people want to move away from research. What I tell them is that we don't have to leave research behind; we have to learn to present it in ways that are productive to the market." According to this research director, different Hispanic traits and characteristics could still be emphasized or downplayed according to whatever product is being marketed or the particular needs of specific corporate clients. Defining Hispanics for marketing purposes thus depends today, as it always has, on whatever audience is being targeted and which product is being sold: the definition arises from the right combination of research, generalizations, and clichés.

This is not to say that when placing so much importance on research, Hispanic advertisers are unaware of its limitations or of their own manipulations of its data.[8] As one owner of an ethnic market research company said when responding to my questions about the reliability of market research, "Figures lie, and liars figure." Indeed, the accuracy of research has long been the subject of criticism in the advertising and marketing industry at large, and Hispanic advertisers were just as quick to point to problems in market research as to show interest in more appropriate and revealing methodologies.[9] A trend that seemed to be in vogue during my research was that of "account planning," involving a more ethnographic/in-depth study of consumers' lifestyles and interaction with particular products. This trend made me—the anthropologist—particularly interesting to the advertising executives I talked to: they offered me jobs and asked me to lecture them on the basics of anthropological practice—which I did—so they could get a better understanding of this industry-wide turn to ethnographic research. Yet, despite a general awareness of its limits, research is still awarded a disproportionate level of legitimacy in the industry, and criticisms of it seldom go as far as doubting its methodological assumption or biases.

Contributing to this trend is the proprietary nature of most research studies, available only through purchase or subscription, or not at all outside the company that commissioned them. Their high costs mean that only the most profitable agencies have access to them; thus, these reports are not readily accessible to anyone interested in corroborating the data, methodology, or statistics that are used to back findings about and knowledges of the Hispanic consumer. For instance, *The Hispanic Market and How to Reach It*, a report of 192-plus pages published by Package Facts, a research agency based in New York City, costs $1,850; the Yankelovich *Hispanic Monitor*, a larger, statistical, attitudinal, cultural, and demographic study, can cost up to $13,000 for the book and $22,000 for the total sponsorship and presentation (all 1998 prices). As a result, only the major findings reach the level of public discourse, be it through the promotional releases put out by the research company itself to be published in marketing and advertising trade journals, or else through the interpretations and interventions of particular subscribers who use the data to back their marketing recommendations. The result, despite the legitimacy that advertisers seem to grant marketing research, is that its production, dissemination, and most of all its interpretation by advertisers are always tied to some type of marketing consideration and thus are neither apolitical nor unbiased. Granted, this is true of all forms of research, although it rings particularly true for marketing research, the costs and proprietary nature of which constrain analyses of its production and of the interests behind it. In this context, determining the accuracy or legitimacy of a research tool is far less fruitful than considering some of the different maneuvers to which it may be subject in practice.

MANEUVERS IN THE MARKET

Marketing presentations assembled by advertising agencies for their clients are considered extremely confidential, because in them advertisers communicate their own "take" or philosophy of the craft of Hispanic marketing. During my research, however, I was able to review a number of these presentations for products as varied as beer, soft drinks, cars, and shampoo, and while each presentation was customized for the needs of particular products, I found that all tended to follow a similar structure and that they addressed similar thematic concerns, which makes them useful introductions to the facts, figures, and general understanding behind the conceptualizations of advertising campaigns for this market.

Specifically, these documents were full of examples of the multiple ways in which marketers interpret and manipulate research in the process of selling the market. One example concerns their projection of the Hispanic market as one that is profitable, that has purchasing power, but that nonetheless remains authentically and culturally Hispanic. Dominant stereotypes of Hispanics in mainstream society revolve around the poor and welfare-dependent population—views that repel corporate clients, who are interested in middle-class and affluent consumers, and have long challenged advertising executives to convince them that Hispanics are indeed a worthy target population. To this end, those selling the market have sought to promote the idea of Hispanics' growing affluence by pointing to the considerable growth in their household incomes during the past fifteen years. According to the Yankelovich *Hispanic Monitor,* for instance, the purchasing power of U.S. Hispanics more than doubled from 1982 to 1993, from $104 to $221 billion, while the Association of Hispanic Marketing Agencies estimates that Latinos now make up a $380 billion market (Riley 2000).

Similarly, images of affluence are always portrayed or alluded to in media kits and reports selling "Hispanics" to prospective advertisers. Telemundo's 1997 presentation video for prospective advertisers, for instance, shows images of affluent and well-dressed Hispanics shopping in upscale boutiques with a backdrop of numbers and figures attesting to the growing buying power of Hispanic consumers. Images of Hispanic affluence, however, are greatly distorted. For one, this image is directly at odds with the economic reality of most Latinos, whose incomes may have increased over the past decade but nevertheless remain low relative to nationwide standards. (Not surprisingly, charts of Hispanic affluence are never matched with income figures for non-Hispanic whites, whose median annual income, at $42,439, far exceeds that of Hispanics [U.S. Census Bureau 1998]). Latinos are still among the poor of this country, with 25.6 percent (versus 8.2 percent for whites) living in poverty and largely trapped in low-wage jobs or unemployment (U.S. Census Bureau 1998). Moreover, images of affluence mask not only the growing inequality between whites and Latinos, but also the inequality existing within and across Latino subgroups. "Affluence" is more representative of the U.S.-born Hispanic than it is of the foreign-born, and also varies greatly along the lines of nationality or according to the contexts in which particular nationalities migrated (the best known example is that of the greater affluence of early Cuban immigrants in relation to the 1980s *marielito* counterpart, who were mostly working-class immigrants, and in relation to Mexican and Puerto Rican populations; see Nelson and Tienda 1997).[10] Income levels also vary along lines of nationality and language use. Hispanics' buying power is lowest among Mexicans, and highest among Cubans; their yearly earnings are $15,072 versus $24,012 respectively (López 1998). While Los Angeles, which is primarily Mexican, may be the largest Hispanic market, its size stems from the strength of numbers not from Latino affluence, which is concentrated in the Miami/South Florida area (Hispanic 1999). English-speaking Latinos and U.S.-educated Latinos also attract higher incomes than Spanish-dominant Latinos. The problem, however, is that these are the very Hispanics who are at odds with dominant generalizations about the market: Spanish-speaking, traditional, and foreign-born. As stated before, the foreign-born, while generally poorer, are considered the most authentic Hispanics, the most likely to be Spanish-dominant and to uphold the traditional values that are supposedly shared by all Hispanics. In projecting the idea of the affluent but culture-bound Hispanic, we thus have one of many mélanges that are constructed in the process of selling the market: a construction involving the higher income of the U.S.-born cloaked in the authenticity of the foreign-born, which only becomes apparent when we ignore the intraclass variation among U.S. Latinos.

Indeed, a consistent problem in marketing research on Hispanics is its lack of attention to issues of class and the reduction of so-called Hispanic traits to culture-bound generalizations. Isabel Valdes and Marta Seoane, in their *Hispanic Market Handbook* (1995; and Valdes 2000), used in many marketing presentations as a resource on the psychographic and value orientation of Latinos, provide one of many examples of this trend. While full of caveats about the dangers of homogenizing Hispanics as one undifferentiated population, they nonetheless engage freely in this type of cultural generalization. In one of many "snapshots" of Hispanic values and cultural characteristics, they describe Hispanics as seeing themselves as part of a group, relying mostly on family, friends, and community, respecting their elders, having obedient and dependent children, upholding defined and hierarchical roles, and characterized by male dominance or machismo, in contrast to Anglos, who supposedly see themselves as individuals, rely on themselves and institutions rather than on family, and stress symmetry and democracy in interpersonal and in cross-gender relationships. While the validity of such generalizations and the sharp dichotomy in values are certainly to be questioned, what I want to call attention to here is the fact that Anglos are class-identified as "American middle class," with class becoming the primary basis for defining them, while no information is provided on the class background dominant in Hispanic samples. In this model, culture is always triumphant over class among Latinos, which makes it irrelevant to identify them by class, since they are all culturally the same, while Anglo-Americans are devoid of culture. As a result, the extent to which so-called Hispanic traits and values are more class-related than culture-based is never addressed. Are lower-class Hispanics perhaps more similar in terms of values or shopping behaviors to their African American, or Asian American, or general market counterparts than to upscale Hispanics? These questions are rarely addressed in research that treats these markets as segregated and isolated from one another.

Hispanics are also consistently presented as the most brand-loyal of consumers, though I was never given a single explanation about why and in relation to whom they are considered more loyal. We are never told if this "loyalty" stems from a lack of choice in brand availability in different markets, or is related to price or to any variable other than to Latinos traditionality and conservatism. And this is not without consequence. If consumption is indeed the one arena where we are told that contemporary citizens are actually heard, then the construction of Latinos and other minorities as brand-loyal ultimately renders them as the most passive, uncritical, and unselective of consumers and hence of citizens.[11]

Yet what is undoubtedly the most highly debated and manipulated issue is the level of acculturation and language use of Hispanics. This has been a constant source of debate and contention given that, since its origins, the dominant view in the Hispanic marketing industry is that Hispanics speak Spanish and thus that Hispanics respond, understand, and connect more efficiently to messages that are transmitted in "their language." This nativist view of language is backed by most research publications on how to market to Hispanics, from Guernica's 1982 report, which argued that "the most universal and culturally unifying characteristic of U.S. Hispanics is their use of Spanish" (124), to Strategy Research Corporation's *U.S. Hispanic Market Study* (1998) and more recent publications which, beyond lifestyles, educational levels, or length of residence in the United States, consider language the primary variable for determining levels of acculturation among Hispanics. This view is backed by the Spanish networks, where the Spanish language plays a symbolic role in corroborating Latino/Hispanic identity. This emphasis, however, is also guided by the corporate clients' marketing plans and priorities for reaching the maximum number of potential consumers. Convinced that Latinos who are English-dominant or bilingual are already being reached through mainstream media, corporations almost always approach Hispanic marketing agencies having already decided to limit their marketing efforts to Latino consumers who are Spanish-speaking. Faced with these pressures, all advertising presentations include a statement explaining that Spanish is the preferred language for all Hispanics, some being more emphatic about Hispanics' use of or proficiency in this language, but all stressing that Hispanics speak Spanish and that they will continue to do so, and that the best way of reaching and connecting with them is through "their language." Even if they do not speak it, Latinos are hence deemed to be symbolically moved and touched by Spanish, reproducing essentialist equations of Latinos with their language.[12] The irony that remains unstated is that such language purity is an unattainable goal in the world of advertising, where U.S. products are being advertised and where product names—all in English—necessarily fill the airwaves with English names and Spanglish phrases.

Yet another vector creating images and knowledges of Hispanics/Latinos are the different Hispanic-targeted media, which also produce and disseminate research through media kits and marketing materials. Primary among them is Univision, which has been a strong supporter of the prevailing view of the Spanish-dominant Hispanic consumer and has long been a strong advocate of research. This emphasis is evident in its media kit, which includes a colorful and handy supplement, "The U.S. Hispanic Market in Brief," a document used by many advertising agencies as a reliable research resource, as well as a "fact sheet" listing the latest Nielsen ratings and the ranking of its programs in different time-slots. These materials stress that 90 percent of U.S. Hispanics speak Spanish, that two-thirds of U.S. Hispanic adults are foreign-born, and that 47.6 percent of the Hispanic population is Spanish-dominant. Having defined the market in this manner, the material goes on to claim that "Univision covers 92.1 percent of U.S. Hispanic households coast to coast," and that Univision has an 87 percent prime-time share of Hispanic households versus Telemundo's 13 percent. In reality, however, Univision's 87 percent prime-time share is not based on the total Hispanic market but on the percentage of Hispanic viewers watching Spanish television, which according to the Nielsen ratings, can range from 25 percent to 40 percent depending on the season. It is only out of this percentage that Univision can claim its 87 percent share of viewers. Similarly, the statement claiming that Univision covers 92.1 percent of Hispanic households is based on the fact that 92.1 percent of these households have access to Univision, not that they actually watch it, although this is not made explicit in the media kit materials. As regards the percentage of foreign-born Hispanics, only among adults is this percentage as high as two-thirds of the population, not among youth, which the same report claims is the fastest growing segment of the total Hispanic population. The point here, however, is not Univision's self-serving manipulation of numbers, but that it constructs the totality of Hispanics out of one or another of its segments. Univision makes a part—its part—into the whole. That is, these statistics not only corroborate Univision's dominance among Hispanic viewers, but also convey that Univision's viewers are the totality of the Hispanic population, hereby defined as the Spanish-speaking, Univision-watching consumer.

The portrait of the foreign-born and Spanish-dominant Hispanic that watches only Univision or Telemundo has not gone unchallenged. This view has received much criticism because of its significance to the other interests seeking also to tap into the market. BBDO's annual study on Hispanics' viewing of English-language network television, for instance, has long noted that Hispanics "watch as much—if not more—English-language television than Spanish-language, even though their viewing preferences differ from those of the general market" (Burgi 1994: 11). Univision's dominance also faces the potential challenge of new media, which are now claiming interest in younger and second- and third-generation Hispanic segments—those who have grown up in the United States watching American sitcoms and who may be less attracted to soap operas or to Latin American programming (more detailed discussion appears in chapter 4).

Specifically, the dominance of Spanish as the defining element of the market has been challenged by radio and print, cheaper and more adaptable media. In what has been called a "magazine boom," a variety of new publications have been launched in the last five years that target Hispanics, many of which challenge dominant definitions of the market with bilingual formats specifically geared to the more "acculturated market" (Nuiry 1996b). In doing so, they are creating different "knowledges" of the identity, needs, and desires of the Hispanic consumer through the same process of generalizing the totality of Hispanics out of one segment or another. In contrast to the networks, media kits for bilingual magazines increasingly stress the bilingual and bicultural experiences of most Hispanics, creating new "knowledges" about these consumers. The media kit for *Hispanic,* for instance, quotes the U.S. census to stress that 22 percent of all Hispanics speak only English, that 74 percent of Spanish-speaking Hispanics "speak English very well," and that 61 percent of Hispanics were born in the United States (*Hispanic* media kit, 1997). For its part, *Moderna*'s media kit, besides detailing the high number of Latinas who regularly use foundation and mascara, emphasizes that 74 percent of its readership was born in the United States and 76 percent prefers to read in English (*Moderna* media kit, 1997). Similarly, *Urban,* aimed at the second- and third-generation youth market through articles on hip-hop personalities, Latino fraternities, and the evolution of graffiti murals, presents its constituency as the young, mobile, professional, English-dominant Latino. Again, the issue here is not whether the numbers are real or not. These conclusions are based on proprietary studies of their readers that are not shared among competing media, or else on similar sources that are given different emphasis and interpretation. The range of bilinguals, for instance, can be easily presented as English-dominant (as *Hispanic* magazine does) or Spanish-dominant (as does Univision). Rather, the point is that in reference to particular constituencies, different knowledges and definitions of the Hispanic population are generated through the same process of generalizing about the totality of Hispanics on the basis of a particular segment of that totality.

However, the proliferation of research and competing generalizations about Hispanics has also backfired in disrupting the consistent and salable portrait of this population for prospective clients. As a director of research in one of the ad agencies explained, most of their corporate clients are "Anglos from Iowa" who are prejudiced against and skeptical about marketing to Hispanics, and who, faced with research that contradicts what they had heard about Hispanics being a homogenous and marketable construct, are more than likely to discontinue any Hispanic marketing effort. She recalled a case in which a "sure sell" was lost because the client got confused after being presented with different statistics and numbers about Hispanics, not only from competing agencies but also from different departments within her agency. Such occurrences have led the AHAA (Association of Hispanic Advertising Agencies) to make the standardization of research a top priority for the organization, although the effort is doomed by this industry's essential function of selling through culture-bound generalizations.

The problems created by the different "knowledges" generated by the rise of research were highlighted during the 1998 annual meeting of the AHAA when a panel for a forum entitled "The Changing Latin Face of New York" included two speakers whose definitions of the New York market were directly at odds. New York's Designated Market Area (or DMA, based on Nielsen specifications) also includes parts of New Jersey and Connecticut, excluding most of upstate New York. Yet as noted by one of the speakers, what clients and advertisers mean by "New York" may vary greatly, as will the statistical portrayal of the New York Hispanic consumer when defined in geographic or market terms. Specifically, portrayals based on New York's statistics, defined in purely geographical terms, will reveal a more depressed picture of Hispanics as consumers than those that include the entire New York media market, which spans suburban Latino populations in Connecticut and New Jersey. As an ad executive stated, the strict geographic definition would suggest that "we are all from the ghetto"—hence the industry's concern with promoting the designated market rather than the geographical definitions of the city. Never mind that only in the imagined community conjured up by marketers are the inhabitants of New Jersey, Connecticut, the Bronx, Brooklyn, and Manhattan Latinos all "New Yorkers."

AND DON'T FORGET THAT WE ALL EAT RICE AND BEANS (OR *HABICHUELAS, POROTES, FRIJOLES . . .*)

So far I have stressed that advertisers and media executives selling to Hispanics are extremely concerned with the promotion and presentation of a comprehensive and generalizable picture of the Hispanic consumer, at least one that is consistent with the particular needs of clients and their products. However, reminiscent of Foucaldian technologies and strategies of power, managing the heterogeneity of Hispanics by exalting and organizing differences has also become a way of constituting the market as a unique and manageable entity. Specifically, the growing recognition of difference among Hispanics by the media and the Hispanic advertising industry alike has been accompanied by the consolidation of an intricate system of typifications to manage and contain this difference, and to screen out what are viewed as nonauthentic Latinos from definitions of "Hispanic," in ways that secure bases of commonalities and the perpetuation of "authentic Hispanics."

A case in point concerns the increasingly popular categorization of Latinos/Hispanics along the axis of language use or level of acculturation by marketers and research strategists. In light of the growing recognition of Hispanics' bilingual and bicultural lives, most advertising agencies and research agencies have developed systems for categorizing these differences in order to present a more complex picture of Hispanics. Accordingly, the use of Spanish is increasingly presented not as a matter of dependency but also of preference, which provides a more fluid understanding of how Hispanics communicate in different settings. Based on a categorization of what is the dominant level of comfort, dependence, or preference in speaking a particular language—with language serving as the paramount proxy for acculturation—agencies can determine levels of acculturation in different segments of the population as well as receptivity to particular media strategies.[13]

These distinctions have not only facilitated the manipulation and selective use of segments of the "Hispanic" population but, most significantly, have provided new axes with which to market differences, such as through social and personality characterizations. One example of this trend is Dieste and Partners' breakdown of Hispanics into psychographic segments: Traditional, Conformists, Recent Seekers, Young Strivers, and Established Adapters. In this schema, levels of acculturation correspond to particular attitudes, language use, and income levels. Accordingly, the foreign-born and less acculturated are perceived as more fatalistic and conformist, whereas the most acculturated are defined by their greater aspirations, success, and income (Roslow and Therrien Decker 1998). Such definitions are obviously informed by the same dichotomies of representation along the Anglo/Hispanic axes that I have discussed throughout this chapter, although when applied to differences among Latinos, their negative undertones become more apparent. The model seems to suggest that the more Latino/a (and hence traditional) one is, the more fatalistic and conformist one also is, and that only through "acculturation" can Latinos rid themselves of such negative traits. Besides the obvious problem of reducing the complex phenomena of acculturation to quantifiable variables that may or may not match the associations drawn by marketers for marketing purposes, I want to stress here that, upon closer examination, the categorization of Hispanics according to language use or acculturation levels often surfaces as a tool to preselect sample groups according to dominant definitions of the market. That is, these categorizations also facilitate the preselection for research purposes of monolingual Hispanics, which are considered the source of authenticity, the ones who update and renew the market, perpetuating the image of the static, unchanged, Spanish-speaking Hispanic who is so attractive to the dominant media, constituted by the Spanish networks, as well as to prospective clients.[14]

Indeed, during focus group sessions, Spanish-dominant Hispanics were commonly chosen as the yardstick for all Hispanics, at the cost of other categories of Hispanics, because marketers and advertisers alike were determined to create a TV ad whose only home would be a Spanish network. As the director of a New York–based market research firm explained, "Most clients interested in research make it clear that it is Spanish-dominant and regular consumers of Spanish media that they are most interested in recruiting. The problem is that they are constantly contradicting themselves. They want people [research subjects] who speak perfect Spanish but who have been here for over 2–3 years and are familiar with U.S. products." She went on to explain what had become their common solution to this quandary: the selection of Dominican participants who "tended to keep the language better," while limiting the number of "acculturated" Puerto Ricans, and keeping some extra subjects ready in the unfortunate case that one of the participants begins to break into Spanglish, or even worse, English. She did not elaborate on the generational differences between the Puerto Rican and the Dominican migrations that, for now, allow some first- or second-generation Dominicans to "speak better" than their Puerto Rican counterparts, providing an example of the unscrutinized culturalist characterizations common in the industry at large.

Yet another strategy with which advertising agencies safeguard the cultural authenticity of the Hispanic market is the selective use of mainland Puerto Ricans as part of the U.S. Hispanic market. As a U.S. Commonwealth, or free, associated state of the United States, Puerto Rico has an ambiguous political status that allows advertisers both on the mainland and on the island to present Puerto Rico both as part of the Hispanic market and as a distinct national market. My previous research on the island showed Puerto Rican marketers recurrently emphasizing the distinctiveness of their market vis-à-vis that of U.S. Hispanics in order to stress the need for nationally distinct campaigns for the nationally distinct Puerto Rican market (Dávila 1997). This distinctiveness was used to fuel the growth of the marketing industry in Puerto Rico and the popularization of nationalist symbols in advertising campaigns appealing to widespread sentiments of nationalism. At the same time, however, Puerto Rican marketers had also begun to situationally present their country as the paramount conduit for the U.S. Hispanic market, as both "Latin" and "American" and hence the best place to test products and advertising campaigns for the U.S. market. This view is represented by Puerto Rican associations like the Hispanic American Leadership, Inc., and is behind the involvement of such Puerto Rican ad agencies as Lopito, Ileana, and Howie in the newly founded Association of Hispanic Advertising Agencies. The growing consolidation of the island Puerto Ricans as part of the U.S. market has important consequences for the nature and scope of the U.S. Hispanic market. For one, it instantly inflates the number of Latinos considered to be "non-acculturated and foreign-born Hispanics" in the U.S. Hispanic market. Most research companies are aware of this and generally omit Puerto Rico from their samples, following the general practice of the U.S. census, which limits U.S. Hispanics to those living in the continental United States. However, this has not curtailed the selective use of Puerto Rican statistics to imagine and present the Hispanic market in Hispanic market reports. Consider, for instance, Isabel Valdes's treatment of Puerto Rico. Despite her argument that Puerto Rico is a distinct case and that it should be treated apart from the U.S. market, she adds the number of Puerto Ricans to the number of foreign-born Hispanics in this country to make projections about the growing importance of foreign-born Hispanics. Similarly, SRC's 1998 *U.S. Hispanic Market Study* of the Strategy Research Corporation distributed questionnaires in Puerto Rico and lists Puerto Rico in its methodology, although it is not explicitly made evident where and how any resulting information was included in the final report. In both these cases, Puerto Rico is summoned by U.S. marketers as an example of the ideal "Hispanic" market: Spanish-dominant, authentic, and contained.

At another level, merging Puerto Rico with the U.S. market is troublesome because it takes as a fact what in reality is a highly contentious issue for Puerto Ricans both in the United States and on the island. Puerto Rico's independence from or incorporation into the United States has been debated throughout the hundred years of U.S. colonization of the island, and its premature resolution in marketing sources is not without political implications: it constitutes, at the very least, a public statement in support of statehood as the only option that would ultimately secure the incorporation of Puerto Rico as part of the U.S. market.

Through this and other strategies, conceptualizations of the Hispanic market have tended to reproduce biases toward the foreign-born and Spanish-dominant Hispanics; consequently, the Latino or Hispanic identity of the English-dominant or U.S.-born Latino is downplayed if not erased. According to one marketer's interpretation of some of the language segmentation and acculturation models that are now common in the industry, "What we know is that there are three kinds of Latinos: the Latino that has just arrived, who is 100 percent Latino; the Latino that arrived as an adult, lives here for over twenty years and continues being Latino; and the one who is born here and becomes an American, even if they seek to identify themselves as a Latino." Or, as yet another one stated, "We have what we call core Hispanics, which is 70 percent of the Hispanic population; of those, 50 percent we call Spanish-dominant, the ones who live their lives in Spanish, and 20 percent we call bilingual. The remaining 30 percent are MELs (mostly English Latinos), who live their lives in English. Like me—I watch English TV and radio and may speak Spanish at home or eat rice and beans, but am in all respects gringo."

Another researcher made similar distinctions, but by differentiating between Latinos and Hispanics. While these terms are used mostly interchangeably, I also heard "Hispanics" used to refer to the unacculturated recent arrival and "Latino" to refer to the U.S.-born or more acculturated consumer. As this researcher explained, "We are really talking about two different types of Hispanics. The Hispanic who is Spanish-dominant, the guy that works hard and at night watches a soap opera and goes to sleep, and the Latino." Interestingly, as he went on to define these different segments, he attached a political personality to the Latino but not to the Hispanic. "It is Latinos that politicians are after," he added. "They are the ones that make noise and that complain if they don't like something" unlike the Hispanics who, according to him, just "watch soap operas, buy products, and work hard." This was not the first time that I heard such distinctions, in which Hispanics were seen as more docile and apolitical, and hence easier to please by advertising, as compared to their Latino counterparts, for in fact, the most marketable Hispanics are those most concerned with material acquisition, not politics. This is the Hispanic that is constructed as the nonpolitical subject, epitomized as the illegal, the alien, the one that "stays home," most afraid of visibility, traits that remain veiled and transposed, never mentioned but always implied in the very category of the "Hispanic."

Stark distinctions between Hispanics and Latinos, however, are not as prevalent in the industry. There is a general and tacit understanding that whether we call them "Latino" or "Hispanic" when we talk about them as consumers, we are referring to an "authentic" consumer not yet "contaminated" by American culture, the one who, according to our discussion above, would more likely be called a Hispanic than a Latino and who remains safe for mass consumption. I purposefully place emphasis on not being contaminated by American culture because the general view is that the more connected Hispanics are to Latin American, not U.S., culture, the more valuable they are as consumers. Latin America is thus largely regarded as the only source of vitality and strength for U.S. Latino culture. A vice president of research at BBDO, a Cuban woman who conducts presentations on the Hispanic market to clients, exemplified this current view:

> Latinos don't assimilate and will not assimilate. With the advances in communications, they are constantly undergoing a process of cultural refueling. They are constantly going back to their countries and recharging their culture and values. The only ones that can't go back are the Cubans, but everyone else always goes back, and that's why we don't assimilate.

Never mind here that her statement ignores the many Central Americans who came to the United States as war refugees, as well as the working poor and illegal Latinos who can't afford such doses of cultural refurbishing upon which, according to her, Latinos' cultural identity is so dependent. She went on to explain why Cubans, who can't "benefit" from the cultural refurbishing provided by a quick airlift to Havana, remain so "Hispanic": they have highly developed family values. Her statement merits attention because, in stressing that Latinos need to travel to refurbish their culture, lest they lose it, it simultaneously implies that there is little of value in U.S.-generated Latino cultural expressions and, most significantly, that advances in telecommunications, not racism per se, are what motivate Latinos to hold their culture dear. For now, I only stress the general bias against the U.S. Latino consumer that is prevalent in this industry and is so much an outcome of marketers' projection of this market as a manageable construct. When I asked whether "Niuyoricans" and second- and third-generation, "acculturated" Latinos would ever see themselves in these images, I was invariably told that "those populations have already been lost," and that it was now up to the English-language networks to target this type of consumer. One creative who was born and raised in Los Angeles and is fully aware that he would not be considered a Hispanic by many of his colleagues in the industry put it this way, "We know that this is not a language issue; it is a culture issue. My attitudes toward my family and toward my parents and neighborhood are all Latino, but then the issue is . . . how far can you fragment the market before it loses its value?"

In these attempts, heterogeneity is consistently downplayed or else subject to a range of "knowledges" for its management and containment according to marketing needs and requirements. A common strategy is to reduce differences not subsumed under the aforementioned issue of language/acculturation to the issue of nationality. As an extension of the dominant view that Hispanics are culture-bound and "turned on by their culture," cultural differences among different subnationalities are often emphasized in research reports and marketing recommendations. Consider, for instance, the industry's treatment of the top Hispanic markets which, in order of size, are Los Angeles, New York, Miami, San Francisco, Chicago, San Antonio, and Houston. The populations in these markets differ greatly in terms of history, times of arrival, acculturation levels, and the heterogeneity of their Hispanic populations. Briefly, the Los Angeles and New York Hispanic populations are regarded as more acculturated than Miami's, which is the prototype of the ethnic Hispanic enclave; affluence is more concentrated in Miami than New York; large populations of Hispanics in the West date from the seventeenth century, whereas most immigration to New York peaked after the 1950s. Similarly, markets like New York City are far more heterogeneous than others, such as San Antonio, where Mexicans and Mexican Americans are 92 percent of the population, whereas there is a greater density of black Hispanics among the mostly Spanish Caribbean population of the east coast than in Los Angeles and San Antonio, where Mexicans and Central Americans represent mixtures of Spanish and Indian heritages. Despite these differences, most of the research strategists I talked to would narrow the issue of diversity to one that could easily be addressed by understanding the specific nationalities that dominate each market within specific regional areas. Following the old dictum of possessive individualism, whereby cultures are seen as distinct and self-contained (Coombe 1998; Handler 1988), regions are associated with particular cultures, and particular cultures with their own traits. This involves addressing the Miami Hispanic market by appealing to the dominant Cuban population, that of New York by pitching to Puerto Ricans and Dominicans, and making sure that any campaign for the West Coast market is undeniably Mexican. Focusing on nationalities, advertisers then rely on studies codifying the language use and cultural trademarks of these groups along the lines of religion, art, political issues, values, and socioeconomic characteristics, among other variables. Isabel Valdes's *Hispanic Market Handbook*, for instance, not only tells prospective advertisers what word each Latin American nationality uses for "beans" (*habichuelas* for Puerto Ricans, *frijoles* for Mexicans, *porotes* for Chileans) or for "bus" (*gua-gua* for Puerto Ricans, *camión* for Mexicans, and *omnibús* for Argentineans), but also which religious practices, sports, or values are dominant and what political issue is most sensitive among these groups. Not surprisingly, however, these culturalist presentations often end up reproducing distinctions and hierarchies among and across Latin American cultures and countries. Readers of Valdes's presentation of broad cultural differences among U.S. Hispanics, for instance, could easily surmise that Mexican American culture is the richest of all, on the basis of her longer discussion and more careful treatment of difference in Mexican culture relative to her discussion of Cuban and Puerto Rican culture. Readers are even guided to see the "discussion of U.S. Cubans" if they want to know about Puerto Rican language and music, subordinating Puerto Rican music to that of Cuba. Mexicans are described as "more group-oriented than other Hispanic groups," are said to "lead all other U.S. Hispanic groups in literary production," to "pronounce all the consonants, unlike Caribbean Spanish," and to be "more active politically" (Valdes and Seoane 1995: 194–202), statements that are obviously loaded with covert value judgments about the richness and complexity of particular Latino subcultures.

Such characterizations are fairly common in presentations and conferences where Hispanic consumers are even psychographically segmented along the lines of nationality. For instance, at a conference in New York City entitled "Direct Marketing to Multicultural Markets," a representative from Bell Atlantic distinguished Puerto Ricans and Caribbeans as "traditionalist" versus the South American "Proud Moderns" who, he argued, were more sophisticated and willing to take chances, and thus more likely to buy products like call waiting, caller ID, and other telephone technologies.[15] In the Q & A period, I noted that class and income levels are likely to be better predictors of who would acquire such additional telecommunications services, but this suggestion did not seem to change the presenter's mind in any way. Despite the fact that Puerto Ricans, given their commonwealth status and long involvement with the U.S. economy, could well be considered the least "traditional" of the Latino subgroups, he was convinced that the reason they did not buy these services was the "traditional" outlook of consumers of Hispanic Caribbean origin.

These differences are not only codified but also caricaturized to subsume regional, class, or generational specificities in highly reductionist ways that can be easily configured into marketing formulas. A common example of this is the reduction of regional and cultural diversity to a matter of music preferences. Adjusting to local tastes and cultural needs thus becomes a matter of using *tejano* music for multigenerational, bilingual Texas, or *rancheras* or *banda* music for rural California, or a mix of salsa and merengue for the New York market—appeals that rely on particularized nationalistic associations that ironically negate the pan-ethnic pretenses of the generic Pan-Latino project.

Evidence of the pervasiveness of this approach is the rise of ethnic festivals since the late 1980s, which have facilitated marketers' appeals to different nationalities (see figures 4 and 5). It is not surprising that the New York City market, with one of the most diversified Latino populations, is home to the greatest number of festivals, events, and parades, from the Cuban Parade in New Jersey to the Mexican, Ecuadorian, Dominican, and Puerto Rican Day Parades, always exploited to reach these subnational markets. Even some of the Pan-Hispanic festivals in the city, like Manhattan's 116th Street Festival, are organized so as to provide segmented marketing opportunities, with each stage platform dedicated to a different type of music, intended to attract particular nationalities and hence particular sponsors.

However, in seeking the more profitable nationwide campaigns, which appeal to the entire U.S. Hispanic market, advertisers are still left with the need to emphasize the existence of essential commonalities that are supposedly shared by all Latinos in order to safeguard the cohesiveness and profitability of this market. This does not mean that TV ads are no longer customized for different regional markets, but that tales of difference are always balanced with those of unity and similarity among all Hispanics, leading back to the all-familiar founding myths of spirituality, *familismo,* and conservatism. Thus, the same advertiser I quoted above as claiming that only the recently arrived Latino is truly 100 percent Latino later said that differences among Latinos were ultimately irrelevant because the Hispanic is a very particular race. It has 50 percent of similarities, in that we are all the same, you and I are attached to our families, we love our families, we respect our ancestors and are proud of them, unlike the American, we are proud of our roots and keep eating rice and beans, but we are 50 percent different in that the Cuban is different from the Argentinean and he in turn from the Colombian . . . what we seek is to tap into that 50 percent that makes us all the same.

I heard a range of percentages of what made Hispanics the same, with the maximum being 90 percent, consisting mostly of their values (which almost always remain implied and unspecified). Whether 50 percent or 90 percent (not that levels of cultural "sameness" could ever be quantifiable), however, it is this need to define what "makes us all the same" that feeds the images through which Hispanics are represented.

Primary among these commonalities is the notion that U.S. Hispanics constitute a distinct nation within a nation. In contrast to the traditional sense of a territorially bounded nation, this "nation" is conceived as a symbolic or "imagined" community (Anderson 1983), shaped and constructed through the media, which would vest it with its own idiosyncrasies and particularities. As the founder of Font and Vaamonte, Cuban-born Pedro Font, recalled, the market had to be seen as a separate nation, "as a country that is separate and apart from the United States" if it were to be a profitable market. "This is the only way to create and maintain the Hispanic market, by considering it as a different entity with a different language and a totally different culture." The concept of a Hispanic nation was mostly used by the founders of this industry, not by its present staff, although most shared the view that U.S. Hispanics constituted a separate entity from both the United States and Latin America, as in constituting the aforementioned "fifth largest and richest Latin American country," and all shared a pervasive need to define the cultural and identity boundaries of Latinos. In this way, even if inadvertently, they too engaged in processes that are similar to nationalism, insofar as they were also concerned with the definition and consolidation of ideas about what is the most authentic or appropriate representation of Latino/Hispanic culture, a whole which comprises a conglomerate of "cultures."[16]

In this "nation," differences among Latinos have to be made as irrelevant and immaterial as are the differences within the U.S. market, an analogy that some marketers have used to convince clients to pay them to find an acceptable image that would lure the Puerto Rican in New York as much as the Mexican in California. As explained by a creative

Figure 4.   Direct marketing through outdoor ads. *Latina*
magazine float in the Puerto Rican Day Parade, New York City.
Photo by author.

at Siboney Advertising, "I always tell my clients that just as they don't
do a different ad for Arkansas and Massachusetts, we don't need to do
something different for New York or California. We find something that
is acceptable for all. It is like a good stew; you need to know how to
cook." In fact, it is to a Hispanic nation that most ads transport viewers, a nation in which there is little reference to the greater U.S. society
in which they live.

However, while the United States is mostly absent from this advertising, it has nevertheless been a key symbolic reference in the marketers'
conceptualization of the Hispanic consumer. Just as it was in the 1960s,
the United States and things "American" have been central references
that have allowed them to project commonalities and override differences
of race, class, or ethnicity among Hispanics. One need only talk to marketers to perceive the strength of these ideas, as I learned after asking
some New York marketers to describe the "average" consumers to whom
they target their ads. They were described, among overtly culturalist characterizations that recycled a view of "traditional" Hispanics in opposition to "Americans," as people who are "conservative, who care about
their culture, who are respectful of their elders and traditions, and who
love to eat rice and beans." Even staff who had been critical of market
clichés repeated this idea in different versions or guises. Feeding this

Figure 5.   Goya float in the Puerto Rican Day Parade. Photo by author.

notion is the unchallenged view that this market is ultimately defined by its culture and that any type of demographic, financial, attitudinal information on Hispanics must ultimately be condensed into presentations that are somehow "cultural." Presentations to clients that do not sound "cultural enough" run the risk of losing their relevance. This view drives the continuous production of research, surveys, and portraits of the Hispanic consumer who, unlike the mainstream consumer, who is targeted in terms of class, generations, or gender, is continually reduced to the issue of "culture."

Part of this trend is the culturalist explanation of behavior and attitudes that may actually apply to any other consumer. That Hispanics love to buy things, but that they prefer to know and trust the person they buy things from, that watching TV is a family affair, or that Hispanics love their families and want to see themselves represented in a positive light in advertising—all these qualities apply to most U.S. consumers, but they were consistently explained to me as a function of cultural uniqueness in the case of Hispanics.[17]

This makes communicating with Hispanic consumers a matter of communicating with emotion and to the emotions. As simply put by Lionel Sosa, founder of one of the largest Hispanic ad agencies in the United States, Sosa, Bromley, Aguilar, Noble and Associates (now Bromley Agui-

lar) in his best-selling book, *The Americano Dream,* "What we're dealing with here is the logic of the heart, not the logic of reason, and the
power of its effect on everyone, but especially Latinos is remarkable. . . .
Like our homelands, we are lush and warm. We are extraordinarily open
with each other. We communicate through a touch, a gesture, an embrace . . ." (Sosa 1998: 112). These views are not different from many I
repeatedly heard that, as simplistic as they may sound, were always
backed by some sort of "research." They are not different from those
that first made Hispanics so attractive for being highly diverse yet essentially culturally unified and thus approachable and marketable. Thus,
after thirty years of Hispanic marketing, research initiatives, and reports,
and after the growing diversification of the U.S. Hispanic population,
old stereotypes are as powerful as they always were, and are perhaps
even more marketable today. In contrast to the early 1960s, today these
stereotypes are supported by and cloaked in the authenticity of research.

Having elaborated on some of the problems of the marketing discourse
on Hispanics, we are left to contend with the fact that in projecting a
sizable market, the Hispanic marketing industry has played a central role
in raising Hispanics' visibility in public life. No other sector in society
has been as invested in emphasizing the increasing size of this population. My point throughout this chapter, however, has been to stress that
this development has been accompanied by an extension of the methods
and measurements that purport to prove Hispanics' abiding cultural
uniqueness and hence foreignness with respect to U.S. society and culture. Underscoring the importance of Spanish—which is a defining element of Hispanic identity but not synonymous with it—has had unavoidable repercussions on the identification of non-Spanish-speaking
Latinos as integral members of this population. This calls into question
the Hispanic identity of most second- or third-generation Latinos, who
are bypassed by advertisers and marketing staff who, in maintaining the
Spanish-centered definition of the market, have tended to emphasize the
role of foreign-born, Spanish-speaking immigrants. The immigrant and
Spanish-dominant Hispanic is viewed as the one who constantly reviews
the market, who gives it its cultural qualities, and who—in contrast to
the "complicated," bilingual, bicultural, perhaps polluted, Hispanic—is
most easily sold to corporate America.

The irony is that in constructing a Hispanic market that is easily marketable—that remains safe, authentic, and ready for mass consumption—
the industry ends up erasing the historical roots of Latinos in the United
States that arise from its very foundation, invalidating the political claims

of Latino populations that are an intrinsic rather than an external or re- cently incorporated segment of the U.S. population. This view therefore reinforces the dominant image of Hispanics as immigrants who are "bur- dens" to the national community and foreign to U.S. society, politics, and culture. These are the Hispanics that we can market to, but also ex- pel or banish, who will remain in their place, within their culture: the "nation within the nation" that is never really part of the "Nation." Ob- viously then, marketing discourse on Hispanics is implicated in perpet- uating this domesticated image and must be analyzed in relation to its likely impact on contemporary Latino cultural politics. But first, let us turn to the visual representation of Hispanics, which presents similar and additional dilemmas.

CHAPTER 3

Images

Producing Culture for the Market

What I eat is not a clear indication of who I am. It is more
important where I go than where I come from. The color
of my hair says nothing of me as a person. I AM NOT A
STEREOTYPE. I love my family. Have values. Like rhythm.
Have faith. But don't categorize me, don't pigeonhole me.
Don't judge me for what I eat, what I wear, by my origin.
Believe in me . . . and I will trust you.

So reads an ad published in *Hispanic Business, Latina,* and *People en
Español,* among other Latina/Hispanic magazines, its final note an ex-
hortation to *trust* Ford Motor Company. Juxtaposed with the narrative
are photographs, images of a woman, an attractive, fortyish brunette,
dressed in relaxed contemporary clothes, alongside pictures of a pizza,
a hamburger, some palm trees, two teenage youths (her children, perhaps?), and three brands of Ford luxury cars, to underscore the seemingly contradictory picture of a contemporary-looking, middle-aged
woman who holds dear her traditional values but nonetheless likes hamburgers and can afford a luxury Ford car (figure 6).

Clearly, stereotypes are a key concern of the Hispanic marketing industry. To sell themselves and their products, those in this industry have
not only drawn from existing stereotypes—after all, the above example
rests on a Hispanic female type that is traditionally at odds with luxury
cars and hamburgers—but have also positioned themselves as the "politically correct" voice with which to challenge stereotypes and educate
corporate clients about Hispanic language and culture. These antithetical processes of reinforcing and challenging stereotypes have gone hand
in hand in this industry, where advertising staff have long had to con-

Figure 6. "Yo no soy un estereotipo." Playing with stereotypes for Ford Motor Company. Corporate image ad for Ford Motor Company by Zubi Advertising, Coral Gables, Florida.

front, reshape, or reformulate all types of Hispanic conventions in order to maintain a legitimate ethnic niche for this market.

At the same time, the categorization, ordering, and simplification at the heart of any process of stereotyping are necessary components of human interaction and communication. What makes stereotypes so troublesome is not that they order and simplify information by reducing complexities to a few limited conventions, but that in doing so, they both reflect and, more important, engender social hierarchies (Hall 1997; Dyer 1993). As a vast literature has clearly shown, stereotypes are never intrinsically negative or positive, but are always historically created and produced in conversation with social hierarchies of daily life (Gilman 1996; Kanellos 1998; Rodríguez 1997). They work by restricting the range of interpretations and therefore facilitating the evaluations that reproduce and valorize the social distinctions at play in the greater society. Even when individuals may interpret these images and ideas differently or imbue them with idiosyncratic meaning, these renditions are by necessity framed within dominant social conventions.

Awareness of such dynamics, however, should not deter us from asking what struggles and interests are contained in the development and dissemination of particular images or why within the world of advertising—so dependent on its ability to interpellate people as consumers—some images are more appealing or commercially viable, despite their apparent stereotypical foundations. This chapter explores these issues by examining some of the images and themes through which Hispanic advertising has imagined, represented, or aimed to speak to Latinas as a generic "Hispanic market." As we will see, Hispanic images have not been static but have changed according to the varied creation and representation of an imagined audience, one that spans different nationalities, classes, and ethnicities, among other variables. These images are also the outcome of the successful incorporation of themes and images that are relevant or recognizable to the generic group known as "Latinos" and to Anglo sensitivities about Latinos. Thus, changing commercial representations of Latinas evoke not only the changing nature of U.S. Latinidad and of its constitution but of the interests and politics that affect its development. What I suggest is that the commercial representation of Latinidad has led to a recurrence of themes and corrective images that, while becoming tantamount to "Latinidad," have further constrained its representation, ironically bringing to the forefront the pervasiveness of racial hierarchies in the very constitution of corrective images.

THE NATION

The construction of a Hispanic market had long been based on the notion of Hispanics as a nation within a nation. However, while fully alive in the minds of marketing staff, "Hispanic" is ultimately a construct whose representation has presented several dilemmas to advertisers, especially to their quest for images that would produce homogeneity out of multiple heterogeneities.

First, as a U.S.-generated category applying to any Latin American or Spanish-background person in the United States, "Hispanic" is a racial category that places its members into a "minority" status within the U.S. race/class/nation conflation.[1] As a result, not only are representations of Latinidad pervaded by dominant stereotypes applied by greater U.S. society to "Hispanics" as one of its "others," but Hispanic advertising is therefore pressed into becoming a generator of "positive" images in order to instill pride in and at the same time appeal to Hispanics as potential consumers. Moreover, as an imposed category, Hispanic/Latina is subject to constant negotiation with regard to the multiple identifications of Hispanics as also Mexican, Colombian, or "Niuyorican." Here, we need to consider that "Latina" and "Hispanic" are composite constructs which are simultaneously tied to, drawn from, and in turn trigger connections to a Latin American country or countries. Hispanic advertising agencies must not only reconcile the multiple diversities among Latinas while showing deference and evoking positive identifications in their visual representations, but also tackle the problem that such representations may trigger particularized types of identifications. Recall our earlier discussion about how advertisements featuring salsa rhythms were perceived as intrinsically Caribbean and hence foreign in the western United States. These are some of the considerations that have added to the need for generic constructions with which to emphasize unity and mutual recognition among the "Hispanic nation's" countries and cultures.

The concept of a unified Hispanic nation, however, has not remained unchanged, nor has its representation always presented the same types of challenges. What advertisers have meant by Hispanic has varied according to factors such as changing immigration patterns of Latin Americans into the United States, which affect the heterogeneity among populations of Latin American background; the number of corporations seeking nationwide advertising campaigns for the totality of the U.S. Hispanic population; and the actual reach of the national TV networks. During the onset of Hispanic advertising as a specialized industry, for instance, when most campaigns were regionally based and developed for local companies and products, ads could easily present Puerto Ricans as the embodiment of the Hispanic nation in the East and Mexicans in the West. Thus Hispanic served as a synonym for Puerto Ricans or Mexicans respectively.[2] Advertisements for Goya Foods, which advertised solely for the New York and eastern markets in the United States until the 1990s, provide a good example of this trend. Founded by a Spanish immigrant in New York City in 1936, Goya's has historically presented itself as a "Hispanic" company that represents and embodies that which is Hispanic. Today, this is done by catering to the taste of the totality of the Hispanic market through the diversification of products, an expansion of its distribution throughout the entire United States, and through advertisements aimed at representing this totality, as I will discuss later. Until the 1970s, however, Goya's version of Hispanidad was publicly conveyed by pointing to the Spanishness of its products, such as its olive oils, advertised in the 1970s as "coming from Andalucia" and being "pure, virgin, and Spanish," or else by alluding to the products' connections with Puerto Rican culture. Constituting most of the market in the eastern United States, the Puerto Rican came to be addressed as the generic "Hispanic consumer." This was especially true for products manufactured in Goya's plant in Puerto Rico, established in the mid-1970s, such as beans, nectars, and sauces. An ad for tomato sauce in the 1970s, produced by Goya's in-house ad agency, Interamerican, also founded in the 1960s, asserted that it was "Made in Puerto Rico with our *criollo* taste and that of Goya" *(con sabor criollo de nosotros y de Goya)*, feeding on the feelings of nostalgia and longing of Puerto Rican immigrants for its *"sabor criollo."* Goya products were also associated with Puerto Rican culture through the use of Puerto Rican personalities, such as singer Boby Capó, who worked for twelve years doing public relations for Goya as spokesperson for its products, and through Puerto Rican folk music in the ads. Some ads for Goya up to the 1970s were aired concurrently in Puerto Rico, pointing to the symmetry between the New York–based and island-based markets.[3]

This was also the strategy followed by other advertisements for a range of products for the New York market, whose bulk consisted of more Hispanic-identified products like those from Goya, Bustelo and Caribe coffee, Banco de Ponce, or products advertised mostly for the regional market. Thus, clients of SAMS, which was the largest Hispanic agency throughout the late 1960s and 1970s, were mostly local companies. These included La Flor de Mayo Express (a moving company), Alameda Room and Tropicana Restaurant, local restaurants and night clubs, Banco de Ponce (Puerto Rican bank), Azteca Films, Argentine Films Enterprises, and Angel Products (distributors of Spanish films), along with a minority of American companies such as Eastern Brewing Corporation (Old Bohemian beer) and the Rice Growers Association of California (Arroz Sello Rojo) advertising for the local market (National Register Publishing 1964).

The depiction of a Hispanic nation, however, became more complicated with the expansion of network TV, which facilitated the conceptualization and distribution of Hispanic advertising and the recruitment of national corporate clients. After the advent of TV, for instance, SAMS acquired the accounts of Colgate Palmolive in 1966, Bulova watches in 1967, Lorillard Corporation (Kent, Newport, True cigarettes) by 1969, and Libby, Mc Neill, and Libby in 1973,[4] and although most national advertisers would wait until the 1980s to advertise to Hispanics, these accounts provided an early taste of campaigns for the totality of the Hispanic market. The first lesson learned concerned the need for campaigns that were not grounded on any particular group but that represented and spoke to a distinct yet unidentifiable construct.

The tropes with which this unity would be conceived have since been varied, depending on a variety of factors: the particularities of different products; whether the budgets provided for multiple campaigns addressing different subnational groupings rather than a single, encompassing approach; and, most fundamentally, the chosen media. Generally speaking, radio campaigns, a more affordable media than TV, have tended to be adapted or conceived with the particular perceived needs of regional markets in mind. This has allowed them to speak to different national subgroups within particular markets, while TV ads have always tended towards generic strategies because they are so costly to produce, test, and circulate.[5] Additionally, the choice between regional and generic campaign types is also affected by trends in the Hispanic industry at large and by the vision or philosophy of particular agencies. Overall, however, the depiction of the "Hispanic nation" for national distribution would necessitate a concise and marketable definition that would help legitimize to clients the existence of a culturally specific market and also generalize tropes of Latinidad among its prospective audience of consumers. Among the most prevalent are the presentation of a neutral or universal version of Hispanidad—the putatively neutral, "non-accented" Spanish and "generic" Latin look—and ambiguous appeals to a Hispanic spirit, way of being, attitude, or morality, which are supposedly shared among all Latinas.

THE VALUES

Let us start by discussing the visual representation of Hispanics' supposedly greater spirituality, centrality of family, and "tradition." Due to their intangible nature, ideas like these have provided some of the most successful references for the representation of Hispanics, allowing advertisements to avoid visual indexes that may trigger national rather than pan-ethnic forms of identification. Primary among these qualities is Hispanics' family orientation and strong family values vis-à-vis the general-market consumer. In this market, the Latin family could well be considered the maximum advertising "referent system," that is, following Williamson (1978), a system of signs and meanings that are known and generalized, and thus can be used to transfer and translate meaning to products. More than any other trope, the Latin family is implicated in and associated with the process of representation, with a cluster of ideas deemed by the industry to be representative of all Hispanics, based on their supposed nostalgia for the past, sense of rootlessness over family separations or relatives left behind, or fixed gender roles within the family.

Of course, the family trope is also dominant here because of advertisers' undifferentiated approach to this market and the nature of companies that advertise to Hispanics. In accordance with the view that Hispanics may have lower incomes but larger families, companies like Procter & Gamble, AT&T, Sears, and McDonald's, and producers of packaged foods and family-oriented basic products like Colgate-Palmolive and Johnson & Johnson have historically targeted this market, rather than companies supplying luxury or status products (credit cards, computers, luxury cars) that are more likely to appeal to an individual's aspirations, although the rise of Latina Internet portals and the growing popularity of Internet marketing are likely to affect this trend.[6] Hispanics are also perceived as an undifferentiated entity, in contrast to the general market, which is segmented according to a range of variables that, though not less constructed, recognize diversity along the lines of taste, lifestyle, age, and gender. This homogenous treatment of Hispanics also contributes to the appeal of the family trope as a way to address gender and generational differences simultaneously within the "totality" of the family.

Moreover, representations of the Hispanic family have changed, and an entire chapter could be devoted to this issue, considering the preponderance of family scenes and of the family trope in advertisements since the industry's beginnings. After conducting a content analysis of ads produced in the late 1970s and early 1980s, I found that most ads revolved around families in kitchen situations with women either cooking or taking care of children. The grandmother and a mustached husband were also recurrent figures. SAMS advertising for Fab detergent, "When I Came to This Country" (1970s), where a grandmother didactically explains to her grandchild that they use Fab because they used it in their country and because it leaves clothes "so clean and fresh," epitomizes this very common type of advertising (figure 7). It shows a grandmother with her daughter and grandchild doing the laundry, a family scene that turns into the ideal opportunity to laud the properties of the cleaning product. Notice here that the product is presented as a family tradition, something they used back home and brought with them. Ads in the 1990s, however, while depicting families just as often, show women in contexts other than the kitchen—playing sports or wearing business attire—and men helping around the kitchen or cooking, as in Goya's ad for its codfish fritter ready-mix.[7] What has nonetheless remained consistent is the use of the family to communicate a range of values that are supposedly associated with Hispanics.

Consider, for instance, a 1998 ad for AT&T's auto-redial feature, meant to communicate that the company gives the "tools to impact your life." It depicts a nervous boyfriend asking permission to marry his girlfriend. The couple is shown waiting anxiously, accompanied by an older aunt, until the father, who subsequently agrees to grant his daughter's hand ("but only her hand," jokes the aunt), is finally reached thanks to AT&T's auto-redial feature. As the creative explained, the ad was based on the view that Hispanics have good family values and a religious orientation, which means that permission to marry a woman must come not from her or from her aunt, but from her father, even when he is absent. The result was a thirty-second "family drama" that evoked not only the patriarchal status of an absent father (whose permission is needed for the scene's resolution), but also the authoritative presence of the older aunt, as keeper of sexual norms and bridge between the couple, the father, and the actual territorial separation of the family.

As in this ad, the family is recurrently used to communicate the supposedly "intrinsic" Latin spirit and morality that are believed to characterize Hispanic consumers, such as the idea that they are motivated by family and collective, not individual, needs and desires. Consider, for instance, Nicorette's ads for the Hispanic market. For the general market, this product was advertised by portraying the decision to quit smoking as an individual one, through testimonials in which people discuss conquering the habit as an act of individual achievement. For Hispanics, however, the tactic was different. As a representative of Publicidad Advertising said, "We realized that Hispanics are mostly influenced by their family. It is a personal decision but one that is taken in relation to others; thus, we use the family and a friend influencing people to quit." Their slogan captures the tactic succinctly: "Por tu Bien y el de los Tuyos" (For your well-being and that of those you love). Figure 8 exemplifies a similar tactic: using the smile and trust of "Daddy's little girl" as the primary motivating force. The advertisement for ITT Technical Schools (1997) also uses the family as a trope to communicate so-called Hispanic values. Whereas most ads for community colleges and other types of postsecondary education for the general market draw on people's individual ambitions to succeed and improve themselves, this ad shows a thankful Hispanic character acknowledging the role his family, friends, and ITT Technical School played in helping him advance his dream and become a positive role model for his parents and community. Interspersed in the

Figure 7.   The grandmother
introduces the little girl to
another tradition from their
home country—the use of Fab.
TV ad by Spanish Advertising
and Marketing Services.

narrative are images of his proud parents, images that would rarely be
seen in an ad for the general market.

In the same tenor, an Oil of Olay Hispanic ad by FOVA features a
woman explaining what "we [Hispanic] women want," which are details,
"like a touch, a caress, or a gentle word." As the creative explained, the
execution of the ad was also based on the view that, unlike Anglo women,
Hispanic women beautify themselves not for "selfish, me-oriented purposes," but in order to please others and obtain their approval and praise.

Figure 8.   The family—and the trust and smile of a daughter—as incentive to quit smoking in "Decidido," produced for Nicorette by JMCP Publicidad.

Avon's Hispanic strategy for 1996–97 is also based on the view that Hispanic women, in contrast to their analogues in the general market (a euphemism for Anglo), are more emotionally expressive, family-oriented, and feminine. As the brand representative in Avon's Hispanic agency stated, "They need to be engaged, not solely informed"; in other words, appeal to their feelings, not their reason. Whereas in the general market, Avon's makeup products were associated with images of independent professional women manifesting a contemporary yet approachable beauty, the Hispanic market ad shows women in group shots of family and friends. A voice-over praises the Hispanic woman for her feminine qualities: "You are always dreaming, you turn life into small smiles, you are alive at all moments, you feel emotions more strongly, you are different, you say what you feel." A final example is the milk ad for the Hispanic market. While the general market ad revolves around comic scenes of milk scarcity, prompted by "Got milk?" the Hispanic campaign features a grandmother cooking traditional milk-based desserts with a caption that reads: "Have you given your loved ones enough milk today?" (see figure 9). This campaign was based on the fear that Hispanics would not get the humor of the original ad and that the maternal instincts of the Latin woman would be offended by the thought of lacking such an important provision as milk.

Obviously, value-oriented ads generally present Hispanics as loving and socially caring individuals, values that Hispanic consumers do believe distinguish them from their Anglo-American counterparts. Compared to the usual U.S. stereotype of Latinos as thugs and criminals who are indolent and lazy, these images are generally positive. Nonetheless, the questions to ask here, as Shohat and Stam (1994: 204) remind us, are for whom, in what context, in relation to what and whom, and with what implications are these images positive? Specifically, I want to emphasize that such representations would make little sense if they were not constructed against the binary Anglo/Hispanic behavioral patterns that have long shaped Hispanic stereotypes. They simultaneously limit Latinas' association with so-called Anglo traits like "individualism," thus reproducing the stereotype of the Latina's collective orientation, in turn associated with an inherent conformism and lack of individual ambition. They are an extension of rather than a departure from dominant representations of Hispanics' "intrinsic" spirit, and of the same nineteenth-century ideas that have since been used to sustain hierarchies of values and dispositions among "Anglos" and "Latinas." Are there no motivated and self-reliant Latinas? Could it be something other than their culture that turns them on? Are they not sophisticated enough to "get" the comedic puns of general market ads? Most significant, the commodification of U.S. Latinas involves their re-authentification by association with the "right" way to be an "ethnic," which requires them to be "exotic," that is, culturally different, but to stay within normative patterns in which the traits of upward mobility are always associated with an aspirational Anglo not Latina world.

Figure 9. Outdoor ads in Washington Heights, New York City. The Johnny Walker Black Label ad reads, "Con el Buen Gusto se Nace" ("One Is Born with Good Taste"), and the milk ad asks caregivers (moms, grandmas, etc.) if they gave their loved ones enough milk today.

Perhaps the most obvious example of what I am suggesting is provided by Budweiser's (1996) "Rebudlución" campaign by Castor Advertising.[8] I say "most obvious" because, while most Hispanic ads have tended to present the Hispanic nation as a nation in and of itself with little reference to the broader context mediating Hispanic experiences in this country, this campaign was ground-breaking in presenting Hispanic men interacting with Anglos in distinctively Anglo settings. As a creative said, the dominant trend in advertising had long been to present "an ideal world, where there are no gringos, no one to think you are ugly; where you don't have to struggle to be heard, where you are not a minority, and where if you go into a bar, everyone there is Hispanic, and everyone is your friend." These ads, however, by showing Hispanics and Anglos in the same setting, display overtly some of the dichotomies that are often drawn between "Hispanics" and Anglo-Americans, and thus present a clear view of the pitfalls of representations that revolve around "positive" images. The campaign, aimed at "inverting" and "Latinizing" the values of American society, shows Hispanics prevailing in stereotypically American situations through their wit, good humor, and intelligence. As if asserting or reassuring Latino masculinity by redefining the meaning of strength, bravado, or power, it revolves around competitive encounters between males. In one ad, we see two slender Hispanics outwitting a group of bulky Anglo-American football players by hitting the football "soccer" style and proving their greater agility despite their small size. In another, some small and slender Latinos prevail over some stocky Anglos in a bikers' bar (figure 10). The ad shows the Latinos at first threatened by the bikers but then victorious after they challenge the Anglos to eat a hot pepper. The pepper makes the Anglos choke, while the triumphant Hispanic dismisses it as "Mexican candy." Violence and bulk have been devalued against the cool wit of the Hispanic (who can take the heat of the habanero). In the background, a voice-over urges viewers to "Rebudluciona las reglas" (revolutionize the rules). In another ad, a Latino enters what the creative described as a "hillbilly" town in Alabama where everyone is hostile to him, but he wins them over by turning his Budweiser can into a "maraca" and turning the hostile scene into a festive one. The Hispanic way wins once more.

Stuart Hall has warned us of the binaries and polarized extremes that characterize stereotypes and the representation of minorities. As he states, not only do stereotypes work by reducing people to fixed types, ignoring the range of variation and difference or the factors affecting any given "type," but these "types" are in turn constructed through binary oppositions that reduce complexity to two extremes. In this manner, positive images take on meaning in relation to their opposites and can simultaneously invoke them (Hall 1997). Thus, in the examples given, the presentation of Hispanics as positive characters is achieved by conjuring and then inverting the social meanings of the stereotypes and social hierarchies pervading their representation within U.S. society. Ridiculing American men as slow, bulky, and less intelligent, not only exalts Hispanic men but also simultaneously associates them with old stereotypes concerning their temperament and abilities. Hispanic cool and wit is related to their definition as "hot and spicy food lovers," full of wit and rhythm, and musically saucy—values which in the real world would never really "win over" the American way. These are roles that also feminize Latinos in relation to Anglo men, who are associated with aggressive sports and the realm of "real men." Ultimately, these inversions and reversals are still caught within the established, polarized binaries between Anglos and Latinos, leaving unchallenged the dominant representational hierarchies. These hierarchies still compel the use of an Anglo figure to establish the Latino's virtuosity, even when only featured as an object of mockery, as in the bar scene above.

On the other hand, unambiguous expressions of Latina pride, not subtly presented through positive images, also convey a politics of irreverence and contingency within the world of advertising, as do presentations of Hispanics in contemporary settings. Recall the discussion in chapter 2 of how marketing research constructs Hispanics as unpolluted and authentic, a view that would inhibit their presentation in situations that may appear too modern or contemporary. Insights into this politics of contingency can be gained by assessing changes in the commercial expressions of nationalism and ethnic pride.

NATIONALISM, NOSTALGIA, AND ETHNIC PRIDE

Hispanics' supposedly fervent love of tradition, their ethnic pride, and their nationalism have been recurring themes in Hispanic advertising. Fueled by the generalized view that a defining trait of Hispanics is their deterritorialized status and therefore their longing to "connect," which most Hispanics have either faced personally or experienced through relatives or friends, advertising has long appealed both to their feelings for their homelands and to their pride as Latinas in the United States. This approach involves associating products with particular countries or with some named or unnamed generic Latina heritage or tradition. References to "our" cooking or values, with "our" standing for Latinas as a finished identity and an inclusive whole are also common.

Again, this strategy is tied to the type of advertiser. Long-distance telephone companies, one of the major advertisers to Hispanics, are renowned for urging people to "make that call" by tapping into people's yearning for their homelands and their past. Bravo's ads for AT&T are a good example of ads that have juxtaposed images of Latin American countries, from Mexican pyramids to South American train stations, that are recognized by viewers as such. Figure 11 represents this trend. It summons the many memories from someone's youth, memories of friends and loved ones that remain behind in one's homeland, nostalgically described as the place where "I opened my eyes for the first time." The voice-over urges the viewer to return to his or her homeland again and again through AT&T. However, other advertisers have also applied this strategy, even composing collages of unspecified Latin American nations as a means of expanding the range of identifications a specific ad can trigger in a given consumer. A good example is Kodak's "patria" ad, which was filmed in

Figure 10.   In "Chile," a Latino outsmarts a gringo biker by eating a chile.
The conflict's resolution is celebrated with a Bud. Ad by Castor Advertising,
New York City.

Puerto Rico but included scenes that replicated lush, tropical, moun-
tainous countryside and colonial urban settings that would evoke any
coastal, urban, or interior Latin American region.

Appeals to people's new, U.S.-based "Latina" or "Hispanic" identity,
on the other hand, have also been common since the beginning of the
Hispanic advertising industry, although they have become increasingly
more prevalent and self-referential, which indicates the growing consolidation of a pan-Latina identity in the world of commercial TV. Ads in
the 1970s and 1980s, for instance, marked Latinas by contrasting them
with Anglo people or Anglo ways, or else through culturally loaded icons
or images: maracas, Spanish guitars, soccer, different foods, a domino
set. As many advertisers were ready to point out, such images were an
important necessity in a context where clients, as Lionel Sosa (1998) explains, "expected the bright colors, the sombreros, lowriders, the adobe
house, the mustached man, and the rose in the woman's hair." As he
noted, advertisers were particularly wary of images that presented Hispanics in contemporary, quotidian situations that they considered were
more Americanized rather than authentically Hispanic. Latinas, in their
view, he argued, needed to be marked and set apart from whites. "You
could not show a Hispanic in a business suit, or wearing a tie." The pro-

Figure 11.   Nostalgia for the country left behind to induce Latinos to make
that call. "Song" TV ad by The Bravo Group.

gressive shedding by Hispanic marketers of overt Latin indexes or direct
reference to "our" traditions as a sales pitch, and the addressing of Hispanics as a unique group without a sharp contrast to Anglo society was
thus not an easy development. It emerged from struggles between clients
who wanted what in their view constituted authentic ethnic consumers
and marketers who wanted to present modern Latina consumers—those
who buy U.S. products but are most of all proud of their tradition, without this tradition being contained in a sombrero.

A telling example of this progressive transformation toward the contemporary Latina is provided by Mendoza and Dillon's advertising for
Miller beer in the 1980s. This campaign attempted to associate Miller
beer with Latinas' values and traditions through the "Miller Beer Anthem" sung against a variety of images meant to index Latina customs.
The first anthem for an ad in 1985 presented Miller beer as an American product that Latinas should drink because it was part of the new
traditions acquired in the United States. It showed images of Latinas dancing to salsa music, playing baseball, boxing, working at La Reina Foods,
going out with their families, watching a vaquero riding in a rodeo, playing "Latin" instruments like maracas and Spanish guitars, and greeting
family at a wedding. Singly and together, these images were meant to instill pride in people's new "Latin lifestyle" within the context of the
United States and its "American way," which was ultimately praised in
the anthem:

> Here where opportunity is so clear, when you know how to strive, and the
> family can be better off, without forgetting our roots. Here where one em-
> braces with sincerity to seal friendships, you sing with joy here, you drink
> Miller ice cold. Miller is of this nation as we are full of heart. Clear and honest
> for all to see. Miller is of this great nation. Miller beer, purity and quality you
> can clearly see.

The second ad, produced just a few years later (1989), however, sheds
any reference to Miller as an American product or to Latinas as being
new to this country, and, instead of the almost didactic collage of Latina
ways used in the previous ad, the new one revolves around a single event:
the family reunion of two *compadres* (fictive kin). As was common
throughout the 1980s, the ad was customized for three different nationalities by showing the *compadres* eating a traditional Cuban, Puerto
Rican, or Mexican meal and dancing salsa in Cuban or Puerto Rican style
or with a rodeo background for Mexicans. In contrast to the earlier anthem, the new anthem more overtly asserts Latina ways, which are directly associated to particular subgroups:

> Things that are clear and from the heart will last a lifetime. Things that always
> keep their value wherever they might be. Clear and pure is my tradition. That's
> the way that I am, I would not change it for anything. That's why I toast with
> ice-cold Miller. Miller has that great tradition from its origin until today,
> always clear and pure as all can see.

Comparing other ads by Mendoza and Dillon in the early 1980s with
those done in the late 1980s and early 1990s further reveals that Anglo

figures, depicted in earlier ads as a contrasting reference to accentuate Latina ways and culture, totally disappear in later ads. Most notably, Anglos are no longer used as authoritative figures who validate the quality of different products to Latinas or who praise their culture, as was a common practice in the late 1970s and early 1980s. Schlitz beer's campaign in the early 1980s provides a good example of this trend. The campaign revolved around a series of scenes where an Anglo, who can't get a task straight (cinch up a horse, fix a car, or pitch a baseball) dares a Latino, an average "Juan," to "give it a try." The Latino succeeds in every task and saves the day, gaining his Anglo peer's praise and of course, the reward of a Schlitz beer. A background chorus sings loudly: "For you who work hard and give it all it takes, for you a Schlitz beer." Today, however, Anglos are no longer authoritative or validating figures; when shown, they are subjects of mockery, as in the aforementioned Budweiser ad. Hispanics are increasingly featured as if living in some Hispanic nation; there is no reference to the larger context in which Latinas live. In this world, the United States may be recognized for its good products and modernity, or referred to as "the new country," but Anglos are never shown interacting with Latinas.

A good example of this approach is the ad entitled "Modern Country/Modern Fab." In this ad (figure 12), in contrast to the product's former advertising strategy, a woman associates using Fab not with the past but with the present, and with her own modernity. As she is shown saying, she buys Fab because she now lives in "the most modern country," where "the most modern things are invented." Another example is provided by the Advil ad "City," where a Latino, astounded with the fast pace of the city, wonders if there is something faster for pain in this country (figure 13). Thus, the United States is only referenced through its products, but because these products are described as superior, new, and modern, this approach concomitantly presents an ironic twist that subverts and qualifies the ads' central message of Latina pride.

In asserting Latina pride, some marketers have even Latinized canonical American symbols, such as the cowboy, jeans, and the Statue of Liberty. Cartel Creativo's ad "Viva la Tradición" (figure 14), for instance, reminds Latinos that "the first cowboys in the United States were Mexican Americans," that "they were called vaqueros," that they invented all we associate with cowboys, and finally that today they wear Wrangler western wear. Cowboys and Wrangler jeans hence become Mexican, not Anglo-American, "traditions." As its artistic creative explained, the ad was a difficult sale; the client was not easily convinced to advertise

Figure 12.   Modern Country /
Modern Fab. Ad for Colgate
Palmolive Company by Siboney
Advertising.

its product with such a divergent representation of the cowboy, but once
filmed, the ad was automatically successful, especially in the Southwest.
Following a similar strategy, Cartel's ad for Tecate (figure 15) shows a
young Latino topping the Statue of Liberty with a Tecate beer banner.
The televised event triggers the pride of his buddies, one vowing, "Te
dije compadre, ya nos tocaba," or "I told you *compadre* (fictive kin) that
our time was coming." The ad ends with the slogan "Tecate llegó para
quedarse," or "Tecate came to stay," as if implying that Mexicans, like
their beer Tecate, are also here to stay. The creator of this spot explained
that his goal was "to dignify Mexican immigration" by linking it to the

Figure 13.   Everything is faster in this country, including pain-killers. "City"
TV ad for Advil by The Bravo Group.

most romanticized symbol of European immigration. Most Hispanic ads,
however, do not pay such open allegiance to Latinidad. Though Latina
pride is always implied, they make fewer and fewer references to Hispanics, their traditions, roots, or values, and instead take Latinas and
the existence of the Latin nation for granted.

Most creatives with whom I discussed these transformations considered them welcome signs of the market's maturation and successful consolidation around a pan-Latina or Hispanic identity. This change has al-

Figure 14.   "Heritage," produced for Wrangler jeans by Cartel Creativo,
asserts that jeans are really Latino.

lowed them to index Latinidad through scenes and situations that are
supposedly shared or recognized as being Latina, such as a soccer game
in the background, a Hispanic personality, or a popular Latin song or
tune. The mere fact that the ad is in Spanish and located in the world of
Spanish TV is enough as ads become less dependent on overt signs and
marks of Latin "traditions" or on overused nationalistic appeals, suggesting the consolidation in the world of advertising of a more contemporary version of the Latina consumer. This trend has also led to the creation of new references that creatives can draw from as material for their
ads, expanding the range of references that are actively mobilized when
portraying "Hispanic" images. Because they must be persuasive to both
their clients and consumers, however, these would necessarily be more
derivative than "new." Typical of this trend are ads for Lincoln and Mer-
cury by Uniworld Advertising, which a creative described as "very Latin."
They revolve not around conga lines or maracas, but around spoofs of
Mexican soap operas and old Mexican movies. These, according to the
creative, are a dominant Latin index in a market dominated by Mexican
cultural products. The "Telenovela" spot for Century 21 (figure 16), for
instance, dramatizes the appalling situation that may follow if a couple's

Figure 15.   "America." Tecate Beer conquers the United States. Ad by Cartel Creativo.

home loan is not approved. Unless they contact Century 21, they may be forced to live, and sleep, with their mother. In this way, ads are increasingly made "Hispanic" not by their direct presentation as such but by their embodiment in Hispanic characters and images. This brings us to the so-called generic "Latin look" and generic, nonregional Spanish, the two most powerful tools used to portray the modern pan-Latina market.

THE LATIN LOOK AND "WALTER CRONKITE SPANISH"

That there is a generic or pan-Hispanic "look" as well as universal Spanish is a view that is shared and taken for granted by almost everyone I talked to in this industry, from producers to creatives and casting directors. This construct dates back to the 1970s and the first nationwide TV campaigns, although it did not consolidate into its present dominant status until after an interlude in the 1980s, when the customization and regionalization of campaigns reached their zenith as marketing strategies. Thus today, even when not everyone may readily know how to define it, or agree with the representativity of this construct, everyone I spoke with

Figure 16.   This spoof of a soap
opera shows a couple confronting
the crisis of having their mortgage
denied and being forced to live with
the woman's mother. Century 21
saves their day. "Telenovela" TV ad
by FOVA Advertising.

took for granted and made constant reference to some sort of generic
"Latin look" that any Hispanic can recognize and identify upon seeing.
But who and what constitutes the generic Hispanic? A casting director
explained, "You know what they want when they ask you for models;
it's unspoken. What they want is the long straight hair, olive skin, just
enough oliveness to the skin to make them not ambiguous. To make them
Hispanic."

What makes anyone Hispanic in advertising, however, is more than
olive skin. The so-called generic look is mediated by the beauty-obsessed
world of advertising, as well as by the demand that this industry be (or
appear to be) representative of its target consumer. Specifically, in contrast to advertising images for Latin American or other North American
audiences, images for the U.S. Hispanic market have to be both aspirational (in the sense of showing beautiful, educated, or accomplished individuals) and also representative. Blondes and Nordic types, which are
common in Latin American ads, supposedly would not work for U.S.
Hispanics who, as minorities, I was told, were looking at ads for representation and confirmation. This does not mean that ad models are indeed representative of U.S. Hispanics—a quick look at Hispanic media
images would surely attest to this—but that there is a concerted effort
on the part of advertisers to cast aspirational models who are still some-

what representative of the "Hispanic consumer," or at least to sell and
stress to clients the need for models who are representative, not just beautiful. However, content analysis of ads filmed in the early 1980s compared with those filmed today confirms what I was told by experienced
casting directors and model agents working in this market: the generic
look has become whiter and thus less representative of the average Hispanic consumer. Early ads showed a greater percentage of darker Latinas, particularly in male models who were never too dark, yet dark
enough to be recognized as ethnic Hispanics. This is what was described
to me as the "dark, mustached, Mexican type," or the stereotypical Hispanic look of the past, that creatives had to rely on in order to convince
clients that their ads were authentic. They have since been able to re-
place this look with the so-called more modern and "representative" Latin
look. The irony, however, is that in supplanting this stereotype, the industry has created yet another powerful one, namely a white one. As with
Vasconcelos's early-twentieth-century dream of Latin American whitening by miscegenation, commercial representations of U.S. Hispanics have
become tantamount to showing whiter-looking, Mediterranean Hispanic
types. In contrast to racial segregation in the United States, Vasconcelos
saw racial mixing in Latin America as the key to the formation of a cos-
mic race, a new and improved civilization stemming from the harmonious integration of its racial components. Vasconcelos's ideas were developed as an anti-imperialist response to the dominant eugenic thought
of the time that rejected mixing as deterioration. His argument was a
simple one: as opposed to Anglo-Americans, whose injustice and inhu-
man materialism had led them to exterminate or exclude indigenous populations from their "civilization," Latin Americans had kindly "mated"
with them and assimilated them into a new culture where "inferior" and
"lower" races could be improved and ameliorated—yet another proof
of Latin America's moral superiority to the barbaric United States (Vasconcelos 1958). This is the same discourse that permeated most Latin
American nationalist ideologies and that reverberates in the marketing
industry's search and casting recommendations for the perfect look; a look,
as Vasconcelos would have it, of balance, harmony, and beauty that is devoid of extreme (ethnic) types. As described by a creative, national advertising campaigns specify Hispanics "with features such as darker/olive-
complected skin and brown-black hair over "extreme" types such as
Nordic or Indian physical types, as well as generic language "whose accent is not traceable to any distinct population and is therefore not offensive to any particular group." Behind these recommendations, how-

ever, stands the practice of casting "whiter" Latinas. As a casting director tired of always being asked for "light-skinned Latinas" noted,

> What they want is a very conservative, anglicized look, a Hispanic in an an-
> glicized garb. Its very much what in the general market we used to call the
> "P and G look," [Procter & Gamble look], the very clean-cut, all-American,
> blond and blue eyes, that was not representative of the United States. That
> was changed a long time ago, but it's not been thrown out in the Hispanic
> market. It's been replicated. They are trying to make the squeaky clean, perfect,
> boxed Latina look, not too dark and not too light.

And when in doubt, she continued, her clients would surely select the
lighter over the darker Latina. Standards of beauty within Latin America which favor whiteness and straight, or "good," hair are very much
at play here, as are those in the United States, especially beauty trends
marked by Hollywood which become dominant in the modeling industry at large. As she insisted, "You also have to consider existing trends
in beauty and looks. My roster is full of Jennifer López types, because
she's hot, and before that I had a lot of Julia Roberts or Jennifer Annis-
ton types. A client will also ask you for an Antonio Banderas type or a
cool Nicolas Cage, and this makes it easy because no one can go through
the entire roster of models." Making reference to Hollywood stars may
facilitate communication between casting director, agency, and client, but
it also translates into the casting of whiter models and actors. There are
after all, few black and Latina Hollywood stars who can be independently recalled as "types." Indeed, there is seldom an indigenous or black
face in Hispanic ads, unless they are minimally included in group shots.
Even ads targeting the Central American and Mexican constituencies in
the West consist of whiter, mestizo types. For nationwide campaigns,
however, it is the generic/Mediterranean look that rules. When more rec-
ognizably "ethnic" types are shown, they tend to be presented as
signifiers of cultural authenticity, never of beauty or generic appeal. Thus
an ad for Banco Popular shows a woman with Indian traits making tor-
tillas only as part of a collage of people to denote its status as the bank
for the people; channel 41's thirty-year anniversary ads present Andean
performers and Puerto Rican folk musicians in authentic garb to mark
their authenticity as performers in order to appeal to specific subgroups
in New York—but they do not speak.

This general lack of nonwhite images coincides with a widespread ret-
icence regarding the issue of racial diversity in advertising. This was evident during the 1998 fall meeting of the Association of Hispanic Advertising Agencies (AHAA), when Felipe Luciano, former member of the

Young Lords, and the only Afro-Hispanic in the audience, brought up the issue of race and representativity during the question and answer period of one of the plenaries. His statement that most of what he saw was insulting and not representative of Hispanics was met with the common argument that "advertising for U.S. Hispanics is far more representative than Latin American advertisements," or that, after all, only a small percentage of Hispanics are black, and this percentage itself does not warrant a transformation of the Latin image.

In fact, even when Hispanic media and advertising staff express interest in transforming this Latin look, they encounter major obstacles in overcoming the dominant image of the light-skinned Hispanic. As explained by the founder of *Latina* magazine, which since its establishment in 1996 has striven for a more realistic portrayal of contemporary U.S. Latina women, even when staff members ask for darker and more diverse Latina models, agencies tend to send the same type: a size twelve if they ask for a large model, and a light-skinned Latina if they ask for a Latina. To cope with this problem, *Latina* magazine has repeatedly shown celebrities rather than models on its covers and tried to profile readers in some of its regular features, which has allowed it to show a more diverse range of Latina women than modeling agencies are willing to provide. Notwithstanding these attempts at inclusiveness, it still took the magazine over two years to feature an Afro-Hispanic model on its cover, the upcoming TV and film actress Gina Ravera, featured in the November 1998 issue. The cover, a response to previous criticism about the lack of African-descent representation in the magazine, however, displayed a half-naked actress, with only her tresses covering her breasts in a sensual portrayal not matched by the rest of the magazine's covers, which had been dominated by wholesome or romantic-looking Latinas or celebrities. The cover hence triggered yet another letter to the editor criticizing the portrayal of women of African descent as "purely exotic sexual beings" (Dias 1999).

The general-market model agencies contribute to the whiteness of commercial Latina media because they operate within the dichotomous black-and-white racial dynamics of the United States, with a limited roster of Latin actors and models. Meanwhile, Hispanic model agencies, while specializing in this area, are confronted with a paucity of opportunities for their "ambiguous" Latin models, such as Afro- and Indo-Hispanic models, who could be taken for blacks or Asiatics, rather than unambiguous Hispanics. Indeed, a casting director I spoke with had few black or other "exotic" types, as she described them, in her photographic ledger, and those she had were rarely booked by Hispanic agencies, who feared that these models might blur the uniqueness of Hispanic marketing as not only a cultural but also a racially specific market. Thus her recommendation for an aspiring black Hispanic actress was simple enough: change your name from Mónica Rodríguez to Monica White and market yourself as a black actress instead. The irony is that, as she also explained, the ethnic/racial ambiguity is more easily accepted when the model is a white Latino or Latina.

The so-called generic Latin look has its linguistic match in "Walter Cronkite Spanish"—unaccented, generic, or universal Spanish, supposedly devoid of regionalism or of traceable accent, which is generally believed to be the most effective medium for campaigns reaching the entire market. This is also the Spanish that most creatives and ad executives I spoke with were convinced they themselves had cultivated, in order to corroborate their own pan-ethnicity and thus their authority to address this pan-ethnic market. In this way, Hispanic marketers acted as a "linguistic community," in Michael Silverstein's (1996) phrase, united by their allegiance to the existence and promotion of a "standardized" language, which they treated as a "realizable asset" that they themselves had cultivated and mastered. This "standard" Spanish was conceived as standard English is in the United States, perceived as correct speech and valorized as an instrument of clarity and rational thought. Most of all, it was regarded as the optimum means to avoid the potential double meanings and malapropisms that could ensue from the various speech patterns and codes of different Latin American nationalities. Their adherence to this construct was apparent in marketers' avoidance of regionally marked terminology, in their boasting about their lack of accent, and in the pride with which they reacted to my inability to discover their national background from their speech.

Yet, like any putative standard form of language, "Walter Cronkite Spanish" is not an empirical fact but a "discursive project," reproducing particular language ideology and social distinctions (Woolard 1998); as such, it is not uncritically accepted by all in the industry. Walter Cronkite Spanish is slightly influenced by English at the level of structure, vocabulary, and grammar, and English's lingering threat to Spanish is one factor that guides the hiring of Latin American–born staff. Moreover, although many advertising personnel have reduced their native Latin American accents as a result of their immigration experience and their involvement in the "linguistic community" of advertising, the origin of their accents is still perceptible under scrutiny. In addition, their nationalities are never shed when they reduce their national accents; in fact, Hispanic marketers are quite adept at "reading" each other's camouflaged accents to expose knowledge of each other's background, a knowledge that remains important for social interactions within the industry at large. In fact, some advertising staff I spoke with admitted that the so-called Walter Cronkite Spanish was a cloak for the "Mexicanization" of the language, a perception that is not at all unfounded. Given that Mexican Americans constitute 65 percent of all Hispanics and that many ads are filmed in Mexico with Mexican actors, ads for the national market often end up with a Mexican flavor which, combined with the central role of Mexican soap operas and programming on the U.S. Hispanic airwaves, further strengthens Mexican language, accent, and mannerisms as the embodiment of generic Latinidad. What we therefore have is the dissemination of a media register of a sociolect of mostly upper-class Mexican Spanish, where Mexican (mostly *chilango,* or from the capital) mannerisms and accents are more likely to be accepted as "representative" of the market, whereas Caribbean Spanish is hardly heard in generic advertisements and is highly edited in the Hispanic networks' programming. For example, both the Cuban Cristina Saralegui and the Puerto Rican Ray Arrieta, popular Univision entertainers, have publicly revealed the pressure they faced to tone down their accents. Cristina, who has achieved considerable influence in this industry, struggled and was able to keep her Cuban accent and have it accepted as a trademark of her TV personality, but Raymond had to shed his Puerto Rican "Ay bendito" after the first filming of his new Univision program *Lente Loco.*[9]

For others, generic Spanish is but a myth that never fully appeals to all Hispanics. This view is most prevalent among radio professionals, who work in a more regional medium and are thus inherently less likely to embrace the generic Spanish idea. According to Eduardo Caballero, a primary figure in the development of national Hispanic radio, "The problem is that the generic Spanish is a myth. It's like Walter Cronkite, who, wanting to reach all, would not reach anyone. That's the problem. It's generic, but it is not absolutely relevant or direct." Connecting to consumers, he argued, involved speaking to their "souls" through their particular type of Spanish, enhancing rather than diminishing accents. Later, we will examine how audiences perceive this so-called Latin look and generic Spanish. From what we have seen so far, we can safely infer that the growing interest in Hispanics as consumers has been paralleled by their being recast into a sellable abstraction that is becoming both more bounded and defined, and more distant from the real heterogeneity of the "average" Hispanic consumer.

"THE NATION AND ITS FRAGMENTS"

As already mentioned, the dominant trend in Hispanic marketing is progressively moving toward a generic "Hispanic nation" and market.[10] The regionalization and customization of campaigns for different national subgroups, however, has also been a common strategy to address this market, even if in decline and in constant competition with the growing consolidation of the so-called generic, or "universal," Hispanic.

Today, such customization has been reduced to the realm of radio and print media, and consists of slight adjustments to national campaigns or of promotions customized for different subgroups. Yet in the early 1980s this task often involved the development of different versions of an ad to appeal to different national subgroups. The irony here is that the few ads for nationwide campaigns done in the early 1970s were conceived in terms of the generic, so-called neutral Spanish, and so, despite the scarcity of nationwide campaigns, the industry had some practice with the generic Hispanic construct, only to abandon it in the 1980s with the growing popularity of the market. This change and eventual recuperation of the generic Hispanic construct is a topic that triggered many explanations from all I talked to. For some, customization and regionalization resulted from growing competition as regional differences became a selling point for new agencies seeking to distinguish themselves in a more competitive market by emphasizing their expertise in the ethnic particularities of different markets. I was also told that this development was related to an overall reaction to the generic campaigns, which were seen in the West as too Caribbean and not representative of the Western-based Hispanic market. Recall that the first ads were devised by a mostly Cuban creative staff and filmed in Puerto Rico. This may explain why, when transmitted alongside the Mexican programming, over 90 percent of which was imported from Mexico until the 1980s, these first ads may have appeared as "foreign" rather than generic in these markets.

Yet another motive for customizing campaigns was the growing budgets attracted by the industry at this time, which facilitated the development of customized campaigns for different regional markets. Amidst the rising interest in the Hispanic market during the 1980s, many corporations began to institute multicultural and Hispanic initiatives, which led to a sudden increase in media budgets for Hispanics.[11] A commercial for Goya's Canilla rice in the mid-1980s, for instance, was filmed three different times, customizing it for Puerto Ricans, Dominicans, and Colombians (along with Central Americans) through particular themes, casts, backdrops, and music, while maintaining the same message in its jingle. While all of the ads were filmed in the Dominican Republic, each aimed to evoke scenes that would reverberate specifically among these other nationalities. The Dominican version was filmed on the famous beach of Boca Chica, and juxtaposed images of a fisherman and a couple eating in a seashore restaurant. The jingle featured a merengue beat. The Colombian/Central American ad showed a middle-class family scene with more Andean/peasant music, whereas the Puerto Rican ad depicted countryside scenes aimed at recreating Puerto Rican landscapes with a backdrop of Puerto Rican *jíbaro* music.

The ads for Campbell's soup by Conill Advertising also exemplify such customization. These ads present the product as the ideal side dish to traditional Puerto Rican and Mexican meals such as *arroz con pollo* and *chiles rellenos,* with Puerto Rican and Mexican models exhibiting the accent and mannerisms of each national subgroup. Even basic products like soap or detergent have been customized for different regional markets. An advertisement for Tide laundry detergent by Conill in the mid-1980s was filmed twice, using two different musical jingles and backdrops. Both ads showed a woman dancing with the box of detergent, but the West Coast version was accompanied by a soundtrack of "Chapanecas," a traditional Mexican song, while for the East Coast market, the *manicero,* a Cuban salsa-like rhythm, was used.

All the advertising executives I talked to agreed, however, that the increase of generic representations was affected primarily by the requirements of corporate clients, who needed easily marketable Latinas. As one noted, "We were selling them the idea that all Hispanics are alike but then pitching them to do two or three different advertising executions. It got too complicated. We had to make it easy for them. They had to understand that advertising for Hispanics is like advertising for the general market. You just don't do an ad for Alabama and one for New York." Indeed, today most advertisers have left behind this regionalized approach to the market and now address Hispanics as a unique "nation-within-a-nation," with more commonalities than differences. Figures 6, 8, 12, 13, 16, 18, and 20 are all examples of this generic advertising approach. This does not mean that the industry no longer targets specific markets; rather, customization is now confined to the less costly and therefore more flexible realms of radio and print media. Most national TV campaigns are accompanied by a radio component using salsa musical backgrounds when advertising for East Coast audiences, *conjuntos* for the audiences in the West, and a Caribbean or Mexican scenario, ambiance, or flavor for East and West Coast audiences respectively. Meanwhile, the continued proliferation of festivals such as Miami's Calle Ocho and New York City's Dominican and Puerto Rican parade, as well as of ethnic-specific promotions, is a sure sign that regional/ethnic appeals will continue to be a vibrant component of this industry.

Vidal, Reynardus, and Moya's (now the Vidal Partnership) advertising for Heineken beer provides a good example of this trend. Though its national TV campaign revolved around nondescript music and artistic shots of beer, lacking any Latin index, it was accompanied by an outdoor ad program customized for particular markets, filled with culturally specific references that could only be identified by inhabitants of particular neighborhoods. A poster placed all around my own Manhattan neighborhood, Washington Heights, in the commercial center of 181st Street, uses street signs of this very street along with signs from bodegas and street lights marking this commercial intersection to associate the beer not with New York, but with this particular neighborhood (figure 17). The agency also customized poster ads for other Latina neighborhoods that similarly mixed and matched important landmarks, be they buildings or signs, into a Heineken neighborhood collage.

Univision's New York channel 41 promotional ad provides a good example of the persistence of this trend. For its thirty-year anniversary, while its ads repeatedly appealed to a common Hispanic spirit, language, and heritage, the channel shot different versions using certain performers to appeal to different Latin American constituencies in the city, singing the promotional song in different national rhythms and often accompanied by their respective "national dances." Thus the Dominican version of the ad, filmed in the Dominican Republic, shows Dominican performer Sergio Vargas playing a merengue version of the song in scenes that intercalated the Dominican Flag and tourist spots. Similarly, the Colombian version shows Colombian performers playing the same song, arranged to a *cumbia* rhythm, and the Argentinian version shows a couple dancing the tango, lest any groups feel excluded or offended. What have not changed, however, are the culturalist types of appeals that reduce different subnationalities to culture indexes and traits, such as a type of food, music, or a festival, which are seen as the greatest inducements

Figure 17.   Outdoor ads in Washington Heights, New York City. The Heineken ad, placed on 181st Street, incorporates the street sign into the ad to associate the beer more closely with the residents of this Latino community.

to Latinas, irrespective of their background. Consequently, differences of class, race, and lifestyle among members of the same nationality are never addressed, nor are those between different nationalities (except in special cases like the channel 41 ads, which were specifically generated for the New York regional market).

The trend towards addressing Hispanics as a totality for nationwide campaigns, however, is not solely an issue of economics. While such ads are easier to sell to Anglo corporations and appear more authentically

Hispanic, this trend is also fed by a generalized view among advertisers that the United States is indeed undergoing a process of Latinization, and that there is a great degree of cross-fertilization among different Latina groups. As proof, creatives pointed to the advent of Puerto Rican *merengueras* (female Puerto Rican singers of an originally Dominican rhythm), to the popularity of Caribbean salsa among Mexicans and Central Americans, and to the sold-out Madison Square Garden concert of Mexican Alejandro Fernández, the *ranchera* singer, in a market where it is Puerto Ricans and Dominicans, not Mexicans, who form the largest Latina population. The result is that advertising is increasingly less particular to specific markets. Thus, for instance, instead of customizing ads for different markets, Goya's new ads translate "beans" as both *frijoles* and *habichuelas* (as said by different Latina populations) within the same ad, and show the national dishes of different Latin American countries next to each other. For the promotion of Malta drink, Goya's ads show children playing both baseball, popular among Hispanic Caribbeans, and soccer, popular among Central and South Americans. Similarly, Tide's ads in the 1990s appealed to a common Hispanic spirit through scenes of experiences supposedly shared by all Hispanics/Latinas. One of their more recent ads shows a recent immigrant learning English and discussing her difficulties but also her will to succeed in this country, which I was told is a "universal" experience that Hispanics have either had themselves, or experienced vicariously through friends or relatives.

Another common strategy for reconciling the need for inclusiveness with the need for specific representation was described to me as the "café con leche" approach, where unity is constructed and projected from references to difference. However, in contrast to the customized campaigns of the 1980s, where different nationalities were segmented and addressed through culture-specific ads, these ads show different nationalities juxtaposed or, increasingly, mingling and socializing within the same ad. Good examples of the juxtaposition of different nationalities is provided by figures 18 and 19. In "Opinions" (figure 18) Campbell's Soup is simultaneously targeted to Mexicans, Cubans, and Puerto Ricans who, while chatting with the Campbell's Soup can, are indexed through language mannerisms and regional accents. In "Family Favorites" (figure 19) these three groups are again addressed together but this time through their national cuisines. The ad juxtaposes different models rejoicing at their respective national dishes, such as Mexican *huevos rancheros,* the Cuban beef stew, *ropa vieja,* and the Puerto Rican *bistecito encebollado con yuca* (steak with onions and garlic cassava). The ad concludes with images of *churros,* codfish fritters, taquitos, and a very pleased man joyfully exclaiming "Ay, ay, ay."

As for ads showing different Latino nationalities socializing, an ad for AT&T by Bravo (1997) recently teamed up the Cuban singer Jon Secada with the Mexican soap opera star Thalia to appeal simultaneously to two distinct Hispanic subgroups. Drawing from viewers' knowledge of U.S. Hispanic media personalities, the commercial shows Secada arranging a song for Thalia in Mexico to laud the clarity of an AT&T telephone connection. In this case, Secada's dark looks are mediated by his fame, which points to another industry trend: when black Latinas are shown, they are mostly media or entertainment personalities like Celia Cruz or Secada portraying themselves. Black Latinas are seldom signifiers of generic Latinidad. Another example of appealing to different nationalities is K-Mart's Christmas ad, which presents shopping at K-Mart as a Hispanic tradition by juxtaposing a Cuban, a Mexican, and a Puerto Rican woman remembering each group's traditional Christmas requirements of *buñuelos, posadas,* and *aguinaldos;* or Conill's Toyota ad, which shows a car driving through a collage depicting different urban, regional, and Latin American settings—a beach which could be taken for Miami or Puerto Rico, an urban landscape which could be taken for New York or Chicago—to appeal simultaneously to different Latina subnationalities. Miller's 1999 beer ad even features an invented word, the hybrid *salsarengue,* to tell consumers not to argue about whether they like salsa or merengue: dance both and drink Miller. The Bud Light 1999 campaign, for its part, adopted a regional Latina montage drawing from the impersonations of comedian John Leguizamo to present Bud Light as the facilitator that reconciles regional differences among Latinas, facilitating the process of Latinization. In a spot named "Banda," Leguizamo is shown in Tex-Mex gear crashing an audition by Projecto Uno, an East Coast hip-hop and merengue band; tension fills the air, but the potential clash is quickly mitigated with a Bud Light. Additionally, music is increasingly described as "contemporary Latin" rather than Mexican or merengue, and images of soccer and baseball are being dropped for more conceptual images. Even telecommunications companies have abandoned any reference to old countries left behind and now feature relatives calling their friends and family, not "back home" but all across the United States. As one creative said, "Where we need to go is to the point where we show husbands and wives with different accents, because we do intermarry, and where we don't need to even make reference to family or soccer." To get there, however, creatives need first to overcome

Figure 18.   Cambell Soup's "Opinions," featuring Cuban-, Mexican-, and Puerto Rican–accented Spanish. Produced in 1984. Ad by Conill Advertising, New York City.

Figure 19.   "Family Favorites" TV ad for Mazola by The Bravo Group.
MAZOLA is a registered trademark of Bestfoods. Used by permission.

a series of obstacles which work against the expansion of the range of Latina images, as explored in the next chapter.

What is indeed obvious is that in the process of projecting corrective images through lavish portrayals meant to make Latinas proud of themselves and their "Hispanic" identity, the industry has generated additional tropes and stereotypes of the Latina consumer which are more derivative than new. These processes remind us of the constraints against which struggles over what it means to be Latina or Hispanic in the media are being waged—the same struggles that overcame clients' insistence on traditional images of Latinidad, although not necessarily the discourses that gave rise to those images. Recall that the view of the white, moral, and traditional Latina hinges on the dominant U.S.-generated discourses about Latin culture that have been rampant in nineteenth-century ideologies of Latin American elites. The association of Latinas with so-called pride-worthy values and images, has functioned also to reduce what can and cannot be representative of Hispanics in this country to very specific conventions. They are therefore increasingly codified around marketable tropes and images that have become more distant from their everyday realities. After all, a great number of Latinas are trapped in poverty and low-wage jobs or unemployment, and the Mediterranean Hispanic does not compose the majority of the U.S. Latina population, nor does that majority speak upper-class, "Mexican" Spanish. Moreover, while the ways in which these themes are represented have not remained static or unchanged—families have taken less traditional roles, representations of Latinidad have become more self-referential, the generic look has whitened—the references around which they are framed have not been altered. Hispanic advertising still responds to the social hierarchies that subordinate Latinas in this country and is still predicated on the need to project positive images, leading it to rely on the same clichés of the good, traditional, patriotic, not-too-dark/not-too-light Latina which, against the always-present specter of Anglo culture, still dominate their commercial representation. Unfortunately, these are the same clichés that, while making Latinas safe and commercially viable for mass consumption, limit their association with some sort of cultural ethos, keeping them unthreateningly in "their place." The dominant racial and ethnic hierarchies at play in U.S. society thus remain unchallenged. They hinge on the existence of a normative white world, where difference is contained and marked so as never to disturb this world. Untouched as well are the existing ethnic/racial hierarchies among and across Latina subgroups, the same ones that make the lighter Latina the more marketable one, that favor the so-called standard Spanish over Spanglish, and that treat certain accents as more representative of Latinidad than others. The preceding discussion warns us of the pitfalls of positive images, reminding us that the need for them and their production are still predicated on, and therefore affected by, dominant frameworks of race, ethnicity, and nationality.

At the same time, the growing popularity of generic, national Hispanic advertising suggests that such appeals, while narrow and exclusionary, have attained some generalized acceptance, helping to partially consolidate a highly heterogeneous population around images of a world where everyone is good, no one is a minority, and "everyone is your friend." In this context, the Hispanic marketing industry becomes a mirror of trends in the advertising industry at large, and of the same processes through which differences are ordered, contained, or partially represented. This is because, far from being merely shrewd fabrications, Hispanic ads are also products of strategies of representation aimed at the partial representation of the "Hispanic consumer," even when this simultaneously involves the erasure and reconstitution of differences (such as those of class, race, nationality, etc.) into his or her very construction. Thus we saw that Hispanic models, though generally white and Mediterranean-looking, are indeed darker than most models in the general market. Similarly, intangible cultural values have continued to be popular as a way of reconciling intragroup differences, allowing creatives to avoid reference to particular groups or everyday scenes connected to particular Latina subgroups in ways that might invoke regional, racial, or subnational, rather than the intended pan-Hispanic identification. It is also to this end that most campaigns are still accompanied by an ethnic-specific promotional or radio component that reminds different groups that, despite the commercial abstractions of Latinidad presented in the TV ads, these campaigns are really addressing "them" as "Hispanics." In these processes, these constructs become self-referential of Hispanic culture, even though this "culture" can only be found in the ad world.

CHAPTER 4

Screening the Image

[Because I'm from] the South Bronx, they would say that
I sounded black, that I didn't . . . speak with the right accent.
I would say, "No one on my block sounds like that." It was
so frustrating. Over and over again, they said I just wasn't
Spanish enough.

These casting directors called my manager and said,
"We told you we wanted somebody who was Mexican.
We wanted somebody dirty. He was white as far as we were
concerned."

I was told that I was reading my hooker role very "white."
[The casting agent] said to me, "You're Spanish or Mexican
or whatever you are. We need to hear the accent."

The director said to me, "You know what? It is not
necessary for you to audition. Let's not waste your time
or mine. Obviously you are a person with culture and
education, but what we are looking for is a Puerto Rican."

> Comments by Latino members of the Screen
> Actors Guild, in *Urban Latino,* 1999

So far readers may think that Hispanic advertising agencies were solely
responsible for the commercial portrayal of Hispanics and for generating the different formulas for their representation. In reality, however,
these images emerge from active negotiations between Hispanic agencies
and their clients, processes in which the agencies' insights and recommendations are often subordinated. These issues repeatedly came to the
surface during conversations with creatives, producers, and other staff
involved in the creation of ads, particularly when discussing their as-

sessments of their work and that of others, and their criticisms of the Hispanic advertising industry, which many saw as implicated in generating its own set of stereotypes about Hispanics. And while most staff I spoke with generally associated stereotypes with the past, as having once been necessary to give cohesiveness to the market, they nonetheless complained that these conventions continue to limit their work as well as the range of representations of what can appropriately be considered "Hispanic." Some even reflected on their past involvement in the creation of such images and regretted having to carry the burden of old stereotypes that now limited their ability to use more complex representations in their ads and—most important from their perspective—to tap into and therefore profit from existing differences among "Hispanics."

Yet criticizing and transforming these images are very distinct matters. In what follows I explore some of the politics involved in the creation of commercial representations of Latinos in order to expose some of the strategies and interests behind these representations and modes of appeal. Through stories told to me by copywriters, producers, creatives, and account executives about their experiences in creating and obtaining approval for their ads from their clients, I intend to examine the kinds of issues that have affected the commercial representation of Latinos and that, to different degrees, are common in the industry at large.

THROUGH CORPORATE EYES

Marketing to Hispanics involves selling an idea to a corporate client, and this process gives us the clearest view of the strategies behind the making of "Latin" images. These clients have the ultimate word and can approve the execution of an ad for this market, even when they may have little familiarity with their target audience. What the clients never lack, however, are their own ideas and stereotypes about the "Hispanic" consumer— ideas which, as I have argued throughout this work, have long been sustained by the Hispanic ad agencies' effort to contain and define their market.

Clients also have the ultimate authority to approve ads for the general market, and this leads to more constrained and predictable ads than would otherwise be produced by their creatives and producers (Lury and Warde 1997). What is unique in ethnic and Hispanic marketing is the extent to which these processes are additionally mediated by issues of race and ethnicity. Consider the following exchanges between Hispanic marketers and corporate clients as told by a creative at Uniworld, an

African American–owned, multiethnic agency that also targets Latinos and Asians. This creative, a native of Venezuela who had formerly worked with Alicia Conill and had been active in the industry for over twenty years, was quite critical of the "illusory" nature of the media's representation of Latinos. As I later learned, this outlook stemmed from his own perspective and experience working in a multiethnic agency, which he was convinced had "stained" his standing as a Hispanic marketer among his counterparts working in Hispanic-only shops, who tended to look down on him for working in a "black" rather than authentically Hispanic shop. He was therefore more than ready to divulge examples of the difficulties involved in challenging Latino images, although his stories were not at all unique within the industry at large. He told me of two cases, one in which his attempt to use images of nonwhite Latinos was either met with resistance by Anglo clients, who saw his choice as possibly insulting to Latinos, or else stalled within the agency in anticipation of their client's censure. In an ad for Kodak, where a father, upon being asked by his son to define the word *patria*, is shown telling his son about his Latin American homeland (depicted as a generic Latin American country), one of the homeland scenes was supposed to include two black, Puerto Rican child models eating *piraguas* (ice cones). The models, described by the creative as "a beautiful girl, black with green eyes, who would have broken all kinds of stereotypes, along with her real brother," were part of his attempt to broaden the range of Latin looks. Yet upon seeing the first shooting, the agency's account manager rejected the proposal, on the grounds that their client would consider it insulting to Latinos, who, as they had learned from marketing studies, do not think of themselves as black. In the end, the models were replaced with two much lighter kids (one of them almost blonde).

Similar processes deterred the same creative from developing an ironic ad for a car company showing a humorous family scene—a son presenting his girlfriend to his family, who ignore the girlfriend in favor of her car. At the request of the client, the ad was modified and the irony softened. Their belief, explained the creative, was that families are sacred for Latinos and that they would be insulted by the humor. The result was a far more conventional ad showing the same extended family greeting the girlfriend, but lacking the humor and the embedded critique of the family intended by the original commercial. Yet another example of the constraints to showing alternative representations of Hispanics on the airwaves is provided by Robles Communications, one of the few (if not the only) independent Puerto Rican–founded and owned advertising agency in New York. Their decision to use music from the Puerto Rican group DLG, which mixes Latin music with urban black rhythms, from hip-hop to rap, in a beer commercial was turned down by the corporate client in favor of a more "folkloric" musical background with hints of *cumbia*.

Thus, authorship of the ads is always shared and negotiated in ways that partly incorporate the expectations of their audience, with creatives acting as "surrogate audiences" who anticipate the needs and desires of the most important segment of this audience: the corporate clients.[1] They and their representatives have the power to censure images that do not meet their stereotypical conceptualization of Hispanics and to constrain diversity within the context of the ads. The most likely moment at which such image censuring takes place is during the initial business pitches of agencies to prospective clients. It is at that point, when an agency is presenting ideas to position particular products in order to sell itself to a prospective client, that it is most exposed to the client's preconceptions of the market. Indeed, discussions with marketing personnel working from the corporate client's side at Procter & Gamble, Coca-Cola, and Johnson & Johnson confirmed that they tended to select Hispanic agencies on the basis of their general feeling about how well agencies "understood the market and communicated with us" during business pitches. Their expectation is that the agency review process will lessen differences in marketing philosophy and outlook between agency and client prior to the start of a campaign, facilitating the synergy between general and Hispanic marketing that is so sought after by corporate clients. Tension is greatest, therefore, in these presentation stages, and clients' views of the market come unabashedly to the surface. An executive from Zubi Advertising in Coral Gables, Florida, recalled situations mirrored by many of her colleagues: when confronted with condescending or stereotypical remarks by their clients on Latinos, they just got up and left, or discontinued their marketing presentations to a prospective client. The instance when she left the presentation involved a corporate client who rejected her pitch to advertise a luxury good (which she declined to name) on the grounds that "you all came in boats" and could never afford the product. Particularly upsetting to this Cuban executive was the social context framing the comment—the height of the Marielito incident,[2] when destitute Cubans came to sully the image of the model Latino earned by original Cuban migrants in Miami. "It just dawned on me that for him we were all *pobretones* (shoddy and impoverished)."

However, it is not only the corporate clients who end up narrowing the representation of Latinos. In their effort to sell a distinct ad to a corporate client, agencies also end up producing ads that are far less representative of racial and ethnic diversity than some of the general market ads that a client may want to use or adapt for the Hispanic market. For instance, the general market version of ads for an income tax preparation company showed people of different races and backgrounds going about their work in a multicultural collage common in mainstream advertising. When adapted by FOVA to the Hispanic market, the ad was quickly transformed, its diversity replaced by the generic Latin look. The creative said his decision to change most of the models was based on the simple fact that "the general market is more used to multiculturalism, but for Hispanics, we are all Hispanics." Thus, while the general market ad included black, Hispanic, and Anglo models, the Hispanic ad showcased the lighter Hispanic models exclusively, along with some of the white models that he thought "could pass for Hispanic." Behind this decision is the already noted tendency to portray Hispanics in a self-contained world, where differences are managed to minimally signal distinctions among and across Hispanic subgroups but never between themselves and non-Latinos.

THE VIRGINAL MOM AND OTHER NEGOTIATIONS

The extent to which the expectations of clients affect the nature of Hispanic advertising is most evident when comparing the presentation of women in advertising with the rest of Hispanic programming. In *La Usurpadora,* one of Univision's most popular soap operas of 1999, viewers were reminded again and again of the protagonist's goodness, morality, and immeasurable sacrifice for her family. She, Paulina, is contrasted with her evil twin sister, Paola, who, bored by her "lovely" family, beautiful children, and handsome husband, forces her twin sister to impersonate her while she goes off traveling around the world with one of her many rich and decadent lovers. While Paola's away, Paulina fixes every imaginable problem in Paola's family, endears everyone with her constant sacrifice and devotion, and, most of all, remains pure and a virgin, refusing to impersonate her sister in the bedroom. And to make sure that viewers perceive her as the good and moral woman she is, Paulina wears only pink clothing and pink lipstick, in contrast to her sister's penchant for scarlet reds, and openly declares her virginity to a friend, the cocktail waitress, who represents a further contrast to Paulina's purity.

This dual portrait of Latina women as virgin or whore epitomizes the range of representations of women in Hispanic television and explains the dominance of the mother figure featured in most Hispanic advertisements. This dichotomy reflects the dual stereotype of Latin women as either the traditional señorita or the overly sexualized, loud, and hot-tempered Latin spitfire that has dominated stereotypes of Latin women in mainstream media (Kanellos 1998; Rivera 2001; Rodríguez 1997). This duality is not at odds with the dominant constructions of gender roles as tied to norms of sexuality. As scholars of gender and nationalism have explained, the way in which women are presented as dutiful citizens in many nationalist ideologies is as repositories of morality and traditionality. Women are vested with the responsibility of maintaining appropriate standards of decorum and respectability (particularly in the realm of sexuality), an association that leads to the idealization of motherhood and their subordinate role within the male national brotherhood (Williams 1996).

This common duality of the virginal/promiscuous female is, however, represented very differently in ads than in TV programming, offering a vivid example of how corporate clients' ideas of Hispanics affect their representation. In TV programming, this binary is confounded or made more limited—according to how one looks at it—by the glamorous sexuality that is required of any female character. Whether a good or evil woman, a Latina is foremost beautiful, white, and alluringly dressed. Thus, the good Paulina may be dressed permanently in pink in *La Usurpadora,* but her skirts were not less short, her dress less tight, nor her lip-gloss less defined than that of her sister Paola. Yet in advertisements, the Latina icon is mostly a mom who is young, light-skinned, long-haired, "soft-featured," and beautiful, but never shown to be as glamorous as are most women anchors, or the women in *novelas* (the serials of short duration that dominate the airwaves), or the talk shows, or the rest of the programming. In advertisements she is most of all the caretaker and guardian of the family, concerns that she keeps always in mind as she selects any product, from soap to yogurt. She's a Paulina without the lip-gloss.

Arguably, this disparity can be attributed to the same factors that have made the family such a dominant trope in Hispanic advertisements, such as the type of companies and products advertised in this market. In beer ads, which cater mostly to men, the glamorous, sexy Latina in a tight dress and high heels, as in the ads for Miller and Budweiser, is just as common. Discussion with creatives and account executives suggested, however, that the virginal but less sexualized representations of women presented in the ads are most of all the product of their client's stereotypes about Latinas and their own standards of female sexual and social propriety. To understand this, we need to recall that whereas Hispanic TV's programming is mostly imported or produced as a potential export to Latin America, advertisements are produced under the assumption that they will address the particular needs of the U.S. Hispanic market, and they are shaped directly by conversation regarding the needs of their clients. As an account executive with whom I discussed my perception of these different portrayals of women explained,

> It's a purely cultural thing. Clients don't understand Latino culture and cannot read the way women dress, or accept that they are concerned about their looks, their makeup, and appearance. We tell them all these things, but they feel that it would sexualize women if we presented them that way. And they get scared. They want women to be conservative and covered up.

This disjunction was corroborated by the head of ethnic marketing at Colgate-Palmolive, a Latina who recounted the difficulties she faced in getting her supervisors to understand the different dress etiquettes held by Latina women. A scene that showed women wearing strapless dresses at a wedding was considered too sexy by her supervisors, forcing her to explain to them that such dresses were common and, most of all, not provocative by Latin standards. Obviously, the argument that Latina women have a "tendency to overdress" or display "emphatic use of color, [and a] steady interest in color cosmetics" is commonly used to attract cosmetic companies to advertise to Hispanics (Roslow and Therrien Decker 1998: 63), and hence it is embraced as needed. What is striking is that in the world of advertising, the issue of better representation for women is reduced to one of appearance and looks, or the quantity of lip-gloss or the mode of dress that can be tolerated without disturbing the virginal innocence that is required of women in TV. Hence, the construct of the fashion-conscious, sexy, and made-up but moral Latina promoted by Hispanic marketers is ultimately still predicated on the same type of concerns, namely, on the threatening sexuality that pervades both Anglo and Latino prototypes of Latinas and is always in need of some sort of accommodation. What differs is the manner in which these concerns are handled when Anglo clients become involved in the process—how they contribute to more aesthetically conservative images of femininity and decorum.[3]

Such disjunctions in perception lead to similar battles between creatives and their clients, with the clients having the ultimate authority. For their part, Hispanic marketers have two powerful tools, research and experience, but these tools force them to constantly perform their Hispanidad in front of their clients. Indeed, pointing to one's individual experiences in order to corroborate the Hispanidad of different trends and ease clients' concerns over Hispanic consumer sensibilities was a common tactic used by people in the industry at large. More than one producer, creative, and copywriter mentioned having used their experiences or made references to their own lives to defend the authenticity of their representation of Hispanics. One example was provided by a creative with whom I spoke at Siboney Advertising who, when advertising a new whitening and tartar-control toothpaste by Colgate, had proposed showing a newlywed couple shopping in the supermarket, where the wife, upon her husband's selection of two different toothpastes, quickly corrects him and picks up Colgate's double-use toothpaste instead. According to the creative, however, the client, concerned that the ad showed the man as a passive fool, being scolded and corrected by his wife, insisted on changing or canceling the ad. His greatest fear was that this scene would offend the always "chauvinist" Hispanic men. In response, the creative insisted on the idea, pointed to research documenting that it is Hispanic women who make most shopping decisions for day-to-day items, and appealed to his own experience, explaining that he had only conceived of a situation that he himself had lived or could have lived with his own wife. The ad (figure 20) was finally approved.

One producer, a dark-skinned Colombian female, pointed, after a client's objection to the inclusion of a dark Latina model for a group shoot on the grounds that Hispanics "are not dark," to her own color, immediately silencing her client. In an ironic reversal, an Argentinean account executive convinced a client to showcase a white South American model by pointing to his own Latinness, irrespective of his whiteness. In both cases, it would be hard to imagine white creatives defending their choice of models by pointing to their own skin or hair. Another example is the ad pitch for tropical fruit yogurt in which a father tells his son how back in his country fruit was plentiful and mangos were just taken from his neighbor's yard. The client, concerned that this scene would evoke negative stereotypes of Hispanics as thieves, was placated when the creative pointed to his own experiences back home and assured him that mango trees were "common property" for Hispanics.

Accusations of inauthenticity are commonly faced by creatives and agencies when attempting to portray alternative representations of His-

Figure 20.   "Honeymooners." Siboney Advertising, New York City.

panics or to create conceptual rather than "culturally specific" ads. At
such times, creatives are often confronted by clients who question what
if anything makes their creations Hispanic, challenging the need to produce Hispanic advertising in the first place. And despite their adeptness
at justifying the Hispanidad of their creations by pointing out the nu-
ances of popular culture that may permeate their creations, I found that

Hispanic marketers were ultimately left with the need to confirm the Hispanidad of their ads by asserting that they were filmed in Spanish and created by a Hispanic, claims that simultaneously reinforce essentialist definitions of Hispanic identity based on the Spanish speaker and/or the "authentic" Hispanic creative. Many creatives I talked to, aware of these circular dynamics, try to reject becoming Hispanic cultural brokers who must constantly corroborate the authenticity of their creations by ridding them, for example, of the cultural basis that is often required of this market. As one creative asserted, "I can speak whatever language and to whomever. I don't have to do Hispanic marketing. I choose it because that's what I want. But just because I have a Spanish surname does not mean that I have to be limited to Hispanic marketing. I can as easily market to Asians or to suburban generation-X kids." Still others insisted that what they do is "publicidad en español" (advertising in Spanish), not Hispanic marketing. As yet another creative said, "I can't do Hispanic marketing because it just does not exist. What I do is marketing in Spanish that can speak across a variety of groups."

An agency's ability to represent itself and its work, however, always depends on the clients' knowledge or their perceived knowledge of Hispanic culture, as well as the leverage this knowledge may provide the Hispanic agency to break away from clichés in order to develop more contemporary ads for Hispanics. Clients that had been advertising to Latinos for some time were generally agreed to be more sophisticated in their understanding and approval of ideas, whereas new clients with little knowledge of the market were perceived to be more interested in easy, safe, and therefore less novel representations of Hispanics. Nonetheless, a constant problem is that Hispanic advertising strategies are often managed at the lower levels of a corporation's marketing hierarchy, by personnel who have limited decision-making power and who are in constant turnover. This type of corporate functionary was described to me as the "most recent twenty-four-year-old who really wants to be out of the [Hispanic] gig and usually leaves within six months." Agencies are therefore always faced with new people whom they need to "convert" to Hispanic marketing and "educate" about the basics of Hispanic culture.

This concern over the need to educate corporate clients, however, must also be analyzed in relation to the position of Hispanic marketers as corporate intellectuals inevitably obliged to create, maintain, and circulate knowledge of Hispanics as consumers, rather than solely as an outcome of the actual ignorance of their Anglo clients about Latinos. This concern was a central component of marketers' self-presentation as "embodiments of Latino culture" or experts in the market with the mission of educating clients about Latinos and their culture, and it was often deployed as a way to reverse the subordinate position of marketers relative to their clients. This stance allows them, for instance, to disregard their clients' expressions of racism or prejudice as mere ignorance or lack of sophistication which could be easily eradicated through education. Connected to this are the real or perceived gaps in background, class, and cultural capital between Hispanic marketers and their clients. I have explained that the industry has traditionally been dominated by Latin American–born, middle-class marketers, who, having lived both in the United States and Latin America often speak more languages and are often better traveled than their Anglo clients. On these bases, many marketers consider themselves more sophisticated, cosmopolitan, and cultured than their American clients, and the job is therefore one of uplifting the Anglo client from his inherent ignorance and unworldliness. As an account executive explained, "Most of the people that work in this industry are just so sophisticated, they have traveled, studied, and seen the world, unlike their clients. Their level is just so low. They come from suburbia and know nothing of the world. It's just sickening." The image of an "ignorant suburban gringo" was a common construct circulated to explain client attitudes toward the Hispanic marketer, particularly signs of racism or discrimination which could therefore be dismissed as due to lack of sophistication, worldliness, or manners. One account executive, after telling me about the horror of a corporate client on a market tour of a Hispanic barrio—the woman was petrified with fear and demanded to be taken back to the office—dismissed her reaction as a sign of crudeness, not of bias or intolerance. The marketer was born in the U.S. to Argentinean parents, was white and not so easily racially recognizable as a Hispanic—as he made a point of telling me his clients had told him numerous times—making me wonder whether his reaction was based on a lack of personal experience with U.S. racism or on marketers' tendency to dismiss negative encounters with their clients in this manner. Certainly he had felt his client's discomfort with the barrio visit, and his interpretation of the event was that she lacked sophistication and worldliness and that had she been more cultured, as he was, she would not have reacted with horror.

Still, as different and socially superior to the client as Hispanic marketers may consider themselves, they are confronted with the reality that clients constantly assert their authority over Hispanic marketers, doubting both their objectivity and their professionalism. A relevant story was told to me by a Venezuelan creative whose decision to include a plate of *frijoles con queso* (beans with cheese) in a cheese commercial was overturned by the client's brand manager, who had not seen the dish during his two-week trip to Mexico and, positioning himself as the maximum authority on Mexican cooking, concluded that it just did not exist. As the creative explained, "What irritated me is that the commercial's production team were all Mexicans and that he was calling from the U.S. to override the plate, even after everyone in the Mexican studio had agreed with me that this plate was indeed part of Mexican cooking." In this case, the client thought that the creative was just lying to get the ad approved, a common accusation faced by Hispanic agencies that are often seen as biased advocates of their ads rather than as objective marketing professionals.[4] An illustrative story was told by a New York–based publicist who had almost lost an account for that reason:

> I made them this whole presentation about how they should target Latinos. I told them about segmentation, acculturation, the whole thing, but they would not sign unless their secretary, who was Hispana, would corroborate my presentation. I could not believe it. If it were an Anglo marketing presentation, they would not endow any authority to their secretary, but we are talking about Latinos. All of a sudden their secretary had more authority than I, even though I was supposedly hired as the advertising expert.

Discussions with marketing staff on the client's side provided analogous accounts of skepticism and ambivalent feelings toward Hispanic marketers. A general view among clients is that Hispanic shops may be knowledgeable about Hispanics, but they are lacking in overall strategic marketing, making them inherently inferior to general market agencies. As explained by a marketing representative at Johnson & Johnson, "Our experience has been that these agencies are strong in Hispanics but not in strategic marketing. When you work with general market agencies, everyone there is pretty business-oriented. You have people who have graduated from the top schools and have a good understanding of packaged goods. You don't find that in the Hispanic shops." The Hispanic shop was unable to please this client, and the company hired an agency that would adopt the same strategy they had already approved for the general market, thus avoiding the perceived risk of working with an agency that lacked the "proper business personnel" for the strategic positioning of brands. Mistrust of Hispanic agencies from the corporate client's side also came in the form of skepticism about the need for Hispanic marketing in the first place. Not only is there skepticism about the need to advertise specifically to Hispanics, but there is also doubt that enough real differences exist between Hispanics and other ethnic groups, such as African Americans and Asian Americans, to merit culturally specific advertising. An advertising executive I sat next to at a multicultural marketing seminar in New York, after I asked his impressions of three presentations on the Asian, Hispanic, and African American markets, provided his own interpretation of this quandary. Insisting that he could hardly discern any real difference among the three markets, he sardonically stated that the issue was tantamount to the general rule of "family, of showing more and more family scenes when advertising to any particular group."

To overcome their reputation as amateurs relative to general market shops, Hispanic advertising agencies are increasingly "professionalizing" themselves to establish their legitimacy as the experts on Hispanics, by forming organizations such as the Association of Hispanic Advertising Agencies and by including lecture presentations for their clients to challenge their perceptions of the market. These strategies, however, can sometimes backfire. Market tours, devised to introduce Anglo clients to the Hispanic market by taking them into Latino commercial districts and showing them that Latinos shop and can consume their products, sometimes reinforce clients' exotic ideas of Hispanics. Consider, for instance, these comments of a market tour leader: "People think that entering these neighborhoods is like entering a war zone. They may advertise to them, but most of them don't even leave the bus. They never stop thinking that our audience is made up of their shoplifters." Hispanic ad professionals, however, are not naive and also use their clients' biases and fears to their own advantage. The market tour leader cited above, aware that his client could not tell a Mexican neighborhood from a Puerto Rican one, admitted that he has often presented the same mixed neighborhood as either Colombian, Mexican, or Puerto Rican according to the needs of his clients, a strategy that has allowed him to sell group-specific outdoor marketing, like signs and wall murals, targeting particular nationalities.

Yet clients' stereotypes and misconceptions of the market are not the only forces affecting the range of representation of Hispanics. Creatives also complained of having to "educate" their mother agencies, the larger entities that have incorporated many of the most profitable Hispanic agencies. A problem here is that the greater agency generally tends to ignore its Hispanic branch when pitching to a client, and initiates involvement only at the request of the corporate client. In these cases, Hispanic agencies must negotiate their positions within the mother agencies, either by justifying the need for an original execution or by adapting ads in ways that make them relevant for Hispanic consumers. In the latter case, the task of the Hispanic agencies is reduced to adapting or modifying a preconceived ad, either through a different voice-over or by changing the models.

Another factor that reduces the involvement of Hispanic shops in the development of ads is the corporate client's demand for synergy between campaigns, whereby advertising campaigns for the same product in different markets are required to be fashioned in close concert with the general market strategy. This is not only cost-effective on the client's side, allowing them to keep their budgets for Hispanic and ethnic marketing to a minimum by leaving marketing decisions regarding original executions to the upper levels of the marketing hierarchy; it also helps ease clients' concern over working with agencies that they sometimes see as limited in strategic planning and product positioning. A direct outcome of the trend is that Hispanic shops are not always allowed to do original executions but are forced to do more conservative executions in line with the already approved general market strategy.[5] As the creative for a Los Angeles shop put it: "You have to remember that we are still talking about corporate America, not corporate Hispanic America." Again, Hispanic marketers are left with the same recourse to convince their clients: the exoticizing of their audience as different and unique. As one stated: "What I tell them is to imagine themselves living in Japan. And to think that all of a sudden there are enough of them that a network develops with programming, and then come the ads. And that everything is in English, in their language. Yet everything is done by Japanese according to their own executions. They immediately know that it is not for them. That it's different." I interrupted this young executive with the argument that Latinos are not as unfamiliar to U.S. culture as Japanese culture would seem to a stranded American, but to no avail; it was only through this exercise in exoticization that he had managed to convince an unyielding client to do an original Latino ad.

Yet perhaps the most recurrent complaint among Hispanic marketers is their corporate clients' general penchant for "safer" ads. As a creative put it: "In this country, images pass through an American system of control; they have to be approved by an American client who likes images that are easy and stabilized in their own little box within their level of understanding and approval. This makes for far more moderate images than they otherwise would be." The result is that even when ads are not done in direct synergy with the general market strategy, creatives still find themselves crafting their ads with their clients rather than consumers in mind, and producing bland and humorless commercials whose spirit and meaning can be easily communicated to their corporate clients.

Consider for instance, the difficulties in translating and selling humor to corporate clients. A recurrent issue is that Latino comic sensibilities are seen as clashing with Anglo ones or with their clients' preconceptions of the Hispanic consumer. As a producer explained, Latino sensibilities, which he saw as highly tolerant of "what is funny, dirty, and has double meaning, as long as it does not poke fun at 'sacred' symbols," contrasted with Anglo ones, which he thought were far less tolerant of parody and mimicry. "If they don't get it, it must not be funny," he went on to say, which means that creatives face the double challenge of making their ads funny and appealing in both English and Spanish. Complicating the issue is the difficulty of explaining differences in humor across Latino subnationalities. Thus, while Latinos may be as moved by humor as the next person, selling humor is far more difficult, leading to its omission in relation to evocations of tradition and/or family scenes.

However, not all clients fit the Latino's stereotype of the ignorant suburban gringo; some clients are not even Anglo. There is always the executive who is married to a Puerto Rican, and makes a point of saying so, or the one who claims to be undergoing "reverse assimilation," becoming more and more immersed in Latino culture by learning Spanish or attaining other bits of the "cultural capital" of Latinidad. Whether this arises from what Jon Cruz (1999) calls "ethnosympathetic interest" or the benevolent reception of marginal culture while ignoring its politics is difficult to ascertain for every case. Certainly these "Latin Anglos" are fully aware of being homogenized into the "stupid gringo" category and resent being patronized by Hispanic marketers. The objectifications of Anglo and Latin culture hence run in parallel tracks, always feeding off each other.

Since the mid-1970s, as part of the establishment of ethnic marketing departments, corporations have been hiring Latinos in their advertising and marketing departments. And just as Hispanic marketers represent themselves or are perceived by others as the "embodiment" and representation of what is Hispanic, Latinos working within corporate America are seen as the Latino experts and are made responsible for the company policy toward the Latino population. In these processes, differences of class or background among Latino corporate executives emerged as key variables affecting the selection of Latino commercial images. One example came to the surface in an interview discussing HBO's 1998 Hispanic campaign, recounted by their head of Hispanic marketing, an Ecuadorian-born and U.S.-educated young woman. When discussing the agency review she conducted to select HBO's new Hispanic advertising agency, she made it clear that she was looking for an agency that would break away from the stereotypical portrayal of the Hispanic consumer, and offer instead something that would speak to her and her own perspective on the market—that of an upscale, affluent, and savvy Latin American professional now turned "Hispanic."

> I am Latin American and maybe that shapes the way I look at advertising, because there [in Latin America] it is very savvy. It wins awards: it's funny and entertaining. Thus I think advertising should be funny. We want to see quality, because people can turn to the next channel and see what everybody who's not Hispanic is getting. Agencies in the Hispanic market still work in the same mode, affecting Hispanic "hot buttons" like the music, the family.

Convinced that most Hispanic agencies underestimate the "savviness" of the Hispanic consumer, she made sure that her review finalists were mostly newer agencies, some with less than five years in the market, and that the winning agency would be noted for its more conceptual and artsy executions and meet her demands for something trendy and new. In particular, she was looking for an agency which her Anglo corporate associates could relate to, one that was, as she described it, more professional and thus less ethnic:

> I'll tell you, there is a handicap to being Hispanic on the client's side. If you work with general market agencies, there are certain things that you would never take from an agency. As a Hispanic person, I think your emotional side comes out, and you tend to attribute some things to culture. You say, "Oh, but, . . ." and you know there should not be a but. What I like about my agency is that they are on top of everything, and when I am not here somebody here that is not Hispanic has to deal with them, and they will feel like they are dealing with just another agency. There is no reason that other people, Anglos in particular, should feel that they are working with a Hispanic agency.

This young executive was not alone in seeking to work with people who would make her Anglo colleagues feel at ease. This preference is behind the emergence of what a Puerto Rican former corporate employee at McDonald's described as the *"blanquitos* who look polished," within the Hispanic advertising world, with *blanquitos* standing not only for a person's whiteness but also for speech, demeanor, and the ability to keep ethnicity "in its place." Although not a *blanquito* by birth, this person, who is now an independent marketer, gave ample evidence of what makes a *blanquito*. Born in the projects and coming from a working-class background, she had received scholarships to attend Columbia and was so fluent in Spanish and English that, she claimed, Cuban marketers thought she was "one of them." What she was pointing to was therefore not solely "whiteness" but also education and sophistication, traits that, as mentioned earlier, Hispanic marketers had appropriated as part of their demeanor.

Concluding the HBO agency-selection process, the executive chose a young agency, recently founded by a young advertising executive from Mexico who was the son of a key Mexican advertiser with ample experience in dealing with corporate clients. His agency projected itself as hip and modern, intent on "raising the bar" of Hispanic marketing by doing work that was, according to Dieste Advertising's 1996 mission statement, "comparable to or better than the work which clients have come to expect from the best general market advertising," an objective that is increasingly shared by many in the industry who seek to disassociate Hispanic marketing from some of the negative connotations that accompany its ethnic status. The end product was an ad replicating a movie, showing a Hispanic attacked by some Chinese martial fighters, who is able to defend himself by turning his remote control feature to Spanish, allowing him to communicate with his attackers (figure 21). The ad, in which the martial fighters stand for the incomprehensibility of English, ends with the final caption, "¿Entiende?" ("Understand?"), urging viewers to not miss out in their movies: to turn to HBO in Spanish. I will come back to this example later because it touches on ongoing debates over what constitutes "quality" in Hispanic advertising, and on the Latin American/Latino divide that is often at the heart of such evaluation. The point I would stress here is that Anglos are not the only ones behind the approval of images; Latinos have their own preconceptions of what is more representative of their market and which agency is most capable of delivering the company's message.

As noted earlier, corporations have also opened special and ethnic departments of marketing to target Latinos, and in sharp contrast to the example mentioned above, most have hired U.S.-born Latinos to work on the clients' side. Regarding my earlier discussion of the ethnic dimensions of hiring practices in this industry, it is not language "purity" but what was described to me as Latinos' more "Americanized" skills in speaking on behalf of corporate clients that are most needed by corporations. These corporate spokespeople for "Latino culture" are therefore often at odds with the image of Latinidad portrayed by Hispanic agencies, which largely neglect Latinos like themselves. Their involve-

Figure 21. Print ad version of the HBO ad, "No te Quedes
a Medias." Created for HBO in 1998 by Dieste and Partners,
Dallas. Copyright © 2000 HBO, Augustine V. Jalomo, Jr.,
Account Supervisor, Dieste and Partners. The ad plays with the
idea that English is as foreign to Hispanics as Chinese.

ment in corporate marketing decisions has therefore been central for
expanding the "Latin look," and launching campaigns that address so-
called acculturated Latinos. A Texas-born Latina, who now owns her
own Hispanic advertising agency, recalled how after one year of working for one of the largest, transnational U.S. corporations, she broke her
company's long-time association with one of the first Cuban-founded His-

panic shops in New York for a San Antonio agency that would reflect
Latinos' acculturation and affinity with U.S. culture. Some of the most
novel and influential Hispanic marketing initiatives, such as that of Sears,
which launched a magazine for this constituency, or Anheuser Busch's
"gringitos" campaign featuring Anglos interacting with Latinos, have
had U.S.-born Latinos making marketing decisions from the corporation's side. However, very few Latino executives have genuine decision-
making power on marketing to Hispanics within a given corporation.
As one explained to me, corporations hire only MBAs, and Hispanics
with the "right" credentials are likely to disassociate themselves from
ethnic marketing. A trend here is that corporate America consistently
relegates Hispanics to community relations departments, where they ad-
vise the corporation about Hispanic issues or debates, or about the best
activity or latest festival they should sponsor, but rarely have influence
or the power to direct the development of original advertising executions. The executive mentioned above, for instance, ended up quitting
her job, frustrated by the company's decision to discontinue a Hispanic-
specific marketing department (it claimed to be adding Hispanics into
their mainstream advertising budget), which she felt would make impossible the already difficult job of advancing her ideas within the company's corporate structure. She now works as a consultant with her own
advertising shop and has learned that all she had done to bring the company "up to date" on Hispanic issues has been lost. As she noted, they
have since hired young Anglos with MBAs who are lost *("están perdi-
dos")*, while she wonders what happened to all the information she gathered during her tenure.

IDENTITY POLITICS

Identity is at the core of the Hispanic ad industry, and identity politics
inescapably permeate the commercial representation of Latinos. Just as
different Latino subgroups have long emphasized differences among
themselves in the process of advancing particular ends within U.S. society, advertising staff have also tended to call attention to differences
among Latinos, thereby questioning the interchangeability or homogeneity of these groups that is asserted in the process of representation.
Behind this trend is the fact that, despite their commitments to a Hispanic pan-ethnicity, most Hispanic advertising professionals see themselves and are seen by others in the industry as Cubans, Mexicans,
Venezuelans, and Puerto Ricans first, and only secondarily as Latinos/

Hispanics. Research has repeatedly noted that this is true for most Latinos, even those born in the United States (Oboler 1995). This situation has been sustained by the historical dominance of some Latino groups over others in the development of the industry, which has both affected hiring practices and associated the industry with particular nationalities, mainly Cuban and later Mexican. Indeed, the few Puerto Ricans who were active in New York City's advertising and marketing industry during the 1970s and 1980s shared many stories of the problems they faced while trying to break into an industry that claimed to be "Hispanic" but was dominated by Cubans. Meanwhile, the animosity between Mexicans in the West and Cubans in the East was the cause of much tension, which centered around different conceptions of the market, as indexed by language, that were developed particularly by Mexicans and Mexican Americans in the West and by Cubans in the East. I myself sensed the suspicion toward Cubans among executives on the West Coast: whenever I contacted people there for phone interviews or information, I was inevitably asked, "Are you Cuban?" One Mexican American owner of a very successful Hispanic advertising agency went as far as to state that Cubans were not really Latinos but "Spaniards who had lived on an island for a while," an image that was certainly based less on his knowledge of Cuba than on the middle- and upper-class Cubans he had encountered in the U.S. Hispanic ad industry.

Agencies are also fully aware that they could be judged not only by whether they were professional or trendy but also on whether they were too "Cuban," "Mexican," or "black." An example was provided by a creative at Uniworld, who told me of a Cuban car dealer in Miami who (he believed) had refused to work with his agency because it was seen as a black agency and had rejected his proposal to feature Jon Secada, the Cuban-born pop star, as spokesperson in an ad. The reason given by the dealer left no doubt in the creative's mind that it was indeed racism on the part of the client: he thought that Secada, who is black, would appeal only to Puerto Ricans but not to the affluent Hispanics he aimed to target, such as white Cubans like himself. This account ended up going to another agency, one which, according to the creative, the client considered more Cuban.

As another creative put it, "The problem is that if you are Venezuelan, nobody cares if you are Venezuelan when you go to Mexico, and if you go to Colombia no one cares if you are Chilean. Somehow, however, upon crossing the boundary and coming to the States, Hispanics become racist against each other. And that is a purely political issue." Obviously, what the creative was pointing to was the effect of U.S. identity-politics frameworks among Latino subgroups and the inequalities engendered when groups find they must define their political, ethnic, and identity boundaries if they are to be considered putative equals. Commenting on how subethnic divisions can affect the public projection of a Hispanic nation within the United States, he went on to tell me about an ad he had filmed in Mexico with Cuban and Mexican actors that was rejected by the Cuban regional brand representative in Miami because it was "not Cuban enough." The irony is that he complained about the very segment that featured one of the Cuban artists. This artist had been living in Mexico, which, presumably, had affected his accent and his acceptance as an authentic Cuban. The creative's expectation that the Cuban actor would be perceived as Cuban merely on account of his background was as ill-founded and as much a function of essentialist ethnic politics as was the account manager's demand for a Cuban actor who "speaks like a Cuban." Both positions manifest the problems affecting the representations of an undifferentiated Hispanic nation in a context rife with identity politics.

Identity politics are very prevalent in the selection of actors and models for Hispanic ads, as well as in the hiring of staff and creatives by Hispanic agencies. Although an actor's age and nationality are confidential information and it is illegal for producers to ask actors about their backgrounds, this information is widely circulated by word of mouth, as are the backgrounds of producers, creatives, and others involved in the industry. One casting director and talent representative I talked to was able to identify the nationalities of many of the actors/actresses in her ledger, though she claimed that she had never asked them about their background or nationality.

This unofficial knowledge, in turn, sparks rumors about the favoring of certain nationalities for work assignments at various levels of the industry. According to the same casting director, Cubans, who generally dominate in production, are biased in favor of casting Cubans when shooting commercials; Mexicans were said to be favored because they are believed to have the most generic accent, while Puerto Rican actors are reported to have the most accented and therefore least salable language skills. A desire for authenticity also pervades the industry in executions that target particular groups. Although models sell themselves as "generic Hispanic talent" who can embody any particular Hispanic nationality, and in some cases imitate a variety of accents, I was told that when a Mexican accent is requested, it is rare for a nonnative Mexican to be booked for the part, just as it is equally difficult for nonnatives to be cast to portray a specific nationality. The trend is that Puerto Rican "types" or accents are cast in New York, and Mexican types in Los Angeles, as if, contrary to their industry's precepts, Hispanics were not and could never be mutually interchangeable. Likewise, Hispanic agencies strive for representativity by hiring staff that cover the spectrum of Latino nationalities, the premise being that each creative or staff member will function as the "expert" or embodiment of his/her particular nationality within the agency. Here, too, attempts at recreating Hispanic representativity are reduced to the issue of nationality—creating a "mini-Hispanic nation" within a given Hispanic agency is therefore never about language, class, gender, or race but about hiring talent that comes from or represents Mexico, Venezuela, or Puerto Rico.

THE REAL OR WANNABE HISPANIC

As evidenced in the foregoing discussion, Hispanic agencies and creatives face a variety of obstacles in producing marketable Latin images. In particular they face minimal budgets that further constrain experimentation and corrections, and thus present added obstacles to the industry in its quest to meet general market standards. A general market budget of $25 million may allocate only $1 million to the Hispanic market, which is a large amount, considering that this industry had accustomed itself to filming ads for $10,000 to $15,000 in the mid-1970s. Lack of funds, however, necessarily translates to issues of quality relative to general market standards. It is therefore not surprising that Hispanic ads have obtained a reputation in the advertising industry as being mostly educational, geared at introducing recent immigrants to new products and consumer practices, rather than being entertaining, innovative, or amusing. In a context where advertising is also seen as artistic, with all the universal values implied in art as a category, Hispanic advertising's ethnic connotations were always an impairment to the creative's artistic aspirations.[6] Most creatives I spoke with, aware of how ethnicity tainted their artistic aspirations, were constantly stretching their budgets to produce the best ads, striving to come up with the most innovative and creative ideas, knowing full well that if they failed, their ads would be seen by their clients or their competitors as signs of their lack of sophistication or of that of the Hispanic consumer.

Thus, the industry is consistently haunted by the specter of its peripheral position and by the need to project itself as undergoing rapid

development and achieving "higher levels of sophistication." Yet issues
of quality and whether ads are seen as patronizing, demeaning, or ade-
quate are not always seen by people in this industry as related to its structural constraints and its peripheral position vis-à-vis the general market.
Within and across the Hispanic agencies themselves, these issues are often blended with issues of authenticity and intertwined with discussions
about quality and about who and what is more representative of the market. Consider, for instance, how agencies reduce differences among one
another to matters of quality and/or Hispanic representativity in ways
that engender further inequalities within Hispanic agencies, rather than
challenge the overall position of the industry. These debates and the ensuing "philosophies" of what constitutes quality advertising are among
the forces that most directly impact the scope and content of Hispanic
marketing.

Consider, for instance, how Hispanic creatives shape their ads as a reaction or in relation to contrasting approaches in the industry, some of
which respond to generational differences or just to differences in outlook. As I mentioned earlier, there are now three generations of Hispanic
advertising professionals: the founding generation, some of whom are
still active in the market; the second generation, most of whom were U.S.-
educated and trained by the founders, and have been pivotal in the industry's growth and institutionalization; and a third generation of creatives who are new to the market but have quickly attained recognition.
Among them, the newer generation of producers and creatives is the most
critical of old stereotypes and of the "flawed and substandard nature of
Hispanic ads," and most vocal about the need to challenge and transform a market which they consider underdeveloped in relation to what
they have experienced back home or in the general market. For many,
working with U.S. Hispanics means confronting their own negative preconceptions of the U.S. Hispanic market, which they see as entailing a
debasement of their creative work. They are quick to recall how, in international and Latin American displays and competitions, Hispanic ads
are consistently regarded as inferior to those made for the Latin American market, where they are looked down on in terms of quality and considered patronizing rather than uplifting to Hispanics. One producer, who
claimed to avoid working on Hispanic productions whenever possible,
explained that "I thought that I would never work in the Hispanic market. They never have the money, and you always have to compromise,
like not show certain issues. I still don't know if this is true, but this is
how you perceive it, and self-perception does not allow things to be tried."

Many of these producers and creatives, like the ad executive for HBO mentioned above, use "Latin America" as the standard for what should represent Hispanics in this country and do so in ways that denigrate past U.S. Hispanic productions as inferior, less artistic, and second-rate compared to Latin American and U.S. general market advertising. The problem with this assessment, however, is that Latin American advertising is produced for a national not a minority audience, which makes a significant difference in terms of budgets and the freedom to tap into local or national humor. Creatives were of course aware of such constraints, particularly when required to make their campaigns speak across groups and nationalities, which they thought guaranteed that their campaigns could never be as funny or relevant as when they were uniquely targeted to each national subgroup. Still, their concerns were also informed by ideas about which groups were more responsible for this "debasement" of the quality of Hispanic advertising. The tale of one account director about one of the tactics used by his agency to convince clients to do more "risky" and exciting advertising for Hispanics is indicative of these dynamics:

> What we decided to do was to show them Latin American–produced ads so they would realize the type of ads that people are exposed to in their countries, which are fun, daring, and exciting. There's this ad, I forget the brand, but it's for pantyliners, where you see a woman going to see her doctor, who is so hot and handsome that she gets sexually aroused. So she's very glad that she is wearing pantyliners. But you'd never see this type of ad in the U.S. Hispanic market. The thing is that this ad was done for the southern cone countries, for Chile and Argentina, which have very sophisticated ads; you couldn't do something like this for Mexicans, who are more traditional, and the problem is that this market [U.S. Hispanics] is too swayed by the Mexican consumer.

The ad described above is as unlikely to be aired on the U.S. general market networks. What is important to stress here is this creative's view that the Latin American market is more sophisticated than its Hispanic market counterpart, and that immigrants from "traditional" countries are to blame. Their self-conceived mission of "uplifting" the quality of Hispanic marketing by bringing Latin American aesthetic ideas and standards to the U.S. Hispanic market thus simultaneously involves judgments about which countries have better advertising traditions than others, or are more "sophisticated," or modern. It is also predicated on the subordinate position of Hispanic to Latin American marketing and on the perceived lower quality of U.S.-based productions. Thus, rather than evaluating their predecessors' productions in terms of the budgets or con-

straints imposed by their corporate clients, newer generations were more
likely to point to the lack of creativity and professionalism of the early
generations to explain the industry's current position. In doing so, many
simultaneously position themselves as more creative, as coming in "fresh"
to rejuvenate the market, covertly invoking the long-lasting hierarchies
that reinforce the Latino/Latin American cultural divide and denigrate
U.S.-based cultural productions.

From their side, older generations of creatives, account mangers, and
directors see many of the new Latin American creatives as uninformed
and disconnected from the reality of U.S. Hispanics. For many, the industry's growing level of sophistication was a portent of its potential demise or total assimilation by the general market. They see these younger,
"fresh" creatives as riding the bandwagon of the industry the founders
struggled so hard to create, a bandwagon that may now be threatened
by its newest riders. As one of these founders said, "There are two things
about Hispanic marketing, selling products and defending our market.
The first thing is defending our market," but this, she thought, is just
what the newcomers were no longer doing. In particular, this creative
was referring to the increasing tendency to "rejuvenate" Hispanic marketing by adopting or imitating the latest general marketing trends, which
calls into question the very need for ethnic marketing.

What all Hispanic advertising professionals share, however, is their
similar positioning as the experts and true representatives of the Hispanic
consumer, and it was from this perspective that they articulated their
views and philosophy for Hispanic marketing. In turn, this positioning
was predicated on dissimilar views of the Hispanic consumer. A creative
who had worked in the New York market for more than fifteen years
dismissed the current adoption of supposedly vanguard and artistic trends
in Hispanic advertising as a "fad," arguing that Hispanic marketers are
ultimately educators—that it is information that consumers want. As he
explained, "I could do the most artsy executions around, but then, am
I selling my product and communicating with my consumer? My consumer may not know how to use a product or may need more information than the general market consumer." In a similar tone, when referring to the HBO remote-control spot described earlier, this creative
claimed to like the ad for its creative and execution value, but wondered
whether it was offensive to consumers by suggesting that they were stupid, and that they would not understand unless spoken to in Spanish.

Another creative bemoaned the reliance on marketing trends that were
at odds with the Hispanic consumer, asserting in the process that he and

his agency were more in tune with this consumer: "Right now the trend is artsy and alternative-looking executions, but some years ago the craze was superimposed typographies. And you had all these ads with very artistic letters, which the Hispanic consumer could not read. We forgot that many Hispanics are illiterate."

The problem, however, is that in defending the use of more conventional strategies for communicating with the Hispanic consumer, these creatives simultaneously upheld an ahistorical vision of Hispanics as unsophisticated consumers who may never have been exposed to supermarkets or to the variety of products they encounter in the United States and who therefore need to be educated about these products and their uses. Yet while this image may have been partly accurate during the inception of the industry, it seldom describes the contemporary Latin American consumer who, as a result of globalization and the deregulation of Latin American markets, is increasingly as immersed in American products as are U.S. residents. Older generations of creatives also positioned themselves as the most knowledgeable and authentic pan-Hispanics, as opposed to the newcomers who, as a former director and agency founder stated, "sell to Hispanics but may not even know their culture anymore. They are all pretty and well-dressed, but what makes them Hispanic? I don't know." From her upscale apartment in New York City, this now-retired advertiser went on to criticize the newer generation of Hispanic marketers who, she argued, "do not even ride the subway or even have children in public schools." Not that she ever rode the subway much, but what this retired marketer was distancing herself from was the increased disjunction between marketers and consumers resulting from the ongoing popularization of the market, positioning herself in turn as the real authority on Hispanics.

From their side, many creatives asserting their intent to change and reinvigorate the market were firm believers in the need to overcome old stereotypes of both the market and the unsophisticated Hispanic consumer. Their vision of the Hispanic consumer, however, was not less narrow. Their argument that Hispanic advertising does not represent the average consumer was often based on their own lack of self-recognition within these images, rather than on their interest in a more realistic portrayal of the Hispanic consumer. Indeed, when discussing the issue of race and the lack of dark Latinos in the ads, many marketers pointed to their own whiteness as proof of the need to challenge the stereotype of the dark Latino, in a gesture that represented more a challenge to their status as Hispanics, and thus as a racial minority, than an argument about the actual racial/ethnic makeup of their prospective audience. Challenging stereotypes hence becomes synonymous with defending the whiteness, affluence, and therefore marketability of the Hispanic consumer, shaped mostly in the image of those involved in ad production. Despite their attempts at professionalization, Hispanic marketers are therefore not much closer than their predecessors to freeing themselves from the traps of corporate Hispanidad and its essentialist politics.

CHAPTER 5

Language and Culture
in the Media Battle Zone

After reading your cover story, "Must Sí TV," by Elia
Esparza, I couldn't help but think—it's about time! As
a Mexican American and a Tejano, I have always been
disappointed with television's lack of recognition of my
culture. Since most TV stations are based in Miami, Mexico
City, New York, or L.A., the views expressed or characters
portrayed on most shows have been based on those cities'
demographics.

> John Barraza, Houston, Texas (1998)

It's great that networks like Galavision are heading in a new
direction as far as bilingual programming goes. But at what
cost? When I was younger, I lost my interest in my roots and
my second language, which is Spanish. I became too assimilated. I realized that relearning Spanish would benefit me in
my job. I had to do something. I didn't have the money to
go back to college, so I watched a lot of Spanish television—
no bilingual television—and read books. I learned how to
speak Spanish better. I believe bilingual television will cause
the younger generation to be cut off from their roots.

> Beatriz Montelongo, Lubbock, Texas (1998)

Once produced, nationwide TV ads are placed in Spanish TV, a world
equally fraught with contention. The letters quoted in the epigraphs, sent
to the editor of *Hispanic Magazine* in reaction to an earlier article announcing the development of the first television programming service targeting bilingual and English-dominant Latinas, provide a glimpse of the

struggles that are commonly waged in this front.[1] At their core is the role of the Spanish language and Hispanic/Latina media as conduits of Latinidad. These are issues that the Spanish-language TV networks have historically drawn from and made central to their self-presentation, and that have simultaneously affected the production and dissemination of the ads.

This chapter examines the politicization and general treatment of language by the Spanish TV networks and what it suggests about the place of language in the imagining of U.S. Latinidad, as well as about the local or transnational location of this identity. My goal is to integrate my former discussions about the importance of language in the Hispanic marketing industry and in the networks into an analysis of recent changes in media forms, formats, and programming in the Spanish networks. Such changes, I suggest, are likely to affect not only the media contexts in which Hispanic advertising and promotions are ultimately placed, but also the manner in which Latinas are packaged and sold to prospective clients in the future. Most of all, these changes reveal how closely intertwined the concept of Latinidad is with specific media developments.

The past few years have seen the growth of new bilingual shows targeting English-dominant Latinas, such as Must Sí TV's *Funny Is Funny* and *Cafe Olé,* as well as a rapid growth in bilingual and English-dominant print media that challenge traditional definitions of Hispanics as a Spanish monolingual constituency.[2] There is also an increase in the use of "Latino/a" rather than "Hispanic" as the new media's main form of address for this imaginary constituency, which directly challenges the dominant business appellation for the market and signals a growing interest in the bilingual, English-dominant Latino. *Latina* magazine, for instance, now speaks to bilingual Latinas about "Workplace *Comadres*" and "*Confesiones* of Revenge," playfully mixing Spanish and English to appeal to the younger Latina (figure 22), while *Urban Latino* addresses the new generations entirely in English (figure 23). Yet nothing provoked more fear and excitement in the Hispanic media and marketing industry during my research than the revamping of Telemundo, the number-two-rated Hispanic network, after its purchase in 1998 by Sony Pictures Entertainment, along with Liberty Media Corporation, Apollo Investment Fund III, and Bastion Capital Fund. The acquisition of a Spanish network by a group of global corporations, and the entry of one of the major mainstream entertainment companies (Sony) into the Hispanic market accompanied by a major revamping of the stations' programming brought to the forefront questions of purpose and intention on the part of the "American" investors.[3]

The Hispanic advertising community was concerned about whether this sale would culminate in Telemundo's "Anglicization" and the eradication of this Latina/Hispanic network space. News about this event repeatedly pointed to the lack of familiarity of Telemundo's new president and CEO with the Latina community and the lack of Latina representation in its management team, questioning the network's legitimacy and authenticity (Mejia 1998). A further cause of excitement and distress was the revamping of Telemundo's programming. Telemundo's sale was accompanied by public announcements about how the network would reshape Hispanic television to provide real alternatives for the Hispanic consumer. This had been a part of Telemundo's mission since its inception, although the network had nonetheless ended up following Univision's programming formula of news, *novelas,* and movies, which placed it at a disadvantage, given Univision's exclusive access to Televisa's programming, the dominant source for Latin American programming. With Sony as a major owner, however, Telemundo now had access to a range of recently released Hollywood films as well as money to invest in original programming. During its 1998 "Up-Front" presentation to advertisers, Telemundo introduced ten new U.S.-made programs with actors and actresses whose U.S. "Latinness" was among their most touted attributes.

As will be evident in this chapter, media initiatives like Telemundo's have fallen short of presenting real alternatives to the Latina consumer. According to its 1998 "Up-Front" presentation, Telemundo's version of original programming for U.S. Hispanic populations would revolve around the reproduction of old American TV shows (*Charlie's Angels, Who's the Boss?* and *The Dating Game,* for example) with mostly imported actors—a far cry from representing the complex experiences of U.S.-born Hispanics—which was soon overturned by one filled with the traditional fare of *novelas.* As a young, aspiring movie producer who has been making her living in advertising stated, "They still treat us as if we were dopes, as if we have not seen these shows or wouldn't know that they are outdated. What they won't do is do a version of *ER* or a first-rate show in Spanish." Her comment suggests not so much that a trendy show like *ER* in Spanish would be an improvement over *Who's the Boss?* but her annoyance at the assumption that Hispanics are unsophisticated viewers and newcomers to U.S. media and to remakes of its programs.

Figure 22. Cover
of *Latina* magazine.
Courtesy of *Latina*
magazine.

Debates about the representativity of any media are of course common in broadcasting; its mass scope is inherently meant to exclude entire segments of its putative audience, be it on the basis of race, class, or
regional background. In contrast to the general market TV networks,
however, the Hispanic networks view themselves and actively promote
themselves as the "spokesmen" for the totality of U.S. Latinos, pretenses
that make even more problematic the real biases of their representations.
In this light, the current media moment is novel and intriguing because
it gives voice to and fosters competing and alternative discourses of Latinidad in the media market, as different outlets seek to carve out a specific
niche and clearly distinguish themselves from their competitors. The
effects of these struggles are already evident in two phenomena. First, as
noted above, we find the increasing use of "Latina" rather than "Hispanic" as the new media's main form of address for their imaginary constituency. Second, there is a growing interest in the bilingual, English-
dominant, urban, Afro-Latina, or the "home girl," as the prototype of

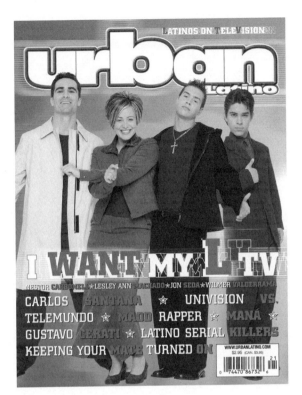

Figure 23. Cover of the more alternative *Urban Latino*. Courtesy of *Urban Latino* magazine.

the Latino/a.[4] Many recent publications have even adopted mission statements evoking Latina empowerment and self-representation and announce that their writers and personnel—unlike Latin American–born writers, artists, and creatives—have indeed "lived and experienced" Latino culture, and are thus able to represent "all sides of our story" (*Urban Latino* Mission Statement).

I will argue that at stake in these developments is the location of Latinidad—with Spanish language and the importation of Latin American programming at the center in the transnationalization of Latinidad beyond U.S. borders, and English language and U.S.-made initiatives as a venue for consolidating the United States as its primary terrain. Additionally, I will suggest that whether starting from the discursive realms of Latin America or the United States, both models are similarly confined by the exigencies of dominant notions of U.S. citizenship. While citizenship is certainly a contentious term, and has received much attention in recent scholarship, my emphasis is on assessing the extent to which assertions of cultural differences intersect with dominant norms of American citizenship that give preeminence to white, middle-class producers of and contributors to a political body defined in national terms. That is, my concern is not with citizenship as a neutral category or with the United States as an apolitical body similarly devoid of cultural meaning, but with how notions of citizenship, belonging, and entitlement are directly intertwined with and predicated on dominant U.S. nationalist categories. Such categories conflate race, culture, and language with "nationality," establishing the hierarchies and coordinates against which cultural and linguistic differences are ultimately evaluated (Ong 1999; Williams 1989). It is therefore these preexisting hierarchies that frame the discourses of Latinidad channeled in the media, along with what the media communicate regarding the Latina community's claim to belong, and in what terms it belongs within the political community of the United States.

I start by analyzing the fare and philosophy of Univision. Univision is the number-one-rated network, with a claimed market share of 80 percent. This network is also the primary promoter of Latinidad as an "ethnoscape," a diasporic community transcending the United States and Latin American nation states (Appadurai 1996). I then turn to an analysis of the U.S.-based approaches to Latinidad presented by Telemundo's 1998 mission and why it may have failed, and then turn to the predicaments involved in both of these modes of representation.[5]

UNIVISION: TOWARD ONE VISION/ONE CULTURE

As stated earlier, Univision's view of its targeted audience and constituency traditionally revolved around the recently immigrated, Spanish-speaking Hispanic, who is traditional and committed to family, to community, and to the *espíritu de superación* (spirit of overcoming). This is the commercial portrait of the Hispanic that Univision has promoted by supporting the dominant role of Spanish for Hispanics. This is also the target audience that Univision had long served with content heavy in imported Mexican programming; until the late 1980s, such imports constituted more than 80 percent of its programming. The proportion of Mexican-produced programming changed in the middle and late 1980s as Univision, in an attempt to target its U.S.-based constituency more aggressively, increased its U.S.-produced programming to 44 percent of the total through a variety of magazine, news, and talk shows, and even *novelas* (López 1995). This move, made under the auspices of its new American investor, Hallmark, was motivated by several factors, including Hallmark's attempts to counter its critics—recall that the sale of Univision had been forced on the basis of its having been under excessive foreign control—as well as the threat of competition from Telemundo, which was also beginning to develop U.S.-made programming. In practice, however, what the network established was a new pattern of importing Latin American cultural products, by importing actors and shows to be produced in the United States as U.S. Hispanic productions. The most noted example is the import by Joaquín Blaya, Univision's first president under Hallmark, of the Chilean Don Francisco and his program, *Sábado Gigante,* to Miami. This example is but part of a trend leading to Miami's appellation as the up-and-coming Latin Hollywood[6] (Aponte 1998). Since the 1990s, Miami has served as the global center for the growing integration of the Latina and Latin American entertainment industry. Most transnational culture industries that target Latinas and many major Latin American entertainment personalities have thus relocated to Miami (Yúdice 1999).[7]

Left unchallenged in this new programming trend is Univision's transnational and transcontinental approach to Hispanic culture, which has so strongly characterized the network's philosophy and operations from its outset. Univision may be selling itself as the station for U.S. Latinas—touted by its channel 41 in New York City as "El Canal de la Hispanidad, una herencia, un idioma, un canal" (The Channel of Hispanidad, one heritage, one language, one channel). Its definition of Hispanidad, however, is ultimately one that more than ever spans the entire Latin American continent and beyond, linking Brooklyn and Los Angeles with Mexico, Puerto Rico, Miami, and even Spain. Not only are these connections financially important for Univision, because they make its programs marketable in both the U.S. and Latin American markets, but they also constitute the backbone of the network's self-appointed role as the keeper and broker of Latin American culture and as a primary conduit between Hispanics and their culture.

This role is particularly evident in Univision's newscasts. As America Rodríguez notes, in contrast to ABC's *World News Tonight* with Peter Jennings, in which U.S. news occupies more than three-quarters of the program, 45.3 percent of the topics on Univision's newscasts are about Latin American countries, even superseding news of U.S. Latinas, which constitutes about 14.5 percent of the news (1996: 66–68). As she notes, this emphasis is part of Univision's "de-nationalizing" mission to form a pan-ethnic identity for Latinas in the United States by making Latin America the symbolic referent, more important as a whole than separated into its constituent countries. Latin America is also preeminently present in Univision's entertainment and variety shows, which always include the latest Mexican soap opera or pop-music star, as well as musical specials or pageants imported from Mexico, Venezuela, and other Latin American countries. Similarly, U.S.-produced shows almost exclusively feature imported talent. Univision's *Despierta America,* for example, modeled after ABC's *Good Morning America,* imported the Puerto Ricans Giselle Blondet and Rafael José and the Mexicans Ana María Canseco and Fernando Arau. *El Blablazo,* a show in which contestants are quizzed on their knowledge of Mexican soap stars and the U.S. Hispanic entertainment gossip, and which is advertised as the only show "where's what's important is not what you know but what you've been told," imported as its host Omar Germenos from Mexico (figure 24).

This close synergy with the Latin America market, in turn, is central in assuring recognition of and identification with the programming among its audience, particularly among the foreign-born and recent arrivals, who are most familiar with similar programming and media personalities from their home countries. After all, Mexico's position as the preferred source of U.S. Hispanic programming is the direct result of Televisa's historical role as the most significant exporter of programming to the rest of the Spanish-speaking world. Since the early 1970s, Televisa has been the mainstay of Latin American *novelas,* variety shows, movies, and other programming, and it is calculated, that in the 1990s, 80 percent of its programming was circulated throughout Latin American and Caribbean countries (Wilkinson 1995: 86). Mexican programming is therefore inappropriately described as a foreign product to Latin American consumers outside of Mexico, although this does not imply that the programming has entirely shed its Mexican identity in the eyes of U.S. Latinas, as we shall see later.

The result is a transcontinental view of Latinidad, in which the latest *conjunto* band from Los Angeles is juxtaposed with the newest pop artist from Puerto Rico, in which guests from TV shows are as likely to be flown in from Panama as from New York, and in which Latin America is constantly reinforced as the central signifier in the U.S. Latina landscape. Univision thus affirms that its mission is to provide a link between U.S. Latinas and Latin America, serving as the primary venue in which U.S. Latinas can connect or reconnect with a world that they may or may not have experienced but that nonetheless, as they are continually told, depicts "Latin America" and thus represents "their" heritage. According

Figure 24.   Univision's personalities Omar Germenos and Pepe Locuaz
of *El Blablazo*. Courtesy of The Univision Network Limited Partnership.

to Univision, being Hispanic or Latina in the United States means recognizing the latest Mexican *"farándula"* (celebrity), or being aware of
the details of Hurricane George's devastation of the Caribbean (news that
is only peripherally covered in mainstream U.S. media), or knowing about
the most recent soccer match, recognizing the latest Miss Venezuela, speaking the "right Spanish," and being familiar with other bits of culture/
knowledge through which Latinas can prove their Latin American prowess
and cultural knowledge to themselves and others.

Such a Latin American–centered approach to Latinidad is, of course,
not irrelevant to U.S. Hispanics. Regarding Latin America as a primary
source of Latina identity is a dominant trend that is evidenced in other
fields of cultural production. Following the nationalist foundation of contemporary representations of culture and identity, in which cultures are
seen as bounded and contained entities, tied to a territory, a past, and a
heritage, it is Latin America rather than the deterritorialized U.S. Latina
culture that has traditionally been valorized as the source of cultural authenticity in Latina/Hispanic culture (Rosaldo 1989; Segal and Handler
1995). In museums and cultural institutions, for instance, I have noted

that this dynamic has led to the differential ranking of Latin American versus Latina art as well as island-based versus U.S.-based Puerto Rican cultural expressions, and to the elevation of Latin American cultural expressions as the most authentic manifestation of Latin culture (Dávila 1999b).

The network's stance is therefore not an arbitrary one, but rather is guided by existing hierarchies of representation that necessarily influence Univision's attempts to become the "representative" medium for Latinas. At the same time, such strong connections with Latin America have generated strong criticisms of the network's lack of attention to the needs and experiences of U.S.-based Latinas, who are marginalized if not altogether absent. In New York City, the Spanish network's Latin American–centered outlook was a repeated concern of some media activists and grassroots groups I talked with, a concern that was also expressed by the focus group participants described in the next chapter. La Comuna, a nonprofit community group in New York City, even called for a general boycott against Univision and Telemundo in 1998. These networks had failed to broadcast Bill Clinton's 1998 State of the Union address, and the group claimed that Hispanics were being deprived of information that was "vital for the growth and development of their community" (*El Diario/La Prensa*, March 2, 1998, p. 20). Similarly, media activists in New York City have voiced concerns like those stated by the first epigraph for this chapter—that these stations reflect the interests of a few people who dictate from Miami what Hispanics should see and hear in the media. During my interviews with members of the New York chapter of the Hispanic Media Coalition, whose members are mostly Puerto Rican, this issue surfaced in their resentment of the dominance of Cubans in the Hispanic media and marketing industry, which they saw as an impediment to raising the visibility of Puerto Ricans. Meanwhile, New York Dominicans have fled to community-access cable channels to develop local-interest shows largely absent in the Spanish networks. Concerns such as these point to the public association of these media with particular Latina nationalities or particularized locations, a phenomenon that impedes their unqualified acceptance as truly pan-ethnic Latina products.

At the heart of these concerns is that the transnationalization of media flows provides little space for material that fully addresses U.S. Latinas' concerns and sensibilities, particularly regarding issues of race and gender.[8] These issues remain hidden and invisible, ultimately rendering these media texts assimilationist in content. Like the black-oriented TV

shows discussed by Gray (1995), Hispanic media thus completely elim-
inate and marginalize cultural differences in the name of "universal similarity," among and across Latina subgroups. Obviously, I am not suggesting that U.S. Latinas could only identify with U.S.-made products
produced by U.S.-based Latinas. An extensive literature has already
shown how problematic and reductionist it is to attempt to ascertain levels of authenticity in different media products, particularly in the current transnational context characterized by new patterns of media flow,
and that literature has warned against dismissing the localized meanings
people find in global texts (Ang 1996; Wilk 1993). On the other hand,
it is naive to ignore the embedded inequalities that are forged by this
common Latin American media market. Relevant here is Toby Miller's
(1999) suggestion for a shift of outlook from what media does to people
or what people do with media to who is involved in its production and
who can participate in the growing transnational division of cultural
labor. When seen in this light, it is evident that the Spanish TV networks'
Latin American–centered approach simultaneously relegates U.S. Hispanics to the level of consumers rather than producers of representations
of Latinidad. Nonwhite Latinas, in particular, are almost entirely excluded
from employment opportunities in the Spanish TV networks. And when
U.S. Latinas do become producers, it is mainly through local or regional
media which never enjoy the nationwide dissemination that the networks
do. As a result, there is little room for probing U.S. Latinidad by acknowledging or showcasing differences among U.S.-based Latinas and
Latin Americans in ways that could facilitate critical dialogue about the
racialization of U.S. Latinas. These issues are rarely part of a Mexican
*novela.*⁹

Needless to say, the flow between the United States and Latin America's Spanish TV market is a bilateral and complex one. U.S.-made TV
shows for the Hispanic market function in a similar though converse manner, reinscribing U.S. Hispanics—or, more specifically, the definition of
U.S. Hispanics produced by the transnational Hispanic media and other
parts of Latin America—as central to the national imagery of particular
Latin American countries. Through shows like *Cristina* and *Sábado Gigante,* Puerto Ricans, Mexicans, and other Latin Americans in their home
countries are similarly exposed to a transnational Latina world of
Chilean, Dominican, and Guatemalan guests, and others from throughout the Americas, as well as to the Nuyorican who may be featured in
Cristina or interviewed in the news, along with new artists, rhythms,
styles, and viewpoints in a mélange to which people are seldom exposed

"back home." This trend is strengthened by the growing transnational nature of all Hispanic programming. Just as Televisa and Venevision universalize their soap operas to appeal to growing markets in the United States and abroad, Univision's Miami productions increasingly have both the U.S. Hispanic and Latin American market in mind.[10] Thus shows like Galavision's *Ritmo Son*, filmed in Mexico with Mexican hosts and featuring Caribbean and tropical music, such as the Dominican group Los Hermanos Rosario and Chichi Peralta, are common, and they are distributed worldwide. Mexican soap operas, for their part, have begun hiring leading men from other Latin American countries and tapping into U.S. Latina themes such as immigration in order to increase their appeal to a wider viewership.[11] This is the case of *Dos Mujeres, Un Destino*, where the lead, Erik Estrada, goes back and forth across the border between two women, and *La Mujer de mi Vida*, where the female migrates to look for work in Miami. The result are shows in which the boundaries of national and transnational become more flexible and fluid.

It is beyond the scope of this work to analyze how these transnational "Hispanic" shows are being consumed throughout Latin America or, even more significant, how they may help disseminate a trans-Latina identity or possibly contribute to the widening of gaps between U.S.-based Latinas and Latin American populations. After all, the widespread distribution of U.S. Hispanic shows throughout Latin America has not been free of contention. In Puerto Rico, TV shows like *Cristina* and *Primer Impacto* are seen as foreign products and criticized for their morals, especially their treatment of sex, and for spoiling the values and quality of life of *"nuestro pueblo."*[12] Similar criticisms have also been raised by Mexican audiences in relation to the hiring of non-Mexican actors in Mexican soap operas. The hiring of Latin American leading men, for instance, faced nationalistic criticism from Mexican actors, who are now threatened by what they see as pretty faces with inferior acting skills. The hirings of Puerto Rican Carlos Ponce, Brazilian/North American Guy Ecker, Cuban Mario Cimarro, and Venezuelan Gabriela Spanic as leads in Mexican soap operas were all criticized on similar grounds. Even Cristina made this issue a topic of one of her talk shows. Particularly controversial was the hiring of Erik Estrada as the lead in the Mexican soap opera *Dos Mujeres, Un Destino*. Estrada's lack of Spanish-language skills became the subject of mockery, as well as the embodiment of the intrinsic faultiness of non-Mexican actors. This event was even featured in a Hispanic ad for Sprite produced for Spanish television by Leo Burnett's Hispanic Division. The ad, an adaptation of the Sprite campaign

"Image Is Nothing," shows Erik Estrada with a voice-over announcing that his Spanish will improve after he drinks Sprite. No improvement results from drinking Sprite; Estrada's "mangled" Spanish worsens as part of the spoof,[13] which draws directly on a perceived discomfort with the transnational flows that now subvert Mexico's media dominance at both the national and transnational levels.[14]

The initial reception of *Cristina* in Mexico included a wave of criticism against Televisa, which was not solely directed at the "vulgar" or sexual content of the show, but also at the fact that it featured a Cuban hostess and was imported from Miami. These responses suggest that the increasing distribution of "U.S.-Hispanic" products throughout Latin America and the transnationalization of media products do affect the public reception and discourse of U.S. Latinas throughout the continent and may be relevant to how locals throughout Latin America think about race, gender, sexuality, and nationalism. These are issues that of course need to be analyzed within particular localized settings and with attention to public reception. For the purposes of this chapter, however, let us briefly consider the predicaments of transnational media products with reference to U.S. Latinas by inquiring into what discourse of Latinidad they promote and what they communicate to and about Latinas in reference to the United States.

THE PRICE OF SYNERGY

Central to maintaining this programming synergy between the Latin American and U.S. market is the Spanish language, which prompts us to consider its treatment and projection by the networks. Spanish has been the most powerful catalyst for the flow of TV shows between the U.S. Hispanic and Latin American markets, helping to consolidate the unity of a transnational, Spanish-speaking media community.[15] Spanish also provides a central political symbol that unifies U.S. Latinas and Latin Americans, as well as a primary vector of Latinness in the United States. It is therefore not at all surprising that Univision and Telemundo have made Spanish central to their operations and self-presentation, treating it as an issue of "cultural citizenship," whereby the maintenance and protection of Spanish are construed as central to Latinas' right and entitlement to maintain their culture in the United States. This is evident in the stations' insistence on using only so-called correct and generic Spanish, in their abstention from Spanglish, and, most of all, in their appropriation of the role of guardians of and instructors in the language within the larger Hispanic community. Expressions like *"tu idioma," "nuestro idioma,"* and *"la herencia del idioma que nos une en hermandad"* ("your language," "our language," "the heritage of language that unites us in brotherhood") are their common discursive devices.

Indeed, the networks' emphasis on Spanish is not ill-founded. They, as well as the entire Hispanic marketing industry, operate in a context where, from the standpoint of many corporate clients, Spanish and culturally specific advertising and programming are not only unnecessary but also an impediment to Latinas' "assimilation" into U.S. society, which should leave them without vestiges of "tainted" culture or language. In the words of an L.A. account executive of Mexican background, referring to his previous experience as brand manager for a major pharmaceutical corporation, "From their [the corporations'] standpoint, our marketing presentations confirm their suspicions that Latinas don't want to be Americans, and what they say is 'Let them eat English,' 'Let them be American.' They can't understand that our wanting to keep our language and culture is not in conflict with our desire to be considered Americans and contributors to this country." In this context, Univision's stubborn insistence on Spanish as the conduit of Latina/Hispanic identity, its resistance to bilingual programming, or to allowing Spanglish or the mixing of languages, must be considered in relation to the station's self-appointed role as public guardian of the language that is seen as embodying Latina identity, an identity that is not only shunned by some, but considered a threat to U.S. national imagery.

What we cannot assume, however, is that language and cultural visibility always equate with social gains or political entitlements. As Santiago-Irizarry (2001) notes in her critique of language visibility as a measure of Latina acceptance, the apparently widespread use of Spanish in public life, such as in urban signs, is less an expression of inclusion than an instrument for organizing everyday life: the direction or containment of populations in their own languages does not equate with their ostensible acceptance or inclusion. Neither should we forget that, as noted by Flores and Yúdice (1993), the commercial use of Spanish is not about the recognition of Latinas but about constituting them as consumers. The question then is whether what Univision airs necessarily fosters an unqualified notion of cultural citizenship as involving the expansion of "claims to entitlements" (Rosaldo and Flores 1997) or whether it also reformulates the frameworks of recognition and debate, destabilizing pervasive constructs of citizenship, nation, and race. Specifically, we need to inquire whether Spanish TV networks actually enlarge the idea of who and what is considered an American, and promote a more complex view of what it means to be Hispanic/Latina in the United States, or whether, instead, it helps validate dominant norms of good American citizenship in ways that reproduce rather than challenge the race/class and gender norms of U.S. society.

Earlier, I argued that the industry's promotion of so-called generic Spanish has been accompanied by the privileging of some accents over others. Mexican upper-class Spanish, supposedly devoid of regional accents, rather than Hispanic Caribbean or South American Spanish, has thus become tantamount to "generic Spanish." What also merits attention, however, is that the stations' preoccupation with language purity has led to the inauspicious containment of language difference among U.S. Latinas, for whom language is not solely an issue of different Spanish accents. Latin American immigrants are also speakers of Portuguese and of a variety of indigenous languages, such as Quechua and Aymara, while for many U.S.-born Latinas the issue of language is one of different levels of competence, ability, and ease with both English and Spanish. As a case in point, Ana Celia Zentella's (1997) study of language use among New York Puerto Rican children notes that neither "English" nor "Spanish" can fully describe the range of language use among Puerto Rican children, whose linguistic repertoire can range across a bilingual/ multidialectal spectrum, which, although differentially valued or stigmatized in relation to the dominant culture, functions as a set of linguistic resources and, in their view, does not invalidate their claim to a Puerto Rican identity. As she and others have noted, Spanglish is at the heart of a wealth of U.S.-generated literary production, some of which has even gained recognition in mainstream scholarly and artistic circles, as well as of music and expressive forms, such as Latin hip-hop and rap, which are central to Latinas' experiences and identities in the United States. Yet on the networks, it is only "correct" Spanish that is reciprocally and symbiotically connected to a Hispanic/Latina identity. Spanish is thus used in a way that "corrects" rather than validates people's linguistic repertoires. Perhaps the best example of this strict correlation of Latinas with Spanish is provided by the promotion of the few English programs for Latinas on Galavision as shows "for the Latino who also speaks English." Not only does this announcement veil the reality of code-switching between English and Spanish, but it also reinforces the notion that all Latinas speak Spanish and that, while some may also speak English, English is ancillary to their use of Spanish, which in their view rightly defines anyone as a Latina.

Yet another problem with the Spanish TV networks' preference for so-called correct language is the fact that it promotes a bounded vision of Spanish that contains difference and keeps it "in its place," reinforcing distinctions between those whose background and education have given them the cultural capital of "correct speech" and those who lack it. While Spanish is indeed regarded in dominant society as a threat to English and to U.S. national integrity, it is relatively better accepted when it is contained by standard grammar, properly spoken, and in "its place" than when left "unbounded" as in Spanglish, code-switching, and bilingualism. Accordingly, unlike the "correct Spanish," which is more likely to be considered a sign of ethnicity not at odds with U.S. dominant ideals of upward class-mobility, Spanglish is more readily associated with linguistic pollution and social disorder as the language of a "raced," underclass people (Urciuoli 1998). Networks have thus historically featured the Spanish that, because it follows sanctioned grammatical rules, can enhance class mobility, or, as noted in one of the epigraphs for this chapter, "would benefit people in their jobs." The Spanglish or "broken English" spoken, for example, by some Puerto Rican or other Latina guests on *Cristina* is covered with a "beep" or corrected by the host's demands that they speak Spanish. I am not implying that all Latinas would like to hear Spanglish on the airwaves; in fact, while Spanglish is embraced proudly by some Latinas, it is generally treated with disdain.[16] The issue is thus that concerns over language purity subordinate the status of everyday language, particularly Spanglish, as faulty speech, contributing to this same disdain among Latinas toward their language and, by extension, toward themselves relative to those who, on account of their background, education, or class, are bearers of "correct speech."[17]

Race, class, ethnicity, and gender are also kept in check in most of the Spanish networks' programming in ways that continually reinforce both Latin American and U.S. racial and ethnic hierarchies, most specifically by prioritizing whiteness. Latin American soap operas are particularly relevant here for their conspicuous display of race and class hierarchies and for their overall dominance in the Spanish networks. Of course, social hierarchies are also overturned, challenged, or mediated in *novelas* both at the level of the narrative itself, as noted by Jesús Martín Barbero (1987), and at the level of consumption and reception, as feminist cultural theorists from Ang to Modlesky have long noted. The point here is that while Latin American soaps may showcase mores and values alternative to those traditionally associated with Latin American culture, such as women having premarital sex or wearing skirts far too short to be considered decent, most are ultimately about the value of the family and the authority of tradition, which are reaffirmed by rewarding the good, the moral, and the worthy (that is, the asexual, pure, and innocent woman, and the remorseful and repentant man), with heterosexual love, marriage, and fortune. This means that transgressive possibilities in this genre are found mostly at the level of consumption, not within the narrative itself, while U.S. Latinas' racialization and subordination in the United States is reinforced by yet more images of whiteness. Consider for instance the treatment of race and ethnicity in most soap operas. In *Mi Pequeña Traviesa* (shown in the 1998–1999 season), the only black character is presented as a happy, good-hearted *negrito* whom the main character encounters upon visiting her deceased mother's coastal home town. In a stereotypical portrayal, the character's appearance is limited to dancing, singing, and serving as the advisor who helps the protagonist get over her depression, actions which lead to public praise for his inherent musical abilities. Meanwhile, the only identifiable Indian character is the maid, who is constantly yelled at and shown comically running away from the *"niñas de la casa."* As anyone familiar with these texts will easily notice, maids are all indigenous-looking or black, and when black, they are meant to portray people from the coast or the Caribbean. Such is the case of the Cuban cook in Univision's *La Usurpadora* or the *abuelo,* the grandfather character, in *Rosalinda.*

While less blatant, U.S.-generated Hispanic shows also promote the whiter, educated, well-behaved Latina and thus keep Latinas unthreateningly contained "in their place." Talk shows like *Cristina* are particularly relevant here because, as a rule, they revolve around audiences and guests, and represent race more frequently than daytime and prime time programming. Moreover, talk shows are particularly revealing because, as noted in Corinne Squire's (1997) discussion of this genre, they display race not only through their more diverse audiences but also by indexing race and ethnicity through behavior and deviance. As she notes, in these shows whiteness is a symbolic reference point: irrespective of their backgrounds, people may appear as "symbolically white" or as "others" to the extent that they distance themselves from the latter by their dress and demeanor or, in the case of the Spanish networks, by their correct use of Spanish. Indeed, not only are the hostesses on the Spanish networks' talk shows blonds or bleached blonds, but the less fluent in Spanish, the darker, the U.S.-born, and those of certain nationalities, like Dominicans, are the ones most often ridiculed and thus "raced" and "othered" in these shows. Such "othering" practices have provoked criticism from spokespersons for the Dominican community in New York City. In 1998, they condemned the talk show *Cristina* for oversexualizing and ridiculing Dominicans and "staining" their image through what they regarded as its selection of *"chusma Dominicana"* (lowlifes) as guests for the show (Atanay 1998). These concerns are similar to those that community spokespersons have raised with regard to their portrayal by the main-stream media, which highlights the Hispanic networks' role in racializ-ing Latinas and furthering distinctions among particular Latina sub-groups along the lines of race or nationality.[18] Arguably, most soap operas and Hispanic shows are implicated in Latin American racial *meztizaje* ideologies which prioritize ethnic commonality over racial differences. The same ideas are also preponderant among Latin American immigrants in the United States, and are also often deployed by Latinas to avoid their racial subordination under the binary constraints of U.S. racial hierar-chies (Jones-Correa 1998). The irony, however, is that even the shows that were initially devised to reflect a U.S. Latina sensibility, such as *Cristina,* end up showcasing and reproducing inequalities among and across Latina subgroups, and that this is undoubtedly tied to the need to maintain their marketability throughout Latin America.

TELEMUNDO: "THE BEST OF BOTH WORLDS"

What I saw was opportunity. A community large in numbers and economic might creating a blended culture the like
of which our country has never seen before. A culture rooted
in American values and pride but with its uniquely Latina tradition and soul that will never be surrendered. A community
ready to express itself in television in an exciting new way.

                    Peter Tortoricci, President of Telemundo,
                    during the station's 1999 "Up-Front"

Ironically, it is Univision's rival, Telemundo, that, despite its announced intention to provide a more complex representation of what it means to be Latina in this country, has most recently and clearly articulated the dominant view of the Latina who stays "in place." This is because, in contrast to Univision's Latin American–centered world, Telemundo's management after Sony's buyout sought to promote the growth of Lati-nos as a U.S.-generated development fueled by "procreation not immi-gration."[19] The network also revamped its image and adopted a new slo-gan, "The Best of Both Worlds," about what it means to be Latina in the

United States, making direct reference to Latinas' partial involvement in the United States and the Anglo world. Yet, what exactly is the "best" of these two worlds that are increasingly encountering each other, and on what basis do we consider these traits the "best" of each world?

A cursory view of Telemundo's 1998 promotional video suggests that it is flan, Chihuahuas, and *guayaberas* that Latinas have to offer in exchange for American collies, T-shirts, and apple pie. With the equivalences Flan + Apple Pie = Telemundo; Collie + Chihuahua = Telemundo; Ketchup + Salsa = Telemundo; Santa Claus + Three Kings = Telemundo, the network's 1998 advertisement touted it as the symbiotic union of American and Latin American culture. Yet, it is the extremely and purposely emotional videoclip of Telemundo's philosophy, shown during its presentation to advertising agencies during the 1998 AHAA conference in New York City, that is most revealing of the new management's vision of contemporary Latina culture. Loosely divided into three sections, distinct images are shown harmoniously blending into one another to tell the story of Latinas' involvement in two cultures, two traditions, and two languages. The Latina world shows Latinas dancing with friends and family to a band of Mexican ranchero-type musicians (whose rhythms are nonetheless more *"salseado,"* as if blending Mexican and Caribbean musical traditions). The words "The Journey" and "The Joy" are superimposed softly over the images, as if reinforcing the feeling of enjoyment communicated by the multigenerational images of young heterosexual couples dancing, and of young children playing and dancing with an elderly grandmother figure. A second section, introduced by the words "The Struggle," "Two Traditions," "Two Cultures," "Two Languages," moves to a more urban environment, and into a transitional state that is now communicated by a Mexican mural and a low-rider car that dominate the scene against which young Latinas, some dark, some indigenous-looking, greet friends and stride around the neighborhood. This is a world where people still know each other and that is still dominated by enjoyment, as depicted by the young Latina girl shown dancing to a more Americanized rhythm, unheard but marked as such by the bouncing of her body. It is also a more sexualized world but nonetheless a world of rules—a young Latino is shown respectfully greeting a young woman who is accompanied by another young man with a kiss to her hand, while openly flirting with a presumably unattached young woman with a cuddle to her face. The third and last section, introduced by the words "The Dream," takes us to a more suburban environment. The opening scene depicts a little girl drinking from a water fountain in a park. This scene is quickly followed by an image of life in corporate America. Here the same models, the old and the young who have traded their hanging-out clothes for business suits, are now walking busily and seriously around a corporate headquarters. The active verbs "Hope," "Climb," "Reach," and "Arrive" are now shown, and a soft, nondescript aspirational tune of violins has replaced the more Latin, rhythmic music, as if to stress Latinas' successful incorporation into a "non-ethnicized" world.

I do not think that I would be reading too much into this videoclip to argue that it embodies the vision of the reborn, Americanized Hispanic citizen in concert with dominant values of American citizenry, as well as the ghetto-to-corporation aspirational image of Latinas disseminated by the Spanish TV networks. As if reminding Latinas, "Yes, keep your culture but keep it packaged," it reflects back to us the hierarchy of values on which Anglo and Latina unity is ultimately predicated. This is far from the station's claim that, as the clip states, it will provide a "world without frontiers, where your words don't need to be translated, that has the best of you on screen, that belongs to you and that you would want to give away to your children, and that is inspired by you."

On the other hand, I recognize that the American middle-class dream does not appear solely in Anglo garb. As noted by Lisa Peñaloza, equating aspirational middle-class images solely with whites simultaneously discredits blacks' and Latinas' claims to upward mobility, wealth, and corporate success (1997). Indeed, Telemundo's promotional finale can be alternatively read as Latinas' assertion of a valid claim to what the dominant culture has otherwise reserved for the Anglo world. This more hopeful reading of the clip, however, is confronted by the ongoing inequality between the Anglo and Latina world that continually hampers Latinas' attempts at class mobility and their claims to equal citizenship. Further complicating this reading is the widespread view, reflected in the videoclip's separation of the world of work from community and pleasure from commitment, that there are some separate Latina and Anglo cultural traits that make success an "Americano" and not a Latina trait.

This is essentially the view promoted by the aspirational books for Latinas published in 1998 by two of the most successful Hispanic media and publicity personalities in the United States: marketing mogul Lionel Sosa and Cristina Saralegui, the talk show hostess. Consider, for instance, Sosa's best-seller, *The Americano Dream*, a guide to "How Latinos Can Achieve Success in Business and in Life," the argument of which grows from the assumption of a distinct cultural ethos among Anglos and Latinas. In contrast to the former, and reminiscent of Oscar Lewis's thesis about the culture of poverty, Sosa's argument is that Latinas' values act as "cultural shackles" and must be superseded if they are to succeed in corporate America. Among these values are those taught by family and church, such as concern with family first, humility, and the belief that there is virtue in suffering, which make Latinas feel inferior and keep them down and back in business and life, over and above the structural constraints or racial and cultural hierarchies at play in U.S. society. Such values originate, according to Sosa, from a shared history of having been conquered and colonized, which has permeated Latinas' language and outlook, making them subservient and hence self-destructive in business and life. His framework defines the most "subservient" Latina subnationalities as those which have experienced the longest history of colonization, as if the experience of conquest and colonization had been inscribed in their genetic makeup and passed on to their offspring. Simply put, the ones to blame are those from the countries whose subjects were taught to be slaves or at least subservient, such as those of Central America and most of the Caribbean except, in his view, for Cuba. In contrast, Latinas originating in South American countries and Cuba, where he claims that Europeans outnumbered indigenous peoples (obviously after and because of extermination), are consequently less subservient and thus better equipped to succeed in an Anglo world. Ultimately, it comes down to an issue of race: in Sosa's view, the whiter Latinas are less docile than those who mixed and tainted their blood with that of subservient populations. The loopholes of this argument are many, the most important being his view that Europeans outnumbered any other population segment in Cuba, which endured the longest history of slavery in the entire Western hemisphere. Thus, we can arguably state that his model is based less on actual history than on his own experience with the mostly white and affluent Cubans of European background whom he encountered in New York when first trying to get into the business.

For her part, Cristina's biography is full of cultural characterizations of Latinas, particularly Cubans, as tropical, warm, and cheerful people, but she makes clear that success comes from discipline, self-improvement, commitment, and *"querer es poder"* (willpower). While she draws fewer comparisons between Anglos and Latinas than does Lionel Sosa, and also associates the values of discipline, persistence, and hard work with Cubans, and particularly herself, it is noteworthy that her family, not hard work per se, emerges in her biography as the greatest force behind her successful media career in the U.S. Hispanic market. Specifically, we see her success riding on the back of the affluent Saralegui family in Cuba, where her Spanish-descended grandparents held absolute control of the printing trade, and where the family bought Artes Gráficas S.A., owners of *Vanidades* and other magazines, which became highly popular in Cuba and Latin America prior to her family's emigration to Miami. As she notes, *Vanidades* emigrated with them from Cuba, in the form of a property registration, which facilitated both its relaunching from New York, where an ex-director of *Vanidades* had already settled, and its continued distribution throughout Latin America. We learn that the Saraleguis, like many other Cubans, did not lose their financial and business partners in Latin America after leaving Cuba; in fact, they received total financial backing from a former distributor of *Vanidades* in Mexico for its re-inauguration in New York City. Soon after the family's migration, therefore, the Saralegui children were able to enjoy private schools, a private yacht, horseback riding, and their familiar, affluent, Cuban lifestyle in Miami. Cristina's hard work and drive thus need to be understood in the particular context that has made so many other Cubans successful in this country, particularly in the Hispanic media.

Returning to our discussion of Telemundo's new mission, a look at its opening programming confirms that the station's philosophy of Latina representation is far more daring than its implementation. Indeed, most of the "new programs" under the new management consist of Spanish derivations of old American sitcoms or game shows, like *The Dating Game* or *The Newlyweds Game* and *Who's the Boss?* while its variety and entertainment shows are no different from Univision's, relying as they do on Latin American specials like concerts and pageants. Moreover, like Univision, Telemundo is directly tied to the Latin American media market and thus promotes the same linguistic programming synergy between the U.S. Hispanic and Latin American media markets. The most noted example of this trend is Telemundo's programming partnership with Televisa's biggest rival, Mexico's TV Azteca, producer of some of the network's most successful *novelas,* such as *Mirada de Mujer* and *Señora.* Thus, Telemundo's original programs have not departed from the dominant trends of relying on imported Latin American talent and filming in Mexico because of lower costs. The Latin version of *Charlie's Angels,* the failed *Angeles* (canceled after a short run), which claimed to showcase "Latina power," is a good example. The artists who played the three female detectives (figure 25) were from Mexico, Argentina, and Colombia, where they had artistic and modeling careers prior to their recruitment for the show, and the episodes were filmed in Tijuana by an American production company.[20] Meanwhile, in an attempt to broaden the appeal of the Latin version of *Starsky and Hutch* (which also failed), *Rey y Reyes* is set in an imaginary U.S. city, "Rio Lobo," somewhere along the U.S./Mexico border, and *Angeles* is set in the "not-so-peaceful town of Costa Brava," an unspecified coastal town in the United States, and thus markedly stripped of history or regional flavor. Shows in the general market media are similarly sanitized of difference or ethnicity, yet when one compares these Hispanic "cop" shows with contemporary general market shows such as *NYPD Blue* or *Homicide,* they appear as overly bland and unspecific. These shows were supposed to take place in the United States, yet most of the street, road, and landscape signs were in Spanish, everyone spoke Spanish, and the characters' Latinidad was devoid of ethnic or national background as a nonissue. While their actual national backgrounds were made public in press releases and magazine articles, and their national accents are perceptible in the show, they were meant to represent "generic" Latinas whose histories and ethnic backgrounds were never developed in the show.

Replacing this original lineup, Telemundo has turned successfully to the already proven format of Latin American soap operas, although, in contrast to Univision, it has diversified its acquisitions, purchasing *novelas* from Mexico's TV Azteca, but also from Colombia, Venezuela, and Brazil's Globo TV, as well as from smaller producers in the region. Telemundo's greatest soap opera hit, *Xica da Silva,* featuring the first black protagonist in Brazilian soap operas and in U.S. Hispanic media, was made by the Manchete network in Brazil, not by Globo, Brazil's number one soap opera producer (Rohter 2000). It also produced shows that seek to reflect more accurately the tensions and experiences of Latinas in the United States. Among them, the 1999 "Up-Front" renewed *Sólo in America,* and introduced *Los Beltranes,* a Latina version of Archie Bunker featuring a racist, homophobic, Cuban bodega owner in Los Angeles, with a Chicano son-in-law and a gay Spaniard neighbor. This show constitutes a novel development, a comedy based on intra-ethnic tensions among U.S. Latinas, and it remains to be seen how this trend will develop. There is also a more flexible attitude toward bilingualism in some of Telemundo's programming. In contrast to Univision's stringent new policies toward Spanish-only advertising and programming, Telemundo's *Sólo in America* (which ran for two years) mixed Spanish and English in ways that would be uncommon in Univision's lineup. However, here too we have evidence of the network's inability to enlarge definitions of Latinidad and the ways in which Latinas are addressed and presented on the airwaves. Telemundo originally claimed that it would reach out to the

Figure 25. The
Latina *Charlie's
Angels:* Colombian
Magali Caicedo,
Mexican Patricia
Manterola, and
Argentinean Sandra
Vidal. Copyright ©
1999 by Telemundo.

English-dominant Latina through bilingual programming, but this goal
has been replaced by a more conservative approach to language difference. Rather than serving as a mainstay of some programs, English appears only in the form of Spanglish, which is selectively used as a "condi-
ment" and mostly limited to comedy shows.

In *Sólo in America,* which revolved around the language and culture
clash between a divorced, Venezuelan, Spanish-speaking Latina mother
and her two bilingual and bicultural teenage daughters in Brooklyn, one
of the main comedic devices was the mother's scolding of her daughters
for their tainted Spanish. The mother is shown constantly reminding
them, explicitly and by insinuation, of the evils of becoming too Americanized, or polluted perhaps? Most important, while the youth are supposed to be fully bilingual, they are shown speaking only short phrases,
and mostly single words in English or Spanglish. The actual meaning of
their speech, however, is almost always conveyed by the context, by an
immediate translation by their mother, or else by a deliberate rephrase
in Spanish. The results are constructions like, "*Mom, I can't believe* que
tú a mí me mentiste" (*Mom, I can't believe* that you lied to me) or "Frank,

no sé porque te abrí la puerta, tu no entiendes *nothing*" (Frank, I don't know why I let you in, you don't understand *anything*) or "*Mom, have you decided,* que vas a hacer? Vas o no vas a Chicago?" (*Mom, have you decided* what you are doing? Are you going to Chicago or not?),[21] where English words or phrases are peripheral to the sentence's meaning. This is rarely how English is used by code-switchers, who are likely to incorporate whole sentences and clauses in English and switch fluently between Spanish and English as appropriate. This situation echoes Jane Hill's discussion of mock Spanish among Anglo speakers of English, although here it is English among native speakers of Spanish whose use is marked by its dual indexicality (Hill 1999). On the one hand, the use of English is meant to convey a symbolic connection with the acculturated Latina, but on the other, indirectly, it implies a debasement of Spanglish and its speakers. For what these shows do for the native Spanish speaker, the main audience for the show, is to digest Spanglish and English; anything that is not "correct" Spanish is never meant to convey the burden of the dialogue but is used as a comedic device. This derisive treatment of Latinas' English and Spanglish speech is also evident on Galavision, Univision's cable network, whose mission, as stated to me by a sales representative, was to "provide programming alternatives for Latinas irrespective of language." So far, this has included only two shows for English-dominant Latinas, "Funny Is Funny" and "Comedy Picante," featuring Latina comedians whose material almost always pokes fun at Latina culture à la Paul Rodríguez and John Leguizamo. Without denying the potentially subversive content of some of this comedic material, it is still worrisome, given that Latinas, along with blacks, have traditionally been relegated to the role of buffoons or entertainers in the mainstream media,[22] that it is mostly or solely in comedy-style shows that English-dominant Latinas who identify as such are heard of or showcased.

THE TERRAIN OF LATINIDAD: TOWARD THE BEST OF ONE OR TWO WORLDS?

Ultimately, despite their claims of Latina representativity, the Spanish networks have shown a limited ability to transform the range of what is accepted and promoted as "Latina" on the airwaves, beyond the Spanish-dominant and trans–Latin American norm. Nonetheless, let us for a moment consider the dissimilar tendencies implied in their programmatic statements in relation to the public projection and perhaps the future conceptualization of Latina identities in this country. Briefly, we are faced

with, on the one hand, the growing interconnectedness of the media environment and the synergy between U.S.-based and Latin American
populations, and on the other, with the possibility of more U.S.-based
bilingual/bicultural media initiatives. As we saw, these initiatives draw
on either a broad definition of Latina identity beyond the realm of U.S.
national boundaries or else on the United States rather than Latin America as the primary reference point for Latina identity, with arguments
about the need for bilingual productions functioning as a means for expanding who and what is represented as Latina on the airwaves. Yet, as
we have seen, neither discursive proposition presents a challenge to normative ideals of U.S. cultural citizenship. This is an issue neither of language nor of the relative connections between the United States and Latin
America that are forged by these representations. As we saw, the dominance of imported Latin American programming continues to limit the
space available for showcasing U.S. Latina sensibilities on race, identity,
or politics. Meanwhile proposals for programs that represent and hence
establish U.S. Latinas as an intrinsic component of U.S. Hispanic/Latina
culture have fallen short of addressing the multiplicity of Latina experience in the States in ways that reflect rather than mock or deride these
expressions, and that do not end up prioritizing dominant U.S. norms
of race, language, and culture. These norms accommodate cultural differences only when neatly "packaged" and in their place. Both of these
approaches are thus closer to each other than the networks' philosophies
would have it: they both prioritize the harmonious integration of Latinas devoid of politics and difference. Most of all, both modes of representation are grounded in the discourse of authenticity which equates
language (be it Spanish or English or Spanglish) with representation,
thereby subsuming, race, class, and different subjectivities and backgrounds under this one issue. And in fact, this is not at all surprising, for
language is to "Hispanics" as race is to African Americans; that which
over and above other indexes of difference marks them as outsiders within
the dominant norms of the white and monolingual U.S. national community.[23] The result is an overemphasis on linguistic difference; that is,
Spanish is reinscribed as the authentic and sole property of Latinas, never
to be part of the larger "national community."

Ultimately, the fact remains that any media developments regarding
the representation of Latinas are likely to be affected more by the numerous interests jumping on the bandwagon of the Hispanic market than
by the ways in which Latina communities conceptualize themselves or
their identities. And to stress this point, let us consider how the afore-

mentioned language and culture "media formulas" could affect Hispanic advertisers, among others whose profitability is predicated on the networks and who are therefore likely to emerge as key players in the culture and language battles that are waged in and through the networks. From the standpoint of Hispanic ad agencies, for instance, the Latin American/U.S.-Latina media synergy presents a threat to the traditional need for culturally relevant ads specifically targeted for the U.S. market. Simply put, if programming imported from Latin America works, why wouldn't advertising? In fact, this lingering concern is very much at the heart of some of the more traditional content and scope of Hispanic ads relative to the TV programming. Contrast, for instance, the beautiful Mediterranean, even angelic, mother figures who adorn advertisements on Spanish TV with the heavily made-up and scantily clad "exuberant" women who work as anchors or sidekicks on most TV shows, from news to comedy shows. Bikini-clad women are rarely seen in Hispanic advertisements but are common in U.S.-distributed Latin American shows like *Bienvenidos,* a Venezuelan show, which, in contrast to the reverent treatment given to family in ads for the U.S. Hispanic market, pokes fun at marriage, family, and religion. Such examples attest to the different sensitivities behind imported Latin American programming and advertising produced for the local U.S. Hispanic market.

Clearly, advertising is a different genre from serials and programs and is required to take fewer risks lest it offend or even repel the consumer. Nonetheless, we have repeatedly seen how the advertising industry, in attempting to maintain the idea of a unique "U.S. Hispanic market," has often had to project a more traditional definition of Hispanidad, one that is more marketable to Anglo clients, than the networks, whose programming is not as dependent on the approval of the corporate clients. Yet, defending the "uniqueness" of the U.S. market and its need for special advertising is likely to grow more difficult for U.S. Hispanic advertisers in an increasingly global context. Already, entrepreneurs working in the U.S. Hispanic and Latin American media markets are forging Latin American advertising networks, a development which encourages the free flow of ads across the border, narrowing the gaps between the U.S.-based and Latin American–based markets. While U.S. Hispanic agencies see themselves as having an advantage in these arrangements, having positioned themselves as the first true globalizers, and thus as more fit to do transcontinental ads for the totality of the U.S. market, this trend also presents an undeniable threat to their current operations.

Meanwhile, the U.S.-centered definition of Latinidad and the growing interest in bilingual or English-dominant programming presents its own set of challenges to U.S. Hispanic marketing as presently constituted. If it is not language per se that makes Latinas "Latinas," then what is to keep mainstream agencies from "jumping on the bandwagon" and targeting Latinas by appealing to culture and lifestyle as they have been doing for so long with regard to African Americans? Already, most advertisements in bilingual *Latina* magazine are in English, and are either the same as or indistinguishable from those in *Elle, Vogue,* or *Vanity Fair,* causing distress among New York Hispanic advertisers I talked to, since this trend represents the end of an exclusively Spanish-speaking setting for their advertisements.

Simply put, language means money for Hispanic media and marketing agencies, and this equation is likely to continue to affect the correlation of Latinas with Spanish, impairing attempts to broaden the media's definition of Latinas, or at least what they sell as "Latinas" to marketers and corporate clients. For now, we are therefore likely to continue seeing claims of Latina representativity reduced to programs that leave unchallenged the flows of media production for Latinas—programs filmed in Los Angeles or Miami but importing talent from Mexico or Puerto Rico—or else that mock English or its Latina speakers. Contestation over the Spanish networks' legitimacy and programmatic content is therefore not likely to end in the foreseeable future.

CHAPTER 6

The Focus (or Fuck Us) Group

Consumers Talk Back, or Do They?

Given the previous critical overview of the commercial representation of Latinos, don't consumers still identify with, feel engaged by, and get pleasure from these productions? What, after all, draws people to images that I have argued scarcely represent them? From the growth of Hispanic marketing, we could easily assume that audiences are indeed attracted by these images. After all, despite the lack of statistics confirming the success of any specific marketing campaign, advertisers have continued to advertise to Hispanics because they have received enough assurance through sales that such advertising is indeed appealing to Hispanics.[1]

Yet how people view these representations and how they consume these texts are questions that remain unexplored and are more difficult to ascertain. In part, this is due to the inherent difficulty of analyzing public reception, a process which is always fluid and predicated on, among other variables, social positioning, context, and place (Silverstone 1994; Mankekar 1999). In fact, recent anthropological research on consumption has shown that people's engagements with these products are not confined to the images alone but extend into all arenas of their lives, so that no single method is inclusive enough to fully discern these multiple practices. Although they should certainly caution us against drawing facile and all-inclusive conclusions from such analysis, these difficulties should not deter us from analyzing people's consumption of media products. Thus this chapter examines viewers' engagements with the culturally specific media products directed at them, not in order to ascertain the authenticity of these representations or to draw decisive conclusions about their effect on consumers, but to elucidate what people's discourses about these representations communicate about them and about how they position themselves by negotiating or resisting the all-encompassing category of identity on which these representations are predicated. These are the issues that I believe are most fruitful to consider, given that as long as Latinos remain ethnic minorities in this country and the Hispanic media continue to market themselves as representative of all Hispanics, these commercial portrayals will probably continue to be mediated by dominant U.S. dynamics of race/class/nationality, and interrogated regarding the degree to which they represent Latinos. I propose here that the key issue is not the authenticity of these images but how peoples' discussions of media texts are enmeshed in wider social issues, so that Hispanic marketing may be experienced either as a medium of marginalization or as a repository of language and tradition, with these images regarded as more or less representative, but always in concert with and hence revealing of people's backgrounds, experiences, and place in greater society.

My exploration of these issues employs a tool from the world of advertising itself: the focus group discussion. Long used by marketers as the principal method of testing their ads and marketing strategies, focus groups remain one of the most important qualitative methods to investigate consumers' mindsets.[2] For Hispanic marketers, focus groups are sometimes even the only qualitative method employed, given their low cost relative to other qualitative and quantitative methods now available for the general and Hispanic market. Recall that advertisers have been generally less willing to spend as much for production and research in the Hispanic market as they do in the general market. My adoption of focus groups as a research tool is thus purposeful, intended to explore the circuitous conundrum of Hispanic commercial representations by exposing the workings and pitfalls of consumer research. At the same time, I am fully aware that, as Ien Ang notes, academic audience research and market research are both about the creation of audience profiles and hence a matter of constructing "positioned truths" (Ang 1996). It is their politics—the kinds of stories they tell—that differ between these different modes of research, according to the institutional conditions of which they form a part. I therefore do not assume that my application of this method will result in "truths"; what I am after are the kind of contextualized stories that seldom come to light through market research about how some Latinos react to these representations. And I stress "contextualized," because, as will be evident below, participants' engagements with the media were always mediated by regionally specific considerations. In particular, New York City's racial/ethnic hierarchies, in which the lowest slots are occupied by the city's largest Latino subgroups, Puerto Ricans and Dominicans, were a dominant reference in these discussions. Specifically, during their discussions of the media, participants would consistently draw on their perception of their place and that of others within these hierarchies while simultaneously communicating particularized identities along the lines of race, class, or ethnicity using the same conventions of Latinidad disseminated by the Spanish and Latino-oriented media. I therefore suggest that, while Spanish and Latino-oriented media have undoubtedly contributed to the process of Latinization or the consolidation of a common Latino identity among different Latino subgroups, they have also helped create and trigger existing hierarchies of evaluation among so-called members of the same group. I provide first a brief examination of focus groups as a research method and then move into some actual groups to explore people's views and discourses about the images of Hispanidad that are directed at them.

THE FOCUS GROUP

The focus group, a discussion group aimed at obtaining perceptions on a defined topic in a permissive and relaxed environment, was initially developed in the 1930s and adopted by social scientists from numerous disciplines, including psychology and anthropology (Krueger 1994). Its extensive adoption by the marketing industry stems only from the 1960s, when consumers began to attain authority in the production process as key agents whose views needed to be accounted for and incorporated into all stages of the advertising process. This outlook gained prevalence with the sudden rise and popularization of account planning in advertising agencies; the planner became the consumer representative, and the consumer was consulted in all stages of the advertising planning and production process (Lury 1994). Since then, focus groups have become a staple in the advertising industry, but their implementation, usefulness, and reliability have been criticized, especially with regard to the haphazardness with which qualitative research using focus groups is conducted and its results interpreted by marketers, as well as the ease with which such groups can be manipulated to support particular findings (Lury 1994; Sherry 1995; Stern 1998). Ultimately, subjective dynamics, issues of race, class, gender, perception, and participants' interactions with the focus group leader and with one another, as well as the authenticity of their responses—do people ever tell you what they really think, or do they say what they think the interviewer wants to hear?—remain as elusive as when this methodology was first developed.

In assessing the affinity or discrepancy among media-generated images of Latinidad and Latinos' reception of such images, I nonetheless decided to employ the same method that marketers use to market to Latinos in order to have them "talk back" to advertisers. I felt that conducting focus groups and learning about how this method is employed by market research companies would also provide me with insights into the Hispanic marketing process while I investigated issues of reception: people's media-viewing habits, their ability to remember particular ads, and their views about what constitutes a more or less representative image of "Hispanic/Latino" identity.

My adoption of the categories prevalent in Hispanic marketing, for instance, proved quite revealing about some general trends in this industry—for example, the regionalized approach to Latinidad adopted by Hispanic marketing research, which veils the everyday realities of most Latinos, whose lives are not spent in homogenous and neatly defined ethnic enclaves. Most focus groups for nationwide campaigns are held in specific regional locations which are considered the major test markets for specific groups: Miami for Cubans and Central Americans, New York for Puerto Ricans and Dominicans, and Los Angeles for Mexicans. Mexicans are thus hardly ever included in focus group sessions in New York, nor are Puerto Ricans and Cubans included in those of Los Angeles, in a neatly defined regional approach to research that impedes understanding of how Latinos interact in mixed-Latino settings. Not surprisingly, the result is the patchwork approach to Latinidad that prevails in Hispanic marketing, with each nationality being addressed through those icons or symbols that are seen to "belong" neatly to it.

A second issue that surfaced during my application of Hispanic marketing standards to my focus groups was the overall lack of attention to issues of class, unless class is included as one of the variables of a given marketing plan, as when research calls for consumers or likely consumers of luxury items. The general tendency is to recruit people for research according to two main variables, language and nationality, in order to gauge their consumption of Spanish media, paying secondary attention to other variables such as age, gender, or class (which the industry defines mostly in terms of income or type of occupation). A likely scenario is that a recruiter goes to a high-density Hispanic neighborhood, be it the

Bronx or East Harlem, or contacts people over the phone in order to select Spanish-dominant Latinos who watch Spanish-language media, ignoring that such a spatial approach and so much emphasis on selecting
Spanish TV viewers already preselects working-class, Spanish-dominant
Latinos. The problem is that studies have found that these Latinos are
the least likely to be critical of Hispanic media and advertising, which
has led to the dominant view that Latinos are "too polite and compla-
cent," and thus culturally constrained, to be the most candid informants.
These so-called "traits," however, have specific correlations with variables of class and education that are not always accounted for during
the research recruitment process. As noted by a study on Latinos and television by the Tomás Rivera Policy Institute (1998), there is a sharp difference in media use and levels of satisfaction with television options and
programming between English- and Spanish-dominant Latinos. Spanish-
dominant Latinos, who rely most heavily on Spanish-language programming, were found to be the least critical of television, a stance that,
according to the research, does not indicate that Spanish TV is more in
tune with the needs of the Latino community, but rather that it is connected to particular social characteristics of the Spanish-dominant Latino.
One issue they point to is that Spanish-dominant and recently arrived
Latinos are less likely to perceive discrimination in a new context, which
would make them less critical of either the Spanish or the general market media. As immigration scholars have noted, an individual's immigration experience inherently involves confronting and acquiring new
frameworks for distinguishing race and class, as well as categories for
discerning inequality through processes of socialization within the new
society (Basch et al. 1994). Moreover, because it is only in the context
of the United States that recent immigrants, who constituted the poor in
Latin America and were considered by advertisers as nonentities, become
reconstituted into "Hispanic" consumers, and hence into a coveted commodity, they are also less likely to be fully familiar with the putative emphasis of U.S. consumer-oriented society on consumers' thoughts and
desires, making them less likely to voice individual preferences in focus
group situations. These are the very dynamics that led a skeptical creative with over twenty years in the industry to describe the focus group
as the "fuck us group." As he noted, "What gets picked [for focus groups]
is a lot of poor uneducated Latinos. And all of the sudden it just hits you.
It is a shame to realize that we [Latinos] are so poor and uneducated.
But we just go on asking all these marketing questions."

Also affecting the demeanor of focus group participants are differences in terms of class and ethnicity between moderators and participants. In contrast to most focus group participants, moderators tend to be highly educated, middle-class, Latin American–born (given the preference for Spanish-speaking facilitators),[3] and often unfamiliar with U.S. Latinos or with the regional/national/cultural differences among the Latino groups they are asked to work with—an ignorance that can affect the overall climate of the discussion. I do not mean to imply that research is most accurate when conducted by members of the same background or nationality as the participants. My point is that class and nationality, or the overall familiarity of the moderator with U.S. Latinos, are seldom taken into account during the process of recruiting facilitators and moderators by agencies and marketing research groups, potentially hindering the reliability of the discussion and its results. I myself was invited to moderate a focus group of Hispanics in Miami by one of the major Hispanic research firms, just on the basis of my business card, which identified me as an anthropologist; no questions were asked about my background or experience in leading marketing focus groups or my familiarity with Hispanics in Miami or anywhere else. I was also able to witness how little knowledge of U.S. Hispanics some moderators have during one of the focus groups I observed during my research. For example, a Chilean moderator questioned the Puerto Rican identity of a female participant after she had identified herself as both Puerto Rican and New York–born. The moderator, seeming very surprised, asked the participant to confirm that she was Puerto Rican, which to me, watching from behind the glass, underscored the moderator's lack of knowledge not only of Puerto Ricans but also of the persistence of nationality as a variable of identification among U.S.-born Latinos (Oboler 1995). The rest of the participants (mostly Dominicans and Puerto Ricans) just laughed about the incident, and I was never able to locate the woman after the focus group ended to hear her views on the matter. I nevertheless sensed that she had been publicly embarrassed. She remained relatively quiet during the group discussion, perhaps more quiet than if her Puerto Ricanness had not been publicly questioned. Let me contextualize this response by noting that the "Latinness" of U.S.-born Puerto Ricans is consistently called into question, as is that of other U.S.-born Latinos, by authenticated notions of Latinidad, although Puerto Rico's colonial status—making the island neither a part of the United States nor of Latin America—renders Puerto Ricans even more ambiguously "Latin." By acting surprised about the participant's self-identification as Puerto Rican, the moderator had openly called into question not only her Latinness

but her Puerto Ricanness. Obviously, one would not expect a moderator, who is supposed to maintain a relaxed and supportive environment,
to voice such a comment. This event shows that, as the director of a Hispanic research company stated, contrary to the dominant view, Latinos
do talk—that is, they are not passive and accepting consumers—and if
they don't, it is most likely because they are either intimidated or "turned
off" by the facilitator, not because they are docile or because of their
"culture." Placing a white, upscale Cuban moderator in a working-class
Mexican focus group or a gringo who spoke heavy, Anglo-accented
Spanish in a Spanish-dominant group were some of the scenarios that,
in his experience, were likely to affect participants' willingness to talk in
a focus group.

Another central issue that may hinder a focus group's reliability is the
highly patterned format according to which the focus group is developed
and used in marketing research. By the time a given idea is tested in a
focus group, its concept, strategy, and possible executions have often already been "approved," having passed through a sequence of develop-
mental stages between client and agency, leaving consumers with few opportunities for real choice or more critical appraisals.[4] A focus group I
observed, sitting alongside the corporate representatives who had commissioned the study, provides a good example. The study was contracted
by a major cable television company seeking to test alternative ways to
target Latinos, beyond their current strategy of dubbing the latest Hollywood releases. It gathered twenty-four Latinos, mostly Dominicans and
Puerto Ricans, who were divided into two groups and presented with
booklets describing the "different" programming options for four channels from which they were asked to "select" their favorite. These included
three that would show the latest Hollywood films along with some Latin
American films, documentaries, sporting events, and concerts, and one
that described the sponsoring channel's current strategy of showing
dubbed Hollywood films and the same fare it offers to the general market, except dubbed into Spanish. However, the programming differences
between the three mixed Latin American and Hollywood film channels
were almost indistinguishable: all featured Hollywood hits and various
amounts of secondary programming, such as sports, documentaries, and
Latin American or Spanish movies. Only one channel would be bilingual
(in the sense that Hollywood movies would not be dubbed), and the real
programming options were so subtly communicated as to make distinguishing between them almost impossible. They were presented in the
same booklet format, and the choices were mixed and matched in such

a way that each channel was almost a reproduction of the others in a slightly different format. The "choice" was therefore not one of concept or strategy, but of degrees, and the issue came down to how much sports, how many documentaries, or how many Latin American movies would consumers like to see accompanying their fare of Hollywood films. Complicating this decision was the fact that consumers were not familiar with the concept of "Latin American movies" or "Spanish movies." Given the lack of general distribution of Latin American movies, consumers could not distinguish what made this option different from the old Mexican movies that dominate the Spanish channels. In the end, the focus group was inconclusive. The premium channel kept its current format, without Latin American movies or original programs incorporated into its fare.

Moreover, questions in focus group situations are framed specifically around a product, with the ultimate objective of increasing its sale. This emphasis greatly limits the dissemination of any information that is not readily marketable or that complicates a facile understanding of Hispanic consumers and their relationships with particular products or reactions to advertising campaigns. This issue came boldly to the surface when I compared the responses given in different situations by one of the five participants in the research for the cable TV channel mentioned above. In that group, participants were asked how much Spanish TV they watched in any given week, with no mention of English TV. To the delight of the corporate representatives and advertising staff sitting on the other side of the one-way mirror, respondents proceeded to mention a large number of Spanish TV shows. A Puerto Rican, unemployed mother of seven provoked smirks among corporate observers when she said proudly that she watched television "all day and every day." Sitting among the marketing representatives, I could see their self-congratulatory delight. Was it because she revealed how much TV, and thus advertisements, participants watched, or perhaps because she matched so well their stereotype of (lazy) Latinas who watch too much TV and can't stop getting pregnant? In later meetings, I too asked participants from this focus group how much Spanish TV they watched, but also how much English TV, as well as with whom and when they watched it. What surfaced was quite distinct from the earlier marketing discussion. The woman who had said she watched TV "all day and every day," for instance, also identified a number of English-language shows she watched, and it turned out that she was not really watching TV but connecting with and getting updates from her seven children, on "their own turf." As she put it: "I ask them what they are up to, and they never talk, but then I sit next to them when they are watching a show and all of the sudden things come up and there's a conversation." She went on to describe her routine, which included particular days to "watch" TV with each of her children. This type of story, however, is rarely given the opportunity to surface within a focus group's very structured, marketing-oriented discussions, and when it does it is screened and edited during its interpretation, ultimately and necessarily reduced to marketing recommendations.

One last challenge presented by focus groups that is worthy of consideration is their internal group dynamic. While this structure does provide space for spontaneous exchange and is most revealing of social dynamics that may emerge across participants, it can also hinder individuals from expressing views which might contradict those of the others. Again, I myself noticed that respondents were more critical of the Spanish media and more willing to say that they liked or enjoyed it during one-to-one interviews than during focus group discussions. During the latter, people would often modify or refrain from expressing their views, particularly after other participants had already expressed some negative thoughts about their favorite type of media. Overall, however, participants in my focus groups took a surprisingly critical stance toward the Spanish media, which I believe was due to their use of focus groups as a forum to voice their wishes for programming, not to the fact that they have inherently adverse views about it. In the end, with the exception of U.S.-born, English-dominant Latinos, all focus group participants did identify themselves as moderate to active consumers of Spanish-language media. But before turning to these issues, let me first provide a brief description of my application of this research method.

My focus groups paid particular attention to the two variables that advertisers are most concerned with when selecting participants for their own focus groups: differences in Spanish-language proficiency, and nationality. In contrast to the "patchwork" approach to marketing research that is dominant in this industry, however, New York was treated as a microcosm of the Latino United States, and as a testing ground for analyzing social interactions across various nationalities, not just Puerto Ricans and Dominicans. This approach was not difficult, given the heterogeneity of New York City's constituent Latino nationalities. Yet by no means am I suggesting that such diversity renders the opinions of New York Latinos representative of the entire universe of U.S. Hispanics. Rather, my aim is to portray the range of issues that color peoples' consumption of these texts; to analyze the opinions of different Latino sub-

nationalities with regard to a common "Latino market," in order to examine how they form their opinions in relationship to each other, as opposed to in isolation, and finally to consider what their opinions may
suggest about how Latinos negotiate the Latinidad that is so promoted
by these commercial representations.

I conducted five focus groups, three of which were Spanish-dominant
groups: one of South Americans, mostly Colombians and Ecuadoreans;
another of Puerto Ricans and Dominicans; and a third made up exclusively of Mexicans.[5] There was also an English-dominant group of youth
(18–25), most of whom were Dominican or Puerto Rican, but also Central American; and a fifth group of bilingual/English-dominant adults (Dominicans and Puerto Ricans), displaying different levels of proficiency in
Spanish, from nonspeakers to bilinguals and active users of "Spanglish"
or code-switching between Spanish and English (Zentella 1997). Within
these groups, attention was also paid to the variables of class and gender.
Thus, while most participants were blue-collar, Spanish-dominant Latinos (ranging from school dropouts to college students mostly working
in service occupations), there were also middle-class and college-educated
participants (education acquired, for the most part, in their country of
origin) in each of the groups.[6] I also included a slightly greater number
of women in the total sample, given that they are considered the
model/average consumers by Hispanic marketers. All the participants had
been in the United States for at least three years, although most had lived
here for over fifteen, and many had been born in New York City, making them all quite knowledgeable of the U.S. media and marketing
environment. Finally, all of my informants self-identified as Latinos/
Hispanics and used these words interchangeably, along with their national identification as Puerto Ricans, Colombians, Mexicans, and Dominicans. U.S.-born Latinos and those with a considerable number of years
in the United States (most of my Puerto Rican, Dominican, and Colombian informants), however, were more likely to call themselves Hispanics
or Latinos than were the Mexican informants in my study, which is not
at all surprising, since most Mexicans are relatively recent immigrants
to New York City, making them new "entrants" into this category.[7]

Contacts with Latino consumers were established through "snowball"
sampling (Bernard 1994) among store owners and customers as well as
in public places (post office, restaurants) in some of the most diversified
Latino neighborhoods in New York City. Among them were Jackson
Heights and Astoria in Queens, the Bronx, and Washington Heights in
Manhattan (where I resided during my research), all of which have a high

percentage of Mexicans, Colombians, and Dominicans, along with Puerto Ricans.[8] The groups were held at Hunter College's Center for Puerto Rican Studies, which provided a central location for people who came from different boroughs in the city, and participants received a small stipend of $60.00 to compensate them for their time.[9] The discussions revolved around open-ended questions designed to inquire into people's general assessments and views of the Spanish-language media, their media habits, and their likes and dislikes in programming and advertising. As is common for focus group discussions, however, each group had a distinct rhythm and dynamic that led to topics as varied as people's views of Latinos' current and future place in U.S. society, social issues, and raising children. For the purposes of this chapter, however, I adopt one more general research practice: deliberate selection. I thus organize this chapter around some interconnected issues that surfaced in most of the groups: views on the authenticity and representativity of Latino commercial portrayals, and the issues of culture, and color, and equality of the representation among different Latino subgroups.

QUANDARIES OF REPRESENTATION

If Budweiser wants to sell beer to Puerto Ricans, then why don't they show a *coquí* [Puerto Rican toad, and national symbol on the island], why show a frog? If you want to sell to a market, you need to reflect it.

> Focus group participant

One of the most generalized beliefs that was repeatedly advanced in different forms by focus group participants was that Hispanic media are representative of U.S. Latinos and that their growth is indicative of Latino achievement and enfranchisement. Again and again, participants would mirror the discourse of representation that the networks are so dependent on, attesting to the extent to which this discourse permeated almost all of my informants' diverse interpretations or evaluations of the media and of the Hispanic marketing industry. Hispanic media were alternately praised, criticized, or excused, but always in relation to their position as an ethnic- or culture-specific product that was unquestionably evocative of Hispanics. The growth of Hispanic media, for instance, was always a cause of pride among my informants, irrespective of their actual opinions about them. This view was succinctly voiced by a Puerto Rican participant who, recalling with pride the rapid growth of the Hispanic media in New York City, insisted that this demonstrated that "they've had to adapt themselves to us, and could not survive if we stop consuming." Not all of the Latino consumers I spoke with agreed that Latinos had finally "imposed their culture" on the United States, or that the structures of U.S. corporate capitalism would unravel if Latinos stopped consuming, but most did express in different guises their feeling that the increased recognition of Latinos as consumers does attest to their growing power and visibility, echoing the ongoing equation of consumer choice with participatory democracy, a common trait of modern consumer society. Even participants who were critical of the sudden popularization of Latino culture in mainstream culture related the growth of Hispanic marketing to the indisputably greater recognition of Latinos. As one of the U.S.-born youths stated,

> They know that by the year 2005 we are going to be the new majority of the country, and of the whole world, and Latinos, especially Dominicans, are migrating more and more every day. And they know that whether we gonna work or sell drugs or work legally or pay taxes or not, you are gonna spend your money. And that's the most important thing, where you are going to spend your money? That's what they are like, "What do Latinos want, what do Latinos want?" That's why they are coming after us.

Nonetheless, people's association of Hispanic media with Hispanic's "coming of age" in the public eye does not make them oblivious to the exclusions generated by these representations. What it points to instead is that discussions of the media were necessarily intertwined with issues of representation as varied as the current and future place of Latinos in U.S. society or their views about what constitutes a more or less factual representation of Latinos. Consider the following exchange among three participants in a group made up of mostly Central and South American, Spanish-dominant Latinos:

TERE: The thing is that we have to adapt to this culture, but without forgetting our own. I feel that the media should always show the true culture, because here one can forget it.

NELLY: Coming here is a great cultural shock. But you cannot educate your children a different way, you have to adapt yourself and celebrate Thanksgiving because your children will want Thanksgiving.

CARLOS: But there is an enormous contradiction in all of this. The Mexicans and we Dominicans, we find everything we need here, like plantains and yucca, things you would not find ten years ago. All of these cultures are arriving and transporting their foods and their traditions, but TV does not show that. TV forgets that all of this is happening and that here we eat yucca and that we are just like we've always been.

NELLY: Yes. The media should not forget it, because we are introducing a new culture here to the Americans. Now you see American ads with words and sayings in Spanish.

CARLOS: That's what I am telling you, that we are imposing our culture.

Besides the obvious pride in the visibility created by the media, this exchange demonstrates that people felt that the images presented should be more representative of Hispanics in this country, and in particular serve as a conduit to their "culture." For some, like Carlos, this would involve showing Hispanics as they "really are" in the States, eating yucca and transporting Latino traditions here. Yet others believed that a more realistic portrayal would be to show life as it was "back home" or to show the "true" culture that may be forgotten here. In fact, it was an earlier statement by a participant that ads should represent Hispanics by showing their culture "back home" that triggered the aforementioned discussion about the need to recognize the United States as Latinos' proper home, one that could even be "Latinized" after their image.

Repeatedly, the media were seen as a repository of language and tradition that should be kept as authentic and thus "non-Americanized" as possible. Consider the following exchange among a mostly Puerto Rican and Dominican, Spanish-dominant group about how they would like to be portrayed in advertisements:

ROSAURA: They should show us more reality.

ANGEL: More typical [típico used here to mean traditional] things, less modern.

ROSAURA: Yes, I personally would like more typical images.

ARLENE (moderator): What do you mean by "more typical"?

ANGEL: Well, they show a bunch of Hispanics, but at the same time they sort of Americanize them in one way or another. I think that if you are showing Hispanics, then you have to show them to be the typical Hispanic. So that if you are doing a production with Mexicans, then you should dress them as Mexicans and in a Mexican background.

ARLENE (moderator): So what you like is that Puerto Ricans be dressed as jíbaros [peasants], is that what you mean?

(Laughter; people overall reject this proposal.)

ANGEL: No, what I mean is that they should be dressed in
          a *güayabera,* and that if you are going to place him
          in the Empire State Building, the Empire State Build-
          ing should be shown to be in 33 street not 42 street.
          They should show that Latinos are everywhere, and
          that's the message they should send. That we are
          everywhere, and that we are here with pride.

Participants in this group went on to criticize the Hispanic media for copy-
ing American TV shows, finding in this practice the epitome of all that
they found negative and lacking in Latin culture and the Spanish-language
TV channels—once again we have the same construct of pollution and
contamination, with the United States blamed for the loss and dilution
of Latino culture. Yet, while they seemed to prefer some sort of "authentic" media space, they could not readily propose alternatives when
asked what types of shows would be more Latin and less derivative of
U.S. shows. What was certain, and what also surfaced in other groups,
was that participants' preference for more "authentic" or realistic portrayals did not necessarily imply "tradition" or anything that would trigger nostalgic evocations of the past. In fact, some of the ads most favored
by participants were humorous, contrary to the marketing truism that
Hispanics don't like humor regarding the things they supposedly deeply
value. People also preferred ads that showed family scenes, but even family was preferred in humorous rather than nostalgic situations. McDonald's ad showing a baby "high-fiving" in joy inside the womb after the
mother eats at McDonald's, or Chevrolet's ad with a young wife who
provokes her husband into falling because she does not want him in her
snapshot of her new Cavalier were the type of ads that participants tended
to recall when I asked them to list their favorite Spanish TV ads.

Language was one issue that participants felt should be kept as untainted as possible. References to "our language," *"nuestro español,"*
particularly among the Spanish-dominant, signaled that Spanish was certainly seen as a central component of their Latino/Hispanic identity and
a reason why they tuned in to the Spanish channels. Echoing the view
of other participants, Nelly, one of the Spanish-dominant participants,
explained, "I watch the *novelas* to brush up on my Spanish. 'Cause we
Latinos speak Spanish and should teach it to our children. That's why I
wish there were more programming for children, so they can learn Spanish and keep their culture." Such comments suggest that many viewers
watch Spanish TV as an educational medium, to "brush up on their Spanish" or even learn it, rather than for entertainment. These viewers had

little tolerance for "bad" Spanish and had a clear and specific conception of what constituted good Spanish: that which was untainted by English. The Spanish channels hence appeared as a medium that not only taught viewers good Spanish but constantly reminded them of the faultiness of their speech. Thus, a discussion of Telemundo's new attempts to show bilingual programming triggered the following debate:

DANIEL: They should not show people that can't speak Spanish in TV.

MARTA: But that's how people speak in real life, we mix Spanish and English.

EVELYN: But it's not done the way they do it in the show, it's fake. You don't say an entire sentence in Spanish and then say "rum and coke" [referring to Telemundo's new show *Sólo en America*, where the kids are shown mixing Spanish and English].

DANIEL: I have not seen that show, but what I know is that I hate it when I see the news and the journalists interview people in the street who don't know Spanish. It's embarrassing. They should choose people better before they allow them to speak.

Spanish and English were indeed mixed in our discussions, and like Marta and Evelyn many validated the use of the Spanglish in daily speech. But generally it was "pure" Spanish most participants wanted to hear on TV. This of course was tied to the overall preference for representations that showed Latinos in terms of a "positive image." In fact, viewers were particularly sensitive about how Latinos are depicted on Spanish-language TV in relation to how people are portrayed on general-market stations. The specter of English media was constant in their assessments of what constitutes a more or less positive portrayal of Latinos, as is evident in this exchange among participants of the Puerto Rican and Dominican focus group:

IRMA: I think that there should be more positive images of Hispanics.

REBECCA: And please not all housewives are disheveled and wear glasses (all laugh).

ARLENE (moderator): But I don't remember seeing any disheveled housewives in Hispanic ads.

REBECCA: Yes, they show them, not as the modern women of the times, but I don't know. When housewives are shown in American ads, you see women who are white and fit. You don't see her having a tummy or anything. But in Latin ads, they show the Latina woman with a ripped robe. They don't show her wearing Victoria's Secret (all laugh).

ELSA: The Hispanic wakes up that way because she is
                  a working woman.

REBECCA (insisting):   There's an ad that shows a woman with eyeglasses
                  and a wig or I don't know what else on. They make
                  her look so ugly.

ELSA: Is that the one in which they show a sick woman?
                  That's the Robitussin ad. The point is that she is sick,
                  that's why she looks that way, because she could not
                  sleep. They can't show her being all made up if she's
                  sick.

REBECCA: Yes, but the one who's sick is the little girl, not the
                  mom.

I was not able to identify any ad that matched the one described by Rebecca. Generally, it is beauty and clean-cut looks that dominate TV's Latin look. Contrary to her recollection of the Robitussin ad, it is the mom, not her daughter, who is shown to be sick, which would easily explain her disheveled state. What I found interesting, however, was this woman's perception, and even conviction, that Latinos were presented negatively when contrasted with the models who decorate the ads in the general market. When seen in relation to these ads, the Latin look, while in reality unrealistically lavish, in her eyes fell short of Anglo images, being always darker and more modest, reminding the viewer that she/he is still subordinate to the "American" consumer.

Here we need to consider that, with the exception of a few, mostly Spanish-dominant, older adults, most focus group participants were very familiar with the fare of the English TV channels, and in some cases said they preferred its programming to that of the Hispanic channels. Indeed, Latino viewers' stance toward Hispanic media is better described as scavenging than devotion, as is evident in this participant's description of her TV viewing habits:

> We have four televisions at home. The bedroom is always on the Latin channels, and the living room one is tuned to the American ones. The kitchen TV is tuned in either channel by whoever is doing the dishes. The kids' television is always used to play games and things like that. I watch the soap operas in my bedroom, but if I see that it's dragging too much, I go to the living room, depending on the day, I already know what American shows I like, I watch two American shows. And then at ten, I go to sleep.

Such multiple involvement with different media venues makes Hispanic consumers fully aware of what they do or don't get from the Spanish channels, providing for comparisons in which the Hispanic channels appear less sophisticated and more repetitive than the general market channels. The overall consensus is that, as stated by a Puerto Rican participant, "English TV takes you all around the world, but Spanish TV keeps you in Mexico." In other words, there is a lot more variety in the English channels, as well as programming for children and the entire family. Latino participants regretted the few options the Spanish TV had for youth and children, which limited the transmission of Latino culture to their children, who were always making fun of the Spanish channels as tacky and old-fashioned. Thus, whereas viewers generally agreed that the Spanish networks were indeed more representative of Latino culture than the American channels, it was the general TV stations that they tuned in to for programming and variety. As one summarized, "There is a difference in that you see more of a spirit of enjoyment in the Spanish television. In the ads, for instance, you'll hear music, or see someone dancing. I don't know, but I feel that there is a difference, not in what they show, but in the way they show it, with a sense of happiness and enjoyment. I feel they identify us more as a people. There is also identification with the language. But they always show the same programming."

This participant was not alone in his ambivalence toward the Spanish-language media. As if communicating their own misgivings about their new subordinate status as Latinos in the United States, participants would often draw comparisons between the U.S. Hispanic fare and that of their home countries, which they rated as better, more informed, and more sophisticated than that of the United States. Such comparisons were drawn primarily by the most recent arrivals, but also by Dominicans and Puerto Ricans, whose recent visits to the islands kept them abreast of their media environment. Always, however, these comparisons were expressed in ways that suggested that people were consuming these media texts not as generic "Hispanic" products but as representative of particular groups and nationalities. This stance was most evident among Mexican respondents who, given the dominance of Mexican programming, seemed to most identify with the networks' programming—so much so that some expressed concern that the programming displayed them for constant scrutiny by other Latino groups and the wider society in ways that made them subject to public derision or even resentment. Consider the following exchange about Univision and Telemundo's programming that took place among a focus group of Mexican participants:

JORGE: Sometimes I think that they are trying to ridicule us. I feel
           that they feature the worst of all countries when there are
           much better programs back home. There are lot of programs
           that are much better in Mexico, but what do they show? *The
           India Maria* or *Eugenio Derbez*, which many don't understand.
           I like some of those programs, but those who don't understand
           them are going to think that we are all silly.

JAIME: Yes, like *Duro y Directo*.

JORGE: These are programs that other people see, and they'll think
           badly of us Mexicans.

IRMA: But some people like those shows. In Provincia, there are
           people who get excited just by seeing a rooster *metido* with
           a cat (referring to the type of themes that are common in
           Duro y Directo).

FRANK: (research assistant and facilitator of this group): But is *Duro
           y Directo* part of Mexican TV? What kind of Mexican TV
           would we like to see?

JORGE: The thing is that there are so many channels in Mexico. The
           channels that feature *Duro y Directo* are *chafas* (lowlifes).
           There you had choice.

These participants then expressed longing for the "good" Mexican programming, for the greater choice and number of channels available in
Mexico, suggesting not only their overall dissatisfaction with the lack
of choice in Spanish-language programming in the United States, but
also their concern about what the shows communicated about "Mexico" to a wider Latino constituency. Some of these participants made
pejorative comments about the "vulgar" content of the salsa/merengue-
formatted La Mega radio station, only to realize that to other groups,
Mexican programming might similarly generate bad impressions about
Mexicans, such as that they are provincial people. Class surfaced as a
key concern of many of these recent arrivals who, regardless of their
work and background—most Mexican participants worked as waiters,
delivery staff, or housewives; were working illegally; and had limited
education—made a point of distinguishing themselves from Caribbeans
as a means of communicating their class image and aspirations.

The exchange above, however, surprised me because, while I was
aware that many U.S.-born Mexican Americans are highly critical of the
Spanish-language networks, I expected recently arrived Mexicans to identify more closely with Mexico's media offerings and therefore to be less
critical of the Spanish networks' fare. Activist groups that work on behalf of Mexican-Americans have expressed dissatisfaction with the Span-

ish networks for providing limited representations of Mexican Americans and for showing programming that does not reflect their U.S. reality, as have other U.S.-born Latinos. Nonetheless, I expected Mexican respondents to be more positive about the Spanish networks, as are other Latin American immigrants who are recent arrivals and who are also exposed to a great deal of Mexican programming in their own countries. Thus, I had envisioned criticisms of the U.S. Hispanic media by Mexican informants to be directed not so much at Mexican shows but at shows they perceived as "Latino," or generic. What surfaced in the discussion, however, was that while some Mexican informants expressed dislike of generic shows—which they thought were too Cuban, and just not Mexican enough—they also regretted the burden of representativity that they believed had been placed on their shows as representatives of Mexico in the United States

Among non-Mexican participants, on the other hand, the dominance of Mexican programming triggered a number of important and interrelated debates. Always, however, participants in all groups gave evidence of being conscious of and attentive not only to what nationalities were being addressed or represented by different media products, but to the dominance of some Latino subgroups over others in these representations. Consider the following exchange triggered by a discussion about differences and similarities between Univision and Telemundo among a group of Spanish-dominant Puerto Ricans and Dominicans:

KIKO:	In my opinion channel 41 (Univision) is a good channel.
LAURA:	"Se siente" [repeating the channel's promotional slogan that Univision "Se siente," or "one feels it"].
TOÑO:	It's a good channel, but all you see are Cubans and Mexicans and that's it. Channel 47 (Telemundo) is more diverse. You see Colombians, and Puerto Ricans, and Dominicans.
ARLENE (moderator):	Yet Univision's newscast has, I believe, about two Dominicans?
TOÑO:	Well, yes. But all they have is a local newscast, and the rest is directed to the west to Los Angeles.
BELKIS:	Let me tell you something, my husband loves sports, but if there is something that he hates it is that they come up with the results of the Chivas Rayadas de Guadalajara [Mexican soccer team] (all laugh).
BELKIS (continues):	What we Caribbeans like is baseball, but you don't see it.

LAURA: I ask myself why is there so much Mexican
                   programming, and I think that it is because it's
                   cheaper. Those canned programs are cheaper.

TOÑO: I think that Univision has a contract with Televisa.

LAURA: But if they [Univision] are supposedly a Latin
                   station, they should also have Dominicans, Puerto
                   Ricans, Argentineans, and Paraguayans.

KIKO: But the issue is the money (all agree, and he con-
                   tinues). Televisa is a multimillion-dollar industry;
                   maybe other nationalities are interested in doing
                   TV but they don't have the money.

TOÑO: Another problem is that we Puerto Ricans only
                   have one show in Univision.

ARLENE (moderator): Which one is it?

TOÑO: *No te Duermas* is the only Puerto Rican show
                   because they took *El Show de Las Doce* away
                   from us.

BELKIS: It's true. I'm with you.

LAURA: Me too, I liked to hear about what was going on
                   in the island.

KIKO: Yes, there's only one show, *No te Duermas,* and I
                   think that they took it away.

TOÑO: Yes they did. *Se durmió* ["It fell asleep," punning
                   on the show's name, "Don't Fall Asleep," to mean
                   that the show is now gone] (the word play makes
                   everyone laugh).

TOÑO (continues): Yes, we need more shows from Puerto Rico. They've
                   erased us.

Toño's concerns that the networks "took away our programs" and
that they "erased us" corroborate that Hispanic shows and products were
therefore not necessarily consumed as "Hispanic shows" but were vested
with particular meanings and associated with particular nationalities,
making us wonder if stations were truly disseminating an uncomplicated
notion of Latinness or rather tearing its seams in the process. Perhaps
the clearest example of this trend was participants' overall preference for
ads that summoned particular backgrounds and cultures over those that
showcased generic Latinidad. Indeed, in an ironic twist, soon after the
aforementioned exchange that was so critical of Univision, all participants agreed that their favorite Spanish TV ads were Univision's channel 41 promotional ads for its thirty-year anniversary—the *Se Siente* campaign mentioned by one of the participants. Far from producing more
of the generic expositions that dominate the networks, they filmed sep-

arate ads that showed musicians from different Latin American countries, some dressed in traditional costume, others in urban clothes; some filmed in Puerto Rico or the Dominican Republic or in distinctive neighborhoods in New York City, such as Queens or the Bronx, and playing rhythms of salsa, cumbia, tango, merengue and hip-hop, encompassing almost every Latino subgroup in the city.

CULTURE AND COLOR

In sharp contrast to the Hispanic agencies' claim that race and color are not issues of concern among Latinos, who, I was told, would always prefer to see light-skinned Latinos in advertising, the whiteness of the world of Hispanic advertising surfaced repeatedly in most of my focus group discussions. Such debates attested to the importance of this issue among Latinos and also revealed those variables which can affect their subjectivities about race and U.S. racism. Briefly, race and racism were of far more concern among U.S.-born Latinos than among recent arrivals, reminding us that immigration and length of stay in the United States are central variables affecting an individual's experience, awareness, or expression of U.S. race and racism. In contrast to new arrivals, those who had spent considerable portions of their lives in the United States were generally more aware of the whiteness of the world of Hispanic television. Some saw it solely as the work of Anglo corporations, which as one stated, show Hispanics "not how we really are, but how they want us to be," a view that is supported by our earlier discussion. Meanwhile, other focus group participants accused Cubans and Mexicans of shaping these images after themselves. This was the view of a Colombian woman, which I believe reflects not so much her belief that Mexicans and Cubans are closer to these images, as her own awareness, and that of other participants, of the dominance of some Latino subgroups over others in the production of these images. On the other hand, others criticized these images not for their whiteness but for their darkness. When recalling the ads that she saw in the Dominican Republic, where blondes are also featured, a Dominican participant insisted that U.S. ads were patronizing because they always showed Latinos as "medium-dark" peoples. As she stated, "They show us like aliens, medium dark, medium brown, always like made of cinnamon," when in fact, she noted, Latinos come in all colors.

Overall, it was Hispanic Caribbeans who were most concerned with issues of color in the media, and who brought this issue to the forefront.

This is not surprising, given the greater African racial influence in the Caribbean—a product of the region's history of slavery—and given also that within the world of Latinidad, it is Hispanic Caribbeans (mostly Puerto Ricans and Dominicans, and to a much lesser degree Cubans) who have been made to stand for "color." Here, we need to recall our earlier discussion about how the world of advertising continually reduces different subnationalities to culture indexes and traits, such as a type of food, a style of music, a festival, or a particular phrase, with the intended or unintended outcome that the various nationalities are differentially evaluated as more or less representative of Latinidad and associated with particular aspects of its makeup. For example, when dark-skinned maids are shown in Mexican soap operas, they tend to be from the Caribbean (as in *La Usurpadora*); or consider the casting of the black Puerto Rican actor Rafael José for the multinational team of *Despierta America,* Univision's version of *Good Morning America*. Yet another example is provided by the short-lived Spanish version of *Charlie's Angels* by Telemundo featuring a multiracial/multinational team of angels—a blonde, a brunette, and a black Latina played by an Argentinean, a Mexican, and a Colombian actress respectively. Echoing what is a common trend in representations of Latinidad, the Angels' skin color is increasingly darker among the actresses originating from the countries closest to the Equator. Spanish TV consistently leaves us with the impression that there are no blacks in Mexico, blondes in the Dominican Republic, or brunettes in Argentina (see figure 25).

Thus, not surprisingly, when one of my focus groups discussed a J.C. Penney ad involving a multinational collage of youth distinguished by the word each uses for "cool" (*macanudo* used in Argentina, *chévere* in Puerto Rico, *padrísimo* in Mexico, and so forth)—a Puerto Rican participant demanded to know why black Latinos, when they were shown, were always Puerto Rican, when Puerto Ricans are of all races and, like the Argentinean, can also be blonde. The interesting thing is that nothing except the word *chévere* marks the black kid as Puerto Rican in the ad. Replaying this ad at home, I also noticed that the same character also says *órale,* said by Mexicans, and the creative who did the ad confirmed to me that the model had been cast as a "generic Hispanic Caribbean," not a Puerto Rican. Thus, this participant's comment is most of all revealing of how much participants' own backgrounds were always summoned as part of their interpretation of the ads. In this case, this informant's awareness of his own racialization and that of

Puerto Ricans, both in greater U.S. society and in the "Latino" community, explains his reaction to the ad, just as earlier another informant had concluded and firmly believed that the Latino housewives shown in Spanish TV ads are always less fair and beautiful than their general market counterparts. His response reveals that, though predicated on appeals to racial and ethnic integration—the ad's punch line is "It does not matter who you are or where you come from. We can all be cool by dressing J.C. Penney"—commercial representations of Latinidad are predicated on assignments of color and race to particular nationalities in essentialist associations that hinder the acceptance of racial diversity as intrinsic to all Latinos, not just some groups, be they Hispanic Caribbeans or Puerto Ricans.

As in this incident, participants were well aware of how certain campaigns and programs are customized to target specific Latino subgroups, and of the stereotypical portrayals intrinsic to such an approach to marketing difference. The media repeatedly surfaced as a vehicle that exposed and, in so doing, helped shape popularly held beliefs among and across Latino subgroups, beliefs concerning temperament, race, values, and traits that are supposedly shared among members of particular Latino subnationalities. Another relevant example is provided by the following discussion about recent programming changes adopted by New York City's most popular radio station, the salsa/merengue-formatted La Mega, to target New York's growing Dominican community by playing more *bachata* and merengue and by featuring Dominican language mannerisms in spoken segments. The overall tone of this station is irreverent—imagine a Latin Howard Stern—sexual imagery and innuendos are common, and, as a result, appealing to Dominicans became tantamount to the DJs using more Dominican slang and accent to call in *mamis* (sweeties) over the airwaves. The discussion took place among a group of Spanish-dominant Latinos, mostly South American (Colombian and Ecuadorian), one Cuban, and one Dominican participant, who was soon turned into the embodiment of Dominican culture and hence of the stereotypes about Dominicans and Hispanic Caribbeans. The discussion started when one of the Colombian women denounced the sexual innuendo that pervades the dialogue between the DJs and their call-in public, particularly after its programming change to increase its fare of merengue. To these comments, an Ecuadorian man responded by evoking the stereotype of the hot Dominican male and the more eroticized Caribbean culture:

MARIA: What I don't like is how they are always talking about sex, as
           if that was what we are all about, and they never talk about our
           culture, or our youth.

ROSA: Yes, women are treated as an object. I feel bad because they are
           always saying "go take their butt," as if it [the butt] is a glass or
           a cup.

JOHNNY: Ay, Mamita [mocking how the radio DJ says the Dominican word
           of endearment, "little mama," that according to its use can stand
           for girlfriend, woman, girl, or lover].

JORGE: But that's Caribbean culture for you. Change the station to Amor
           and you'll see that they speak different because they are not from
           the Caribbean.

ROSA: No, I don't think that's true.

JORGE: Yes, they are more open. The señora is from the Caribbean, right
           [addressing the Dominican female participant]?

SANDRA: [another participant responding on her behalf] Yes, but she said
           earlier that things are not like that in Dominican Republic.

The Dominican woman had previously explained, in relation to a similar insinuation of Dominicans' unrepressed sexuality, that Dominican
culture is not the way it is represented in the Latin media and that such
profanities would not be heard in the Dominican Republic where, she
claimed, a Commission of Public Entertainments would prohibit them
from being aired. Such objections notwithstanding, the issue continued
to surface, with the salsa-merengue radio station serving as the indis-
putable proof of Caribbeans' lustfulness versus South Americans' more
"restrained" sexuality, which one would encounter on another station.
The interesting point here is that these distinctions were made by contrasting merengue/salsa-formatted La Mega with the pop-formatted
Amor, La Mega's sister station aimed at a pan-Latino constituency
through baladas and pop tunes less directly associated with any particular country than are salsa and merengue with Puerto Ricans and Dominicans, respectively.

Such comments were also intertwined with issues of class, which were
similarly indexed and negotiated in relation to various media and in reference to particular nationalities. Specifically, while all groups admitted
liking and listening to La Mega, it was common for people to make claims
about their status and class for themselves and others by shunning or
taking issue with the station's vulgar and offensive content, or else by
being more or less open about their listening to this station. The former
stance was embraced by many, irrespective of nationality, although relative to Puerto Ricans and Dominicans, who constitute the station's main

target groups, Central and South Americans were more likely to shun
the station. In so doing, Dominicans and Puerto Ricans were often treated
as the embodiments of the very qualities that they shunned in the station, as seen in the discussion above. It is also noteworthy that the women
who distanced themselves from La Mega's sexually filled content, including the Dominican woman above, were among the middle-class college graduates in the group, who did not represent the views of all Latinas. The "Mega Jacuzzi" an evening programming segment where a male
DJ takes calls from women as he supposedly lies naked in his Jacuzzi, is
always brimming with Latina women eager to join the DJ's sexual play,
filled with details of how he undresses and caresses them. This exercise
demands both their submission as sexual objects and their agency. After
all, these women represent a direct challenge to the demure sexuality that
dominates media images of Latinas, which revolve around the sexy and
attractive but virginal, maternal, and pure Latina—the beauty to be seen,
not heard, much less if she is openly displaying, or in this case, broadcasting, her desire and sexuality.

Interestingly, the same participants who shunned La Mega would later
reveal that they did in fact listen to salsa and merengue, and appeared
to be quite familiar with the station's programming. Obviously, then, their
negative comments did not necessarily reflect their listening habits, but
their generalized association of salsa/merengue stations with Dominicans
and Puerto Ricans, conceived as a less-educated and unsophisticated Hispanic population. This stance also evokes the white audience's relationship with black music and black people, which is one of pure consumption but at a distance.

Indeed, in most of the discussions, Puerto Ricans and Dominicans became the embodiments of Americanized polluted culture against which
other New York Latinos would distinguish themselves as more moral,
respectable, and authentic. Consider the following exchange between my
assistant, Frank Nuñez, an Ecuadorian graduate student, and a Mexican
informant who had been living in New York City for about four years,
concerning why the informant identified himself as Hispanic.

FRANK: Do you identify yourself as a Hispanic or a Latino?
ESTEBAN: I identify myself as a Hispanic. The Hispanics are those that stay
           here for a season, just for some time, and then go back. Latinos
           are those that live here. Hispanics speak Spanish, more Spanish
           than English, and Latinos don't.
FRANK: And so who are the Latinos in New York?
ESTEBAN: Well, my view is that the most vulgar ones are the Dominicans,

the Puerto Ricans are more open. We Hispanics are more
reserved. We have shame in a lot of things, but they are very
seasoned, and you see that in the way they dress. We cover
ourselves more. But the Dominicans show it all. We have shame
and get embarrassed.

This Mexican informant was not the only one who made distinctions
like this to distinguish himself from Hispanic Caribbeans. Other Mexican participants, like some of the Central and South American participants, were just as ready to voice their concern over their class status
and aspirations as compared to those of Hispanic Caribbeans, particularly Puerto Ricans, who are positioned at the bottom of the city's ethnic and racial hierarchy among New York Latinos. To contextualize these
responses, I summon the work of Robert Smith (1996) and Philippe Bourgois (1995), who have analyzed interethnic relations between Mexicans
and Puerto Ricans in New York City. As they note, Mexicans and presumably other recent arrivals to the city hold negative perceptions of
Puerto Ricans, which are invariably informed by Puerto Ricans, historical subordination in the city and their close relationship with and similar status to African Americans, which have stigmatized them as the ultimate marginal minority. Bourgois notes that these dynamics are affected
by Puerto Ricans' longer experience with the city's ethno-racial economy, which has made Puerto Ricans less willing than most recent Latin
American immigrants to tolerate exploitative working conditions and
lower standards of employment, which they know have not led to their
upward mobility. This stance, in turn, directly feeds their image as indolent or lazy among their newcomer counterparts. What is seldom noted
about interethnic relations among Latinos in the United States is how
value estimations between Latin American immigrants are drawn not only
in terms of each group's particular place within regional or U.S. national
hierarchies, but also of established taxonomies of place, nationality, and
authenticity at play in both Latin America and the United States. Thus,
what I found striking was that Esteban would so readily connect Hispanics to Latin America and Latinos to the United States in a distinction
that is less revealing of this informant's views about Hispanic Caribbeans
in New York (in L.A. this statement could well be made about Chicanos
by any recent arrival, irrespective of nationality) than of the superior status of "Hispanics," defined here as those who have connections to Latin
America and have kept their Spanish, relative to what he considered as
the "Americanized" and hence polluted Latino. Also of interest is how
frameworks of place, temperament, and region are mobilized to construct

hierarchies within Latin American countries and cultures among and across Latino subgroups. Notice that in order to distinguish himself from "those" other Latinos in the city, he identifies himself as a "Hispanic" not only according to the dominant definitions of the market, implying Spanish dominance, but also drawing from long-held Latin American beliefs regarding temperament, weather, climate, and race. Specifically, his ideas regarding Dominicans and Puerto Ricans are founded not only on his perceptions of their subordinate position in New York's racial and urban topography, but on distinctions that Latin Americans hold regarding the value of particular countries and cultures as functions of race, political economy, or climate. Esteban went on to explain that Hispanic Caribbeans were bound to dress the way they do and to feel less ashamed about nudity, exposure, and openness, both because they were "raised near the beach, in a warmer climate," and because they had been in the United States for a much longer time. He himself, he argued, would perhaps end up dressing that way if he stayed in the States. Another Mexican informant used a hierarchy of attributes based on geography to explain disparities among Latinos in the United States: "It's not that I think that I am the greatest thing or anything, but I come from a continent, not from a piece of land surrounded by water [as Caribbeans do]." While the value ranking of such hierarchies varied according to by whom and on what basis they were made, it was obvious that among New York Latinos, the subordination of Hispanic Caribbeans was not due solely to their already low position in the city's racial hierarchies but was also based on evaluative frameworks of Latinidad that other Hispanic immigrants bring with them from their home countries. Specifically, Hispanic Caribbeans were always peripheral to the rest of the countries of Latin America, reproducing the political-economic configuration of the area, favoring the more Europeanized, more putatively white, and more modern "national" countries.

I previously noted that the specter of English TV was present in focus groups' discussions of the Spanish-language media. It was also present in the way people communicated their real or presumed class standings. Many participants subscribed to cable television and made a point of mentioning the roster of channels they had access to and the "educational" magazine shows that they watched "back home." Typical of what Ang (1986) has called the ideology of the mass media, entertainment programs are generally judged inferior to educational shows, and people made a point of conveying their status as enlightened Latinos by mentioning the educational shows they watched on cable or by making distinctions among Spanish TV programs. Even soap operas were subject to this type of distinction. A graduate student from Colombia, who works part time tending children and housecleaning, for instance, was full of praise for the Telemundo soap opera *Mirada de Mujer*,[10] a Mexican production that broke the mold of the virginal and naive role model by featuring an empowered older women who shuns her unfaithful husband to find happiness with a younger man. She made the overt point of clarifying that it was this progressive *novela* that she watched, not *La Usurpadora*.

A revealing instance of how people communicated social hierarchies, class standings, or racial identities through their relation to media took place in the group comprising U.S.-born, English-dominant youth. This group was composed mostly of Puerto Rican youth along with two Dominican participants, a Honduran young woman, and a young man who self-identified as half Spaniard and half Venezuelan. All were U.S.-born, English-dominant Latinos, but most of the Caribbean Hispanics were dark or black, while the Honduran and the Spaniard/Venezuelan were white. Some of the participants were college students, others high school dropouts or service workers. Whether due to issues of race, or to their overt college student status (they came directly from a class at Hunter College), or because they were clearly outnumbered by the Dominican and Puerto Rican participants, the Venezuelan and Honduran participants immediately distanced themselves from the rest. They made this manifest by taking the position of "enlightened" Latinos who criticized all genres of media programming, particularly the musical styles favored by the rest of the participants. One of the first things that emerged in this discussion was the Caribbean youths' pervasive indifference to and dislike of most of the Hispanic media, favoring instead urban lifestyle, hip-hop formats. This was not surprising, given the historical connections and intersections of Puerto Ricans with African Americans at the level of popular and everyday culture, itself evidenced in hip-hop, with which Puerto Rican and Dominican youth were always involved (Flores 1996, 2000; Rivera 2001). The non–Puerto Rican participants, however, dismissed hip-hop as offensive and vulgar, triggering a discussion about the real nature of Latino culture:

ARSENIO: I'm going to say something that may offend people, but I think
           that these stations proliferate ignorance. This is the stereotype
           that exists about our community, and they make billions, I
           mean billions, exploiting the stereotypes that we are all about
           the ghetto, that we are all violent and ignorant. (At this point he

> is interrupted by the group, some of whom had clearly been offended.)
>
> ERICA: Hip-hop is like reality, real life (voices of agreement).
>
> PETE: This is how we grew up, how we live.
>
> ERICA: That's right. You should take it, not as a compliment, but as assertion that we have our own space, a home base.
>
> PETE: It's something that we as a people will always go to, as opposed to say, country music. You should be proud that hip-hop is at Hot 97.7, and that it is in a lot of places. It started in the Bronx, and the ghettos, and the street, and it is a form for us, like, of getting out of the ghetto as well.

Note that all these participants made reference to some sort of "community" that they were all part of, although in contrast to Arsenio, most of the youth validated hip-hop and the urban scene as a legitimate site of that community by pointing to hip-hop's entry into greater society as a sign of the things that Latinos have contributed to and should be proud of. In so doing, the Puerto Rican and Dominican participants defended hip-hop as a reflection of their everyday realities, which they conceived in terms of alterity and marginality with regard both to mainstream culture and to the other dissenting Latino participants, who were presumably not part of and could not understand "their" experience. Participants went on to identify hip-hop artists whom they had discovered were Latino, such as Fat Joe or Big Punisher, or African Americans they had thought were Latinos, pointing out the mutability and cross-fertilization between black and Latino youth culture, and thus highlighting the contributions of Latino artists to rap and hip-hop. In doing so, they were branding the non–Puerto Rican and Dominican informants as "outsiders."

This expression of Dominican/Puerto Rican complicity in hip-hop culture, however, does not mean that other Latino nationalities have not taken part in hip-hop culture[11] or that there is no tension between the New York Dominicans and Puerto Ricans. Despite their similar positions in the city's ethno-racial hierarchies, Dominicans and Puerto Ricans have dissimilar histories which have affected their immigration into the city, their legal status, and their relation with each other. On the one hand, Puerto Ricans enjoy the "advantages" of being U.S. citizens, but must bear the stigma of their status as colonial subjects, while Dominicans have the "privilege" of belonging to a recognized nation-state, despite a long history of dependency and imperial entanglements with the United States. These differences have prompted mutual resentment about the relative advantages or obstacles these groups face as they compete for jobs and resources. An additional source of contention is the racialization of Dominicans by Puerto Ricans, which is greatly influenced by the intense discrimination suffered by Dominicans who have migrated to Puerto Rico in search of jobs and easier access to the United States, only to become the racialized "other" against whom Puerto Ricans construct themselves as culturally superior and white (Duany 1990; Duany et al. 1995). Martin, a college student who was recruited but was never able to attend a focus group, and who is the child of a Dominican-Puerto Rican marriage, explained the strains of this animosity as follows: "This tension has always been present. I remember back at school I was always forced to decide whether I was Dominican or Puerto Rican. They would always provoke me by saying , 'Hey, there is a fight between Dominicans and Puerto Ricans, on which side will you fight?' They wanted me to choose sides." He has since overcome this predicament by identifying himself as Latino, and whenever possible emphasizes his mixed Dominican and Puerto Rican background. He also pointed to his Puerto Rican girlfriend and to the many similar unions and marriages with which he is familiar, as if to augur the development of a better relationship between these groups. Whether or not this state of harmony is achieved, the fact remains that these two groups remain in close contact with each other and serve as the embodiment of a Latino underclass in the city, as evident in the aforementioned discussion of hip-hop and rap. These genres may have received general acceptance in mainstream society, but are still largely associated with blacks and Puerto Ricans and with negative stereotypes of violence and the ghetto, and hence are looked down on as an illegitimate Latino musical genre by most other Latinos.[12]

As in this incident, discussions of the media by young, U.S.-born Latinos provided clues to alternative definitions of Latinidad beyond the dominant definition of Latino/Hispanic that emphasizes knowledge and mastery of the Spanish language, whiteness, and direct connections to a specific Latin American country. Of course, U.S.-born Latinos themselves have internalized such definitions and gave ample evidence of their awareness that they lack or may be perceived by others to lack the "appropriate" cultural capital of Latinidad. While I was recruiting participants, more than one English-dominant youth declined to participate on the grounds that they spoke no Spanish, until I explained that my study included all Latinos. Another recruit (who failed to appear in the focus group), had identified herself as a second-generation Puerto Rican and a Latina, but was ready to add that she might not be the right person for this study because she neither spoke Spanish nor watched the Spanish-language channels, as if qualifying her own authenticity as a Latina on the grounds that she lacked the right language skills. Others overtly expressed their ambivalence about their own Latinness. The following statement by a black Dominican woman in her early thirties indicates how many of my dark-skinned Latino informants negotiated their identity in contrast to the Mediterranean view of Latinidad that is promoted in the Hispanic media: "I have had to redefine what is Latino, and I generally don't identify with Latino culture. I identify with Dominican and West Indian culture, and I say that I am Petromacorisiana" [from Pedro de Macoris, in the Dominican Republic]. Other dark, black, or mixed-raced Latinos were also ambivalent about calling themselves "Latinos," except that, rather than reject Latinidad, they asserted instead an anti-Hispanic version of Latinidad rooted in a mixed, black and mestizo culture that, more important, was grounded in the United States rather than Latin America. As one young Puerto Rican participant explained, "I don't have Spanish blood, so I am no Hispanic." Another noted, after I asked what things they would like to see more of in the media, "My idea would be to have a Latino network. You know, Latinos that migrated have a different view of the world, and they think different from the way we do here. So if you are gonna make a show, it is not going to be successful unless you have a script that is written toward our mentality, which for the New York–based Latino is different. I'm not gonna laugh at the same shit these people laugh at. They laugh at different shit, and it is not funny. You know what I'm saying: it is different. We are a significantly different Latino."

Putting down the Spanish TV networks was a common way for U.S.-born and English-dominant Latinos to try to reverse their peripheral position within the dominant canon of Latinidad. Through this stance they asserted their greater sophistication in relation to recent arrivals and older generations of Latinos, while also advancing a U.S.-centered definition of Latinidad that they saw as more sophisticated than what they described as the tacky and traditional view of Latin culture that prevails on Hispanic TV. As one young participant stated, "I am embarrassed by the Spanish TV networks. It's offensive, they sexualize women, their butts are always out. The women in *Primer Impacto* [a Univision magazine show], for example, all look like painted prostheses." Most of all, such comments brought once more to the surface that U.S. Latino sensibilities about race and gender are markedly different from those of Latin Americans. That they are not reflected in the Spanish-language media is evidenced in the following discussion:

FELIPE: The problem is those *novelas* in Spanish television. They are all white. It's like, I'm a dark-skinned Puerto Rican. And in these stations they are all white. They all look South American. They are racist (all interrupt).

ARLENE (moderator): Let's hear one at a time.

FELIPE: If you watched TV, you would think that Latinos are all white or looking like fucking, I don't know . . .

TRINY: That we all looked Mexican.

FELIPE: But Mexicans are Indian-looking. It's all ridiculous.

TRINY: Yeah, we all have different elements in us, we have whites, Africans, you know, we are a mix of all those people, but even in commercials, all you see is white people eating Goya beans. It's crazy.

JENNY: Yes, we are a mix. You know . . .

TRINY: You don't see a lot of dark-skin Latinos on *novelas*, just the housemaid (all interrupt).

FELIPE: I feel that they misrepresent us. And I don't like to watch it.

ARLENE (moderator): How about you, Manuel, what do you think?

MANUEL: No, I don't like it. It's boring, all they give is soap operas.

HERB: Just for older people.

MANUEL: I was catching myself the other day. I am twenty-five, you know, and I was thinking that every time I pass my sister [i.e., any Latina] on the subway, I catch myself looking at their ass, I just do it (all laugh).

MANUEL: 'Cause all you see is women in bathing suits every time.

SANDY: Like in *No te Duermas, caliente* and with the big butt.

HERB: *No se ve más* (You don't see anything else).

MANUEL: Always is like hoochy mama, you know, something like that.

The ironies in this interchange were more than conspicuous. Here are those who had been described by other groups as the most vulgar of Latinos using the same arguments about sexuality and TV's lack of morality to put down the media products associated with the recent arrival and thus the supposedly "authentic" Hispanic. Still, discussions among the youth did not revolve around the Spanish-language TV media for much longer. Their media universe is much wider than that of any of the other groups, as is their awareness of discrimination, inequality, and the stereotypes to which Latinos are subject in this country. Thus, the discussion of the sexualization of women on the Spanish-language TV networks soon led to a discussion of the portrayal of Hispanic women in MTV's hip-hop videos as the "hot Puerto Rican mammy" as well as to the stereotypical portrayal of Latinos in public service ads in the subway, and to the controversial Taco Bell Chihuahua, pointing to the many ways they are consistently reminded of their subordinate social position in this country. Consider the following discussion about the ads most liked or disliked by this group of U.S.-born youth:

VANESSA: I like the Taco Bell commercial because it's funny.

MIGUEL: It caught my eyes.

ERICA: Some people are offended by it.

VANESSA: Some people are offended by a dog?

ERICA: Dinky, the Taco Bell dog, some people are offended by the dog. The reason is that, look at the dog, the dog is supposed to be representing Latinos and Mexicans because tacos are Mexican and the dog Chihuahua is Mexican and blah blah blah. That is why they get offended is not because of the dog (laughs).

VANESSA: I'm sorry, but the first time I saw it I was on the floor. They are trying to call your attention, and a person saying it is not going to be as funny as a dog.

FELIPE: Seriously, what I get mad about is the stuff I see in the train. You see a Planned Parenthood ad, and they put "She said she is pregnant, and I was crazy scared and da da da . . ." and I am on the train and I am, damn, you know! That's the stereotypical attitude, why can't it be any other girl. A lot of Latina girls get pregnant, that is statistically correct, but . . .

VANESSA: But then why can't it be a Latina girl if that is statistically correct?

FELIPE: But I see another one, for HIV, and it is also two Spanish boys. I'd seen another ad that says, "Help us stop drug dealers," and then you see like a shadow, and you know that shade is a Latino, you just know it, the way he is standing like this (makes a threatening gesture). And it is not only Latino and black people, there are white people dealing drugs too. (All agree.)

VANESSA: I like the Taco Bell dog (laughs).

The exchange above reminds us of the fluidity and hybridity of Taco Bell's Dinky and of the multiple responses that the ad campaign triggered

(Limón 2001). Erica evokes the view of many Latino activists and intellectuals who experienced or are familiar with the caricaturization of Mexican and Latino culture in the 1960s and found it demeaning and offensive, while Vanessa saw it simply as a "funny ad." What are certainly less ambiguous are the public services ads mentioned by Felipe. Many companies, such as Goya, Star Media, and Radio Unica, advertise products to Latinos in the New York City subway, but, as noted by the youth above, the bulk of subway ads targeting Latinos are not commercial but public service advertisements. These ads urge Latinos to use condoms or to get educated and advertise social services that associate them with unprotected sex, drug abuse, and AIDS, and show them forever needy of social services. This observation was further documented by Steven Francisco, a native New Yorker and Columbia undergraduate I met while giving a talk at Clara Rodríguez's seminar on Latinos and the media, who subsequently wrote his term paper on this issue (Francisco 1999). This student brilliantly noted the ironies of such ads in a context when such services and government funding are being scaled back. He, like the focus group participant above, noted the disparity in the representation of Latinos in subway advertisements: that blacks and Latinos are equated with urban poverty. Francisco found also that while subway advertisements for products like Star Media and Radio Unica revolve around the whitened Latin look and present a Hispanicized version of Latinos, similar to that which dominates Spanish TV, public services ads draw on images of marginality. They also show more black Latinos. This disjuncture in representation reminds us that consumption may be whitened, but poverty is always colored; and, as a corollary, that white Latinos do not need social services, that the "good"/white Latino consumes commodities, not social services.

The foregoing exchange also shows that discussions of the media lead not only to critical assessments but also to the expression of particularist forms of identification, be it along the lines of race, class, or nationality, destabilizing in this manner the neatness of Latinidad as an all-encompassing category of identification. It is important to recognize, however, that this category was always a central point of reference in all the discussions that participants used as needed. Nowhere was this more evident than when we turned to the Anglo/Hispanic divide and to the culturalist definitions circulated in the industry about Hispanics.

I did not show any visual materials in my discussions, relying instead on people's recollection of media and advertising images, but I did share at the end of the discussions some charts depicting the broad cultural characteristics of Hispanics and Anglos that inform the dominant frameworks around which these representations are shaped. I shared some of Isabel Valdes's charts which depict Latinos as more spiritual, familiar, pessimistic, communally oriented, concerned over hierarchy, and highly decorative in their homes than Anglos, who are more individually oriented, motivated, and egalitarian. The responses were quite revealing: in relation to Anglo-Americans and Anglo culture, everyone immediately self-identified as Latino or Hispanic and was suddenly willing to generalize about the cultural attributes that are or are not shared by all Latinos. Not everyone agreed on what those attributes are or was as accepting of those broad generalizations. While most were ready to identify themselves with the more positive traits used to define Latinos, such as being more family-oriented, more concerned with home aesthetics, and with their peers, others were insulted by some of those characterizations. For instance, Valdes's assertion that Anglos are more egalitarian outraged many participants who have experienced racism and prejudice in this country, as did some of the descriptions that generalized about Latinos' behavior. Still, all arguments for or against Valdes's generalizations were framed in relation to notions of a generalizable Latino culture, bringing to the forefront the fact that, despite all their previous misgivings, participants ultimately identified themselves with the same category that merged them with that "other"—whether called Latino or Hispanic— that everyone had been trying so hard not to be.

Summing up, separately and collectively, participants' responses suggest that, despite their criticisms of the category and its representation in the media, they have in fact internalized, or made theirs, particular dynamics and conventions of commercial Latinidad. As we saw, commercial representations were actively used by participants to assert their own and others' place and level of "belonging" to this category or to distinguish particularized forms of identification along the lines of class, race, morality, and nationality and even to assert who among them is more or less "American" and hence more or less entitled to representation within U.S. society. The irony is that all of these insidious distinctions fall short of challenging, and in fact reinscribe, the preeminence of whiteness and of the "non-ethnic" as the abiding reference against which each of them is rendered suspect. And my guess is that participants already knew that; thus their spontaneous embracement of the category of "Latino" or "Hispanic" at the end of the discussion.

CHAPTER 7

Selling Marginality

The Business of Culture

Although the $200 billion Hispanic market is not a mono-
lith, several values serve to unite Hispanics. They include
the importance placed on the family and children, the desire
to preserve their ethnicity, an emphasis on aesthetics and
emotions, a devotion to religion and tradition, and a strong
interest in their appearance.

Asia is huge, with billions of people, but, for historical
reasons, its peoples have many cultural similarities, which
simplifies our task. One of these is the family or group focus.
In collectivist or "we" cultures, the family or group culture
is far more important than the individual, while the individual dominates "I" cultures like the United States.

When marketing to African-Americans, keep in mind that
they value self-image, style, and personal elegance. . . .
Family and religious values are very important to most
African-Americans . . . The marketing implications of
feeding, sheltering, and entertaining participants at black
family reunions, which are increasing in popularity, are
phenomenal.

The preceding quotations, all drawn from a single multicultural market
booklet (Rossman 1994: 48, 91, 142–43), bring to the fore an issue that
summarizes and draws together the central concerns of this work. Although family values and religiosity are associated in popular culture with
good old Americana, it is ethnic consumers who are most often presented
by marketers as family-oriented, traditional, and brand-loyal, which, in

marketing, serves largely as synonym for conservative consumers. We have examined these issues in relation to Hispanics, yet it takes only a glance at how Asian and African American consumers are discussed and represented in marketing magazines and trade journals to realize that Hispanics have ample competition for the prized place of the most family-oriented, most brand-loyal, most religious, and most rapidly growing minority group.

That ethnic marketers would strive to highlight these qualities in their consumers is not surprising given that the family values and morality of minority populations have historically been under scrutiny by the dominant society as compelling proofs of their stability and worthiness as targets of advertising compared to the white consumer. U.S. minorities are all subject to stereotyping as low-income, unskilled, uneducated, crime-ridden, unemployed, and, in some cases, as perpetual foreigners, and, whether more or less family-oriented or brand-loyal than other market segments in the United States, they are always required to prove their worth and compensate for their tainted image.

These dynamics became evident during the Invitational Summit on Multicultural Markets and Media, where representatives of the African American, Asian American, and Hispanic consumer markets presented brief statements about why advertisers should target their particular constituencies. The presentations were almost identical, with each speaker exalting the rate of growth of their respective populations and underscoring their family orientation and distinct culture, each almost contradicting the previous presenter. From the audience, the performance, display, and even competition between presenters was far too evident. After all, no two groups can be the number one minority group in 2020 or be the most family-oriented. So indistinguishably are these populations treated in U.S. marketing that they are increasingly conglomerated into a single category: the "ethnic" or "minority" consumer. Variously called multicultural, ethnic, or urban, this phantom conglomerate has become the target of more and more agencies, as evidenced in the change in mission of many black and Hispanic agencies to encompass multicultural or ethnic marketing.

Indeed, minority populations exhibit some similar sociodemographic characteristics, such as greater youth and rapid growth in relation to the general population. Census projections that the nation's combined minority populations will soon surpass the "majority" have made it almost a cliché for mainstream marketers to tout minority consumers as the untapped and golden opportunity for savvy marketers, or even as the emerging majority market (Los Angeles Times 1999). They are also more regionally concentrated in urban centers of the United States, which makes them relatively easy to target through regionally concentrated advertising. Marketers continually rejoice that they can cover the majority of the U.S. Asian population by targeting California or New York, or almost the entire Hispanic population by focusing on the five largest DMA markets. At the same time, the reason for the seemingly great size of the minority consumer population, who, despite their supposedly massive numbers, are never called anything other than a "minority," is that African Americans, Asian Americans, and Hispanics are each undifferentiated identity constructs, encompassing a wide-ranging and highly diverse population which may or may not actually consider itself part of the "same group." We have already discussed the problems and inequalities hidden in the all-inclusive category "Hispanic," and the Asian and black/Asian-American markets are not less of a fiction. Asian Americans include a range of languages and nationalities, the top five being Chinese, Filipino, Japanese, Korean, and Vietnamese, which include widely different histories and backgrounds—from the Taiwanese business man visiting the United States on a two-month business trip to the garment worker or the descendant of a nineteenth-century Chinese immigrant. Similarly, the African American market[1] exhibits wide cross-cultural and generational differences, although blacks of any nationality as well as U.S. African Americans from different classes and backgrounds are considered as part of the same market. However, aside from any other similarities, it is their minority or ethnic status and putative "difference" from general market consumers that these disparate populations have most conspicuously in common, leading us to inquire what their portrayal as culturally specific "markets" suggests about them in relation to U.S. hierarchies of race and culture.

This concluding chapter argues that ethnic marketing in general—not solely Hispanic marketing—responds to and reflects the fears and anxieties of mainstream U.S. society about its "others," thus reiterating the demands for an idealized, good, all-American citizenship in their constructed commercial images and discourses. Like other forms of representation produced in a context of inequality and domination, ethnic marketing is self-referential and more revealing of those who produce the representation than of those who are its subjects. Accordingly, it is not the actual difference of the "ethnic consumer" that sustains ethnic marketing and customized marketing efforts but contemporary U.S. so-

ciety's demand for exotic and segregated others. Only the general inability
to consider racial and ethnic and sexual "minorities" as part of U.S. society sustains marketers' stubborn insistence on the fiction that the general market, like U.S. society, is white, heterosexual, and ethnically untainted and feeds the need for ethnic marketing to affirm "respect" for or
appreciation of minority populations. The same can be said about gay
consumers, who are addressed in a similar fashion as a "special market"
through images that reinscribe normative notions of sexuality and exult
couplehood, commitment, and family values.[2] All of these marginal others need to be repeatedly reminded that they too are part of the United
States and that their contributions "enrich" or "empower" this country
because, regardless of their history or citizenship status, they remain "foreigners" or virtual foreigners vis-à-vis the "general public" by the nature
of their race, ethnicity, and culture, and the values and behaviors that
are ascribed to them by such differences. Ethnic marketing hence functions as the interlocutor for these populations in relation to mainstream
America, and as a site that regulates, mediates, and positions the immigrant alien, the raced, and the underclass into their respective places
within U.S. racial and ethnic hierarchies, while creating myths of peoplehood for these populations where docility, foreignness, and spirituality are triumphant.

MARKETING AFRICAN AMERICANS:
MARKETING "BY ANY MEANS NECESSARY"

African Americans have been part of the commercial imaginary of this
country since well before the turn of the century. Not only were they
once advertised as property, but U.S. advertising has long drawn from
images of blacks to advertise both products for the general market and
specialized products for blacks as an ethnic market. Soap and hair products, skin lighteners, hair straighteners, and other products through which
blacks were told they too could aspire to images of whiteness were among
the first products targeted to African Americans through black newspapers in the early 1920s, to which music companies and basic consumer
products such as clothes and groceries were added (Kern-Foxworth
1994). Weems's study of the rise of the African American consumer market attests that by the 1940s black consumers were represented as a block
by companies such as Interstate United Newspapers, Inc., a consortium
of newspapers devised to rally advertisers to the black press, and that
major corporations throughout the 1950s hired blacks intermittently as

ethnic marketing consultants (Weems 1998: 34–55). Only after the 1960s, however, amidst the ongoing equation of economic empowerment with political enfranchisement and the rise of consumer boycotts during the civil rights period, did marketing to blacks attain its present status as a specialized industry. The top black-owned agencies, such as Zebra Associates (established in 1969) and Uniworld (1969) in New York, and Burell Communications in Chicago (1971), were founded at this time, as were the ethnic marketing initiatives of many U.S. corporations. Since then, like many independently owned Hispanic agencies, black advertising agencies have been bought or instituted as branches within global advertising agencies as part of a growing interest in multicultural marketing in the advertising industry.[3] In contrast to Hispanic marketing, however, African American marketing has lagged in its development as a specialized industry, a situation that leads us to consider some key variables distinguishing African Americans from other U.S. minority consumers. Foremost is marketers' view that African Americans constitute the only "indigenous" minority in the United States,[4] a status that places them closer to mainstream culture, sharing both language and media symmetry with the "general market." Unlike Hispanics and Asian Americans, who may exhibit language differences, African Americans' language symmetry has led to the widespread view among marketers that they are "dark-skinned white people" and not distinct enough to merit culturally specific marketing.[5] In addition, while black print media and radio stations have existed since the 1940s, the African American market has historically lacked a national TV network that would serve to unite blacks as a common, nationwide market. Some stations, like Fox, have at times slanted their programming efforts toward this population. The cable network BET (Black Entertainment Television) addresses blacks, and UPN (Universal Paramount Network) and WB (Warner Brothers) TV networks have designated programming blocks targeting African Americans, but these developments stem only from the 1990s and have never included a nationwide TV network comparable to what Hispanics have in Telemundo or Univision. Most important, African Americans are recognized trend setters in mainstream culture, a role that further negates the need to target them as a unique group, as doing so would miss the opportunity to reach simultaneously the general market. As explained by a chief officer at Uniworld Advertising in New York City,

> The truth is that black agencies were created because of pressure; it was civil rights pressure. No one believed that there was truly a need to use our services. Because mainstream agencies told clients that since black people spoke En-

glish, they really were a part of the domestic populations. We've been here a couple hundred years, you know. So from that point, if it were not for federal pressure, and affirmative action, the growth of black agencies would never have happened, and there is still resistance up until today to use black advertising agencies. . . . And you have the crossover, so, for example, you have Sean Puffy Combs and Russell Simons, who have become mainstream icons, so the mainstream agencies say, "Well gee, we can use them as spokespersons to reach the total market."

This situation poses a contrast with marketing to Asian Americans and Hispanics, whose consumer base is identified as having "their own language" and "their own culture" that is not as generalized in U.S. society, although the ongoing popularization of Latina culture poses questions about their likely mainstreaming in the future. The result is that African Americans constitute the most commodified U.S. minority population, with "things black" and representing blackness incorporated or heavily showcased in general market campaigns. From baggy clothes to labels that show, Michael Jordan, and Motown music, a variety of icons of blackness have been used to advertise soft drinks and burgers (*Discount Merchandiser*, October 1998), thus providing a spurious yet optimistic public view of the incorporation and leading position of African Americans in mainstream society.

From the perspective of black-owned advertising shops and those involved in specialized African American marketing, this development has presented its own set of contradictions: the more "hip-hop rules," the more black agencies have had to struggle to maintain their niche market. During the interview referred to above, the same executive noted how difficult it is for black agencies even to tap into their icons, lacking both the advertising budgets needed to hire the black superstars as well as access to network television. Both he and the executive director of Chisholm Mingo, with over twenty years working in this market, were skeptical of the growing interest in urban markets, which they believed would lead advertisers to whiten black culture for white consumption and rid hip-hop and urban cultural expressions of their origins in black culture and among black people. Reclaiming it, they both stated that "urban culture is really black culture," even if mainstream culture hesitates to credit them with its creation. More optimistically, other black agencies have tried to capitalize on the resurgence of urban markets, by presenting "South Central Los Angeles, Harlem, the south side of Chicago, this basement where the furnace is being stoked" (Jensen 1999) not as a niche market but as a mass market setting trends for the rest of the world and positioning themselves as the true experts on this global market.[6] Whether they can compete with global advertising agencies who are also tapping urban markets and have bigger budgets and greater access to media, however, is another matter altogether.

Yet, more than the mainstreaming and monopolization of black culture by the mainstream advertising industry, it is the historical prejudice against blacks and anything black in this country that presents the greatest impairment to the African American marketing industry and to culturally specific advertising for U.S. African Americans. Just as with Hispanics, the overall media image and low incomes of African Americans relative to whites make them doubtful consumers in the eyes of marketers, while stereotypes about blacks' morality, values, disorganized families, or behavior have added to the obstacles black marketers must overcome to convince corporate clients of the advertising worthiness of their target populations. It is not at all surprising that in marketing articles on the African American market, the rising buying power of the African American consumer dominates discussions, even though when read closely, the same articles are likely to attest how far it actually trails behind that of whites. Thus, a *USA Today* article stating that black buying power is expected to surpass $500 billion in 1999 ends with the less optimistic truth that "the typical black household has less than 20 cents of wealth for every $1 owned by the typical white family" (Belton 1998). Discussions of African Americans make constant allusions to the legality of such income, that black buying power is "money from salaries and wages," implicitly referring to the association of blacks with crime and illegality against which commercial portrayals are ultimately shaped (Poole 1999). Responding to the stereotype of blacks as destitute and unemployed, articles repeatedly note that not all blacks are poor, by highlighting the rising black middle class with incomes over $50,000 that is increasingly "affluent, educated, and professional," and ready to be tapped (McLaughlin 1999). And if the affluence of the black middle class is not convincing enough, marketers can always point to the West Indians and Caribbean Americans, immigrants from Guyana, Trinidad, Jamaica, and other parts of the Caribbean, who are among the most affluent and educated blacks in the United States. This population is presented as a family-oriented group that has a rich cultural life and travels frequently (to see relatives in the Caribbean), and hence as the embodiment of African Americans, diversity and wealth.[7] Most of all, blacks are said to be "hip and primed to shop" (Fisher 1996); we are told that they enjoy shopping more than other leisure activities, and watch 60 percent more television than their general-market counterparts. As one such article reminds us, "The consumer mantra of the 1980s, "Shop 'til You Drop," is alive and well with black Americans. Even those without large incomes are willing to spend money to enhance their personal image" (ibid., 52). Through such images, blacks are consistently described as obsessive and uncritical consumers, who lack the sophistication of whites to choose their purchases wisely, veiling the social inequality in which consumption is always implicated (Chin 2001).

African Americans, however, are only avid shoppers in some product categories. They are believed to outspend whites in groceries, clothes, and accessories such as panty hose, hair and nail accessories, TV or radio equipment, but to spend significantly less on housing furnishings, home maintenance repairs, and insurance (Treise and Wagner 1999), a pattern that is more suggestive of marginality than economic fortune. That blacks are spending to "look good" and improve their image also speaks volumes about U.S. racism, according to which the most subordinated members of society are most concerned to fix, control, or "compensate" for their putative lacks through style, appearance, makeup, or accessorizing. Such constraints involve engaging in consumption in order to meet dominant and unattainable cultural dictates and standards (Weitz 1998) or else challenge those standards by establishing alternative fashions or stylistic trends (Austin 1994). Advertisers are well aware that African Americans are willing to spend more for quality and are more likely to shop in malls and specialty stores; after all, they are buying not only products but also respect and equality (Gray 1998). This is particularly so considering that, as Regina Austin tells us, blacks have historically been condemned and victimized in activities that whites take for granted, such as shopping, selling, and consuming, through poor service and suspicion. Among other issues, she notes how black consumption is seen as deviance or as an expression of their alienation. Buying status through goods, a practice common to everyone, gains added meaning, she notes, when African Americans are believed to be unusually gullible consumers and hungrier than most for status (Austin 1994). Elizabeth Chin (2001) has documented the numerous tactics adopted by malls and shop owners to restrict access to black youth and customers: they establish clothing bans, exert extra surveillance, restrict public transportation access, and even play music that would be unappealing to minority groups. For black youth, she notes, establishing their right to the mall as a public space is a constant struggle as consumption and consumption sites are always bound up with social inequality. In this context, and ironically, the same articles aimed at presenting blacks as affluent shoppers and at distancing African Americans from their position of marginality, when read against the dominant stereotypes of blacks circulated in larger society, simultaneously reinscribe and attest to the same marginality that marketers try so hard to veil. They also support the same ideas about blacks' shopping pathologies by presenting a consumer who exhibits a putative "untamed consumerism" and quest for luxury in personal care, clothes, and small-ticket items that never amount to the general consumption of whites, who have the necessary disposable income and whose shopping patterns are never made into an issue. Whites have the money and hence the right to buy free of suspicion or surveillance: who, after all, has ever read in marketing trade magazines that whites are the greatest consumers of any particular product?

The resilience and endurance of the black family and black community values are also central concerns for marketers trying to lure advertisers to African American marketing. In contrast to stereotypes of the black family as disorganized, marketing reports continually remind readers of the heterogeneity of black families, that nuclear families abound and can even be encouraged by marketing events such as the sponsorship of "family of the year awards" (McKenzie-Kelly 1998). The importance given to the family by marketers is evident in the abundance of family theme campaigns, advertising, and sweepstakes, suggesting that behind the expansive discourse about the variety of black families lies a disciplining message that "rewards" and promotes nuclear families as the ideal. Hence we have promotions like Quaker's Aunt Jemima's Pancake Syrup, where winners of a sweepstakes in a predominantly black community could get a free family portrait, or Quaker's sweepstakes awarding a "family reunion" at Chicago's gospelfest, a free, outdoor, gospel music event sponsored by the company, among other family theme promotions aimed at "highlight[ing] the reality that there are in fact many successful black families in America, while tapping the aspiration of all blacks to have families" (Brewer 1993).

While numerous articles provide statistical information about blacks' buying power or the great number of black consumers, there is a notable lack of generalizations about black consumers' attitudes and cultural values in the marketing trade literature, relative to the amount of such information that circulates about Hispanics and Asian Americans. Marketing news is likely to discuss the buying power of African Americans, repeat that they are an untapped market, that they are brand-loyal, or spiritual, like to shop, or are into style, but one finds fewer cultural generalizations about African-American consumers than about other minority consumers. Depending on how we look at this lack of cultural generalization, we could argue that it stems from the relatively undisputed place they hold as Americans in relation to other groups. Although subject to the starkest discrimination of any U.S. minority group, African Americans are U.S. citizens and publicly recognized as part of U.S. national identity and black/white racial imagery. They are hence less "exotic" than Hispanics and Asian Americans, who, despite their citizenship status, remain potential or suspected aliens. Marketing descriptions of African Americans are hence considerably more nuanced than those of Asian Americans, who represent the primary example of the exotic consumer. Alternatively, lack of discussion of black cultural values may arguably hide a disregard of African Americans' culture; don't they too have a "culture" that can be identified and that is worth discussion? Renato Rosaldo's equation of cultural visibility with enfranchisement, where power and culture are considered to be opposed to each other, is relevant to this discussion. He notes that "full citizens lack culture and those most culturally endowed lack full citizenship" (1989: 198), underscoring that the higher one moves up the socioeconomic and racial/class ladder, the less "culture" one is deemed to have. The social hierarchies upon which these assessments are grounded, however, remain unchanged, and individuals previously marginalized because of their "culture" can either pollute or dilute it, but can never experience the same loss of culture as those who attain full citizenship within the context of a given nation-state. African Americans still have "culture" and are distinct in the eyes of all marketers, but the fact that the nature of those differences is believed to be less identifiable denotes a perception of its denigration or pollution relative to that of other minority groups, whose culture is clearly more "colorful" or exotic. That which is "colorful" in African American culture—that is, directly identifiable as black—has historically been cleansed from such identifications and co-opted for public consumption; hence, we have the preoccupation of the African American marketer with the "urban markets" phenomenon.

For all the talk of congruence between African Americans and mainstream culture, however, marketers I talked with operated under the assumption that African Americans live in a parallel yet distinct public sphere of communication to that of the general market. As one African American advertising executive noted,

> What is unique about this market is the importance of hearsay, what we call the "word-of-mouth" communication. People are not getting information from the local or national media. People may not necessarily trust it and instead operate under a different matrix of communication that influences every sector and spreads throughout, and we know where to go to start the word-of-mouth communication.

I heard similar references to the importance of this distinct word-of-mouth domain of communication from black marketers at Uniworld in New York City, making me wonder whether this construct serves as language does for Asian American and Hispanic marketers: as proof of cultural distinctiveness, and hence as justification for the need for culturally specific advertising. This alternative domain of communication is used by African American marketers to justify the need, for instance, for event promotions and direct marketing, tactics with which to influence the public buzz and word of mouth about particular products. Such comments help corroborate impressions that, despite the mainstreaming of black culture, the public spheres of communication remain segregated and that, while black culture continues to be marketed for general market consumption, blacks, like Hispanics and other minorities, lack access to the media and to the vehicles that affect public discussion and debate not only about themselves but about society more generally. It is this lack that leads to the establishment of alternative domains of communication, as well as marketers' dependency on their existence or promotion.

MARKETING TO THE MODEL MINORITY CONSUMER

Advertisers have been convinced that to ignore African-
Americans is discriminatory. And because the Hispanic-
American market is huge, they know they'd be stupid not to
address it. Asian-Americans, however, have been the "quiet"
minority and need to let marketers know that by the end of
the century they will probably number 12 million, 40 million
by the year 2050.
                                                                    Tong 1994: 6

On the other side of the spectrum are Asian Americans, a "model minority" and, increasingly, model consumers. Although the least developed of the three ethnic markets in terms of the number of specialized advertising agencies and advertisers targeting it, this consumer segment has received a lot of attention since the 1990s and is increasingly appealing to advertisers, given the relative affluence generally associated with it. Like other minority consumers, Asian Americans are said to be the fastest growing minority. Their rapid and sharp increase since the 1980s—108 percent from 1980 to 1990—mostly from immigration following the 1965 abolition of the national quota system in U.S. immigration law, is repeatedly mentioned as a sign of this group's impending economic might (Taylor and Stern 1997).[8] They also comprise the most disparate and varied markets, encompassing diverse nationalities, languages, and cultures, each with diverse histories in the United States, making some wonder if they share anything "beyond rice" (Boyd 1994). Consider Marlene Rossman's marketing breakdown of Asian populations as encompassing "(1) Filipinos, the largest and arguably the best-assimilated Asian-American group; (2) Chinese, who tend to divide into two groups, identified by the Chinese themselves as American-born Chinese (ABC), who are well-to-do and quite assimilated, and 'fresh off boats' (FOB), who are blue-collar, conservative, and patriarchal; (3) Japanese, including both those who have lived in the United States (especially California) for generations and foreign-born Japanese, often on assignment, most of whom live in the New York region; (4) Koreans, who tend to cluster in large metropolitan areas and are often small-business owners; (5) Vietnamese, who are the fastest growing Asian group, one-third of whom live in California; [and] (6) Asian Indians, often highly educated professionals, who are not as geographically clustered as the other Asian groups" (Rossman 1994: 87). This breakdown echoes the ways that Hispanic marketers associate various Latina nationalities with particular traits such as conservatism, affluence, and cosmopolitanism, or with levels of assimilation, creating hierarchies of value and exclusion. The breakdown of Asian Americans, for instance, omits Cambodians, Laotians, and other Southeast Asian groups who are the poorest and hence the least advertising-worthy of all Asian groups. What is worth noting about this breakdown, however, is the amount of heterogeneity that is acknowledged to exist among Asian Americans, which is recognized as extending to the different constituent groups' preferences for colors, numbers, and their general cultural attitudes. Marketers are told to learn that "the color white signals a wedding and happiness to Filipinos; but for the Japanese, white—together with black—is a color for mourning. Chinese and Japanese see red as the color of prosperity, luck, and good fortune. South Koreans prefer blue, because red evokes unpleasant reminders of North

Korea's communism" (Von Bergen 1997). This awareness of differences borders on and is sometimes accompanied by the exotification of the Asian consumer, as described by a cofounder of Asian Television Sales, a rep firm specializing in Asian TV and radio: "Too many ad people still view this market as made up of people from Mars. . . . We get a lot of dumb questions, like "Do they drink water? And I'm not talking designer water, but plain H_2O" (Petersen 1992).

Somehow, though, marketers have found important commonalities within these highly diverse populations to overcome advertisers' fear of targeting this different and "exotic" market. Among them are Asian Americans' family orientation, respect for elders and authority, hardworking disposition, high level of education, and, most of all, the affluence of the immigrant population. Confucian values are often emphasized as the basis for their high esteem of education, values that (while more specifically Chinese than generally Asian) are seen to be indigenous to Asian culture but are then assumed to be magnified by the immigrant experience and inculcated in subsequent generations. The statement of an executive creative director for a New York–based agency specializing in this market exemplifies the industry's dominant portrayal of the Asian consumer: "Not only are Asian Americans a highly educated, affluent market, they usually come to America with an initial fund to start a business and thus have higher spending power than other ethnic markets. . . . The Asian market is an aspirational group who are family-oriented and for the most part came to America to give their children a better life; . . . cultural values such as respect for elders in the family and a strong work ethic define what's important to the Asian American" (Santoro 1996). Indeed, the greatest percentage of the U.S. Asian American population is foreign-born— according to the census, 73 percent in 1980 (Espíritu 1992)—and is the product of immigration following the discontinuation of national quotas mentioned above. What is significant is the emphasis placed on Asian Americans as immigrants with good intentions, who are respectful, stay in their place, and, most of all, come with money ready to spend or invest in the United States. The dominance of the construct of the affluent Asian immigrant is even evident in the kinds of companies targeting this market: telecommunications, airlines, insurance, and banks/financial services, as well as electronics, and upscale foods and beverages (*Los Angeles Times* 1999)— a stark contrast to the basic goods, soft drinks, and beer that are advertised to blacks and Latinas. Further, Asian Americans are said to be "linguistically isolated," and, like Hispanics, they are described as showing an overwhelming preference for media in their own language (Gitlin 1999).

This very affluent, highly educated, yet culturally and linguistically isolated Asian consumer, however, is far from representative of all Asian Americans. While the greater cultural and linguistic isolation of recent arrivals cannot be easily denied, affluence and linguistic and cultural isolation are antithetical conditions for any immigrant. Those who arrived after 1965 are indeed more educated and urban than previous Asian immigrants, yet poverty does exist in this population and is concentrated especially among those with the least English skills who are trapped in low-wage employment or underemployment. Language isolation breeds exploitation, which makes linguistic seclusion, far from a matter of choice, a trap for reproducing a docile labor force that is virtually shunned by the mainstream labor market (Lee 1994; Takaki 1989). The myth of the affluent immigrant thus represents only a subsector of the post-1965 immigration that is highly educated and has capital, such as the affluent business elites from the Philippines, Hong Kong, Taiwan, and Japan who top the income charts for Asian Americans (Campanelli 1995). It does not represent all Asians, particularly the political refugees from Laos or Cambodia, or the Asian immigrant women working in the low-wage garment industry. What is more, while some Asian groups from Taiwan and Hong Kong do outrank whites in income, Asian Americans as a group still have higher poverty rates than their white counterparts, 17.9 percent versus 12.4 percent for whites (Lee 1994; Rossman 1994). Looking closely behind the model minority consumer, we also learn that, among immigrants, even professionals are subject to downward mobility and occupational downgrading in the United States and that, despite their higher education, they are yet to receive equal income compensation for their human capital resources (Hang Shin and Chang 1998; Takaki 1989). Finally, as is true for other minority consumers, income figures for Asian Americans are often based on household not individual income, which begs the question of whether they indeed have higher incomes or whether this appears to be so because they have larger households or because they are concentrated in urban areas where incomes are higher because of the higher costs of living. Most significant, this image of Asians as affluent recent arrivals hides the long history of Asian American groups residing in the United States since the mid-nineteenth century, such as Chinese and the Japanese Americans who, during World War II, were incarcerated and would likely resent being grouped with the "recent arrivals," however affluent they are said to be.[9]

Moreover, we are told that Asian Americans are not interested in assimilating, hence the emphasis on culturally specific marketing in the first place. As one article notes, "Unlike other ethnic groups in this country, Asians are reluctant to assimilate; while they enjoy what America has to offer, specifically the ability to gain respect and wealth through hard work—they do not recognize themselves as a unified market and will never adopt an American "melting pot ideal" (Campanelli 1995: 51). Ethnic marketers make similar anti-assimilationist statements about Hispanics, although unlike the latter, where the English-dominant Latina is recognized even if only as a problem to conquer, older generations of Asian Americans are almost entirely invisible in comparison to their newly arrived, supposedly more affluent counterparts. Like bilingual Hispanics, they are invisible because they are "less profitable" as a target market. This is the same reason why Filipinos, who are among the most numerous of all Asian American groups, as well as Asian Indians, considered among the most educated, are less likely to be targeted through culturally specific advertising or considered as part of the Asian American market. English is a generalized language in both countries, and these populations have the highest index of English use, making them less dependent, according to marketers, on ethnic-specific marketing. Recall the predicament faced by African Americans and bilingual Latinas: one who speaks English is one who becomes "cultureless."

The irony is that, despite addressing their constituencies as "Asian Americans," marketers are aware that not all Asian populations see themselves in this manner and that it is the native-born Asian American, not the recent arrival, who is most receptive to ideas of U.S.-based, pan-Asian ethnicity to begin with rather than being vested in nationalistic and group-specific modes of identification. As Yen Le Espíritu notes, the concept of Asian American pan-ethnicity was forged in the late 1960s as part of civil rights struggles led by students, activists, and middle-class intellectuals, and it is often at odds with the ideas of recent arrivals who don't share the same history or political outlook (Espíritu 1992). While Espíritu notes that the persistence of racial lumping continues to subject all Asians, despite their educational and economic gains, to racial prejudice, the greatest challenge to the consolidation of any common identity or political goal among these disparate groups has been the difficulty of superseding interethnic differences, most felt among the newest arrivals. Indeed, marketers profit from these distinctions and, despite referring to all Asian populations indistinguishably as Asian Americans, marketers target them by nationality, developing language-and culture-specific creative executions for different Asian subgroups. Kang and Lee Advertising in New York City, for instance, has creative teams specializing in

Korean, Japanese, and Chinese language and culture executions. Pan-Asian advertising, which addresses all groups simultaneously, is also developed, although its use of English makes it less attractive to marketers who fear losing the linguistic distinctiveness that makes Asian American marketing profitable in the first place. Thus, the affluent and transient Asian immigrants—the Chinese cosmopolitans, the investor-immigrant, and the professionals—are the ones who, given their class, property, and symbolic capital, can have the lifestyle that resists regularization (Ong 1999) and remain the model "Asian American consumers." Advertisers extol these flexible lifestyles of affluent Asians, whom they characterize as having a "goal-oriented outlook in the United States, such as the Japanese [who take] a deep breath when they leave Japan and exhale only upon returning" (Steere 1995: 9). They are perpetual transients, who neither see themselves as nor aspire to be "American."

Still, marketers make a point of appending "American" to all Asian immigrants, which would never be so easily done for any Haitian, Mexican, or Pakistani immigrant, even if they too came with spending money. For unlike the latter, Asians have accumulated "cultural" capital in the public eye: they have become the living embodiment of the equation of citizenship and entrepreneurial capacity. As Aihwa Ong reminds us, the dominant association of self-discipline, consumer power, and human entrepreneurial capital with whiteness, so common in Western democracies, renders these attributes important criteria for awarding citizenship, or even potential entitlement, to nonwhites, making Asian Americans seem more compatible with U.S. citizenship ideals in the public eye. The lingering irony is that while Asian Americans are indeed generally recognized as the model minority and as having the human capital or symbolic resources for citizenship—the stuff all "Americans should have," such as hard work, entrepreneurial attitudes, and so forth—they remain suspect as potential aliens in U.S. national imagery (Tuan 1998). Being neither white nor black, they, like Latinas, fall into the cracks of U.S. racial hierarchies and national boundaries, particularly when displaying the same linguistic purity and authenticity that is so cherished and promoted by ethnic marketers. Thus, marketing discourse about Asian Americans reinscribes the same dominant discourse that marginalizes them in greater society. On the one hand, emphasis on the affluence of Asians unwittingly reinforces the fear of "Asian peril" evident in the public discourse on Asian business investments in the United States, which places Asian Americans on the fine line "between patriotism and betrayal" (Ong 1999: 180). On the other, marketers' penchant for Asian American authenticity eradicates the involvement and "Americanness" of the older generation of Asian Americans, furthering in the process distinctions between these populations and recent immigrants. After all, disassociation from and prejudice against recent immigrants remain a common response by those who are asked to prove their patriotism and address greater society's lingering fears of their potential betrayal.

SENSITIVE PEOPLE, DOCILE CONSUMERS

Especially, I want them to know that we're Americans.
We're just like they are. Many of us spoke only English
growing up. And if we're bilingual, of course that's a
positive. I want them to get to a place where they're not
afraid of us—where they see us as more than their gardener,
where they see us as their colleague, as their teacher, as their
friend, and their neighbor.

Lydia Ramos, producer of the NBC
special *Nueva America*

As we have noted, there are important differences both internally and across each subgroup of "multicultural consumers." Some are recognized to be more affluent, or more marketable, or as having more or less "culture" than others in ways that echo the dominant discourses about each group that are at play in greater society. Ethnic marketing hence surfaces as a medium where different minority groups' positions within U.S. racial hierarchies are mirrored and engendered. The differential construction of each ethnic market, however, is predicated on similar processes which suggest the role played by marketing in the discursive construction of ethnicity and marginality, and it is to these processes that I now turn.

First, we examine the selective manipulation of marginality in the construction of the affluent yet authentic ethnic consumer. In all three cases, ethnic marketing fed off these groups' marginality, insofar as it was this position that justified the need for ethnic marketing, at the same time that successful marketing required the distancing of these populations from their marginal position. As we saw, this involved emphasizing the wealth, buying power, and hence advertising worthiness of these populations by highlighting the subgroups that were deemed to have the highest cultural and economic capital, according to the dominant variables of each market, such as middle-class blacks, or the affluent, Spanish-speaking Hispanic, or the educated, middle-class Asian immigrant or business person. These subgroups nonetheless remain culturally pure by maintaining their language and "tradition," according to current marketing definitions. Ironically, affluence in each market segment is most prevalent among those who are least likely to be linguistically or culturally isolated and hence are least dependent on ethnic marketing. In the end, marketers' idealization of "authentic" ethnicity cannot fully veil its economic and social costs, nor the reality that ethnicity and affluence are antithetical concepts among U.S. minorities. Those with the most economic capital are also most likely to resist their incorporation, treatment, and regularization as minorities by distinguishing themselves from their racialized counterparts, those who, unlike them, do have visible "culture." These are the same dynamics that lie behind the ambivalence of the English-dominant Latina in Hispanic media, and her emphasis on distinguishing herself from the recent immigrant, or the ambivalence of affluent Cubans toward the second-generation, poor Nuyorican. These are also the dynamics in focus groups that fueled the contempt of some recent Mexican immigrants toward Puerto Ricans and Dominicans, whom they saw as lacking in morals and cultural values. In each case, individuals were making distinctions regarding the putative value of their culture or their "Latinidad" on the basis of different criteria that nonetheless recognized the preeminence of a sanitized version of Latinidad, characterized by "good" Spanish and the maintenance of some named or unnamed Latina traditions, but within the dominant U.S. canons of middle-class values and lifestyles. Similar attitudes are also documented among African Americans: "Middle-class blacks are found to respond less favorably to Afrocentricity and are often offended by black slang" (Morton 1997). These issues also feed the proclivity within segments of older generations and U.S.-born Asians and Hispanics to engage with the same dominant, anti-immigrant sentiments in society, disassociating themselves from recent working-class immigrants as part of their quest for upward mobility, or else to simply claim their rightful status as members, not "aliens," within U.S. society. Simply put, "ethnicity" clashes with the unending plea by U.S. minorities, evidenced in this section's epigraph: "We're Americans. We're just like they are," not threats but "colleagues, teachers, friends, and neighbors." The irony is that such distinctions, like those we saw earlier being used by Latinas to distinguish who among themselves is more or less "American" or "Latina" and/or who belongs and is more or less entitled within U.S. society, fail to challenge and may in fact reinstate whiteness as the definition of the "real American" and as the dominant reference against which everyone else is extraneous to U.S. culture.

To focus on these dynamics of differentiation among racialized minorities, particularly those between U.S.-born and older generations and recent immigrant populations is not to reify these distinctions. I am fully aware that drawing strict boundaries between these groups is particularly difficult and problematic, given that the migratory experiences of populations now integrated as minorities in the United States have been directly tied to U.S. political and economic exigencies and the need for a racialized labor force, as well as mediated by previous U.S. involvement in the "sending" countries through direct occupation, continued intervention, and neocolonialism. Yet, to ignore distinctions arising from the growing inequalities of transnational connections and flows based on the unequal and exploitative conditions of these relationships, such as those between the United States and Latin America, is also problematic. As we saw, such inequalities inform ideas of authenticity, belonging, and spatial claims and even the contempt of some Latina/Hispanic groups for others, even when supposedly included in the same "group." These are dynamics that, I have argued, marketing helps to forge and expose through its promotion of an idealized construct—the isolated and authentic ethnic consumer—which promotes not only essentialized and static definitions of identity but also, and most problematically, disdain for the cultural expressions of the U.S.-born or based or for anyone who clashes with such essentialized definitions. These populations, as we saw earlier, remain the lingering threat to the language purity, media habits, and authenticity of the consumers that ethnic marketing so depends on.

We also saw that marketers' selective manipulations of ethnic populations into unlikely constructs, such as that of the "affluent yet authentic ethnic consumer," by obliterating histories and differences among and across ethnic groups has important social and political implications. By selectively embracing the affluence, authenticity, and cosmopolitanism of ethnic populations, the marketing industry ends up propagating myths of affluence and cultural authenticity for U.S. minority populations, obscuring poverty, marginality, unemployment, and racism, and cleansing the constructs of "Hispanic," "Latina," "Asian American," "black," or "African American" from any tainted attributes, leaving them polished and remade for public consumption. The cartoon in figure 26 succinctly captures this by highlighting the range of Latino political demands veiled from public view, while the "ideal Latino," Ricky Martin, shook his booty. Whether this process may eventually lead to a greater consolidation of these pan-ethnic categorizations, with ethnic marketing fostering greater pride in ethnic identifications, helping to bridge dif-

ferences of class, background, race, and generation among ethnic populations, and facilitating common political projects or outlooks remains
to be seen. A more likely scenario is that such sanitized images will do
little to effect such positive identifications. As long as these groups remain racialized minorities, claims like those of focus group participants
seeking to disassociate themselves from "that other Hispanic" in order
to establish their rightful claims to U.S. society are likely to hinder common associations on the basis of authenticity, values, language, or culture among members of "the same group."

Another outstanding dilemma is that the widespread dissemination
of myths of affluence and upward mobility, or of the "coming of age"
of particular populations, is ultimately an illusion and a hindrance to
any real politics of equality. If Latinas are hot, does this mean that someone who is not "making it," is experiencing individual failure not social
inequality? If the consumption indexes of blacks and Latinas are supposedly growing exponentially, does this mean that poverty, unemployment, or steady employment are no longer issues? After all, people who
are consuming must be making money; should we then care if they do
so by holding three jobs, by working at the periphery of the informal
economy? Or should we care that their income still lags behind that of
whites? If the household incomes of Asian Americans are above the U.S.
average, who cares if they are channeled into some professions, absent
from others, or if their success comes at the cost of a greater human investment than whites make? Ultimately these questions bring to the fore
that marketing discourse is not without political and economic repercussions. It prioritizes consumption over income, and spending over employment or economic parity, veiling the ongoing segmentation between
those with "real" jobs and income, and those who lack it. In this context, the only reference for social parity becomes spending, or the putative buying power of individuals, calculated through disembodied bulk
estimates, never to be contextualized against the consumption rates of
the truly powerful groups in society.

The commodification of ethnicity also presupposes the re-authenti-
cation of U.S. minorities in terms of the "right" way of being an "ethnic."
As we saw, one underlying assumption of ethnic marketing is that each
group has a distinct, identifiable culture that is unique, bounded, and
separate from U.S. culture, which is simultaneously constructed as homogeneous, white, and "mainstream." Indeed, like ads for Hispanics,
ads for African Americans and Asian Americans revolve largely around
exhorting these consumers to be proud of their culture, a culture tied to

Figure 26.   "The Ideal Latino: Why Can't You Be More Like Ricky Martin?"
©2000 by Lalo Alcaraz/www.cartoonista.com. First published in *L.A. Weekly*.

countries left behind, seen to belong neatly to them, and that is not the
product of interaction or slavery, conquest, or exchanges based on class
or on common experiences shared across ethnic groups. Hence we have
the preponderance of promotions such as Hallmark's launching of Ma-
hogany, an Afrocentric line of greeting cards; or campaigns that appeal
to a common African legacy; Heineken's use of two "authentic" masks
from the Ivory Coast to acknowledge black history month, urging consumers to "feel the ancestral honor"; or AT&T's ad that shows a family
viewing a photograph of Egyptian pyramids on an AT&T desktop system (Morton 1997); or McDonald's sweepstakes honoring African American heritage, whose grand prize is a trip to "the motherland," Kenya
(Carmichael 2000). Similarly, for Asian Americans we see the increased
sponsorship of lunar, harvest, and prosperity festivals. In this authenticating context, there is little room for U.S. experiences of cultural hybridity, or for even imagining interracial and interethnic identities, which
clash with marketers' stipulations of appropriate (marketable) ethnicity.
   One outcome of such distinct and authenticated representations is the
unending competition they foster among and across groups regarding

their relative worth and marketability. Previously, I discussed the ensuing debates over what becomes "representative," embraced, or rejected within each ethnic subgroup and how it devalues fluidity and hybridity over fixity and authenticity in cultural expressions (as in marketers' disdain for Spanglish). But we also need to consider the repercussions of these issues across U.S. ethnic groups. The fact that multicultural marketing ends up pitting one ethnic group against another in terms of who is advertising-worthy and who is not, and that it calls on each group to define and distinguish itself from others, means the gains of one group (in terms of public exposure or advertising revenues) amount to a loss for another. Meanwhile, the dominant market values of brand loyalty, family values, and consumption prevail, *ipso facto*, as it is around the same values that ethnic groups are required to prove their worth.

Finally, by calling attention to marketers' penchant for essentialized identities, I am not suggesting that hybridity and interethnic and interracial identities are free from commercial appropriation and better able to challenge marketers' authenticating grasps. After all, the marketing of U.S. Latinos (an unstable and heterogeneous construct) has shown us that no one is ever too mixed or "complex" to be fully out of their aim. As we saw, marketers willingly destabilized this identity and evoked more or less of its complexity according to the logics of profitability, reminding us that they are likely and well equipped to continue rendering hybridity along racial/ethnic/culture lines into appropriate (marketable) ethnicity.

Also problematic are the potential repercussions of marketing discourse on the political claims and modes of debate of ethnic populations. In marketing discourse, "consumers" must prove their value and advertising worthiness through behavior, attitudes, and consumption. Of concern is whether this discourse promotes a "politics of worthiness" and the assumption that people are only entitled to visibility, rights, or services from society after they have proved their marketability and social worth. Considering that the preeminence of ethnic marketing discourse has been accompanied by the privatization of public life and social services, from schooling to welfare, as well as by a reduction of government regulation of and involvement in the involvement of minorities in U.S. society, we may well be confronted with the problems of such a "politics of worthiness" for the economically marginalized and disadvantaged. Not that I am blind to the fallacies of regarding the state as "guarantor of rights" and to the problems of U.S. distributive policies for women and racial minorities. However, I would posit that, unlike earlier policies prompted both by civil right demands and by the state's needs to ac-

commodate dissent, contemporary policies encourage a view of any social or political demands that disavows the existence of some fundamental
entitlements that are communally shared and not questioned by any in
society. The fallacies of "universality" in political rights and democratic
freedoms are not even a pretense when the old "meritocracy" discourse
becomes revamped into a politics of marketability and worthiness. At
the same time I do not deny that consumption is a central arena in which
we could direct our attention to issues of citizenship and politics. Against
the increasing privatization of civic society and preeminence of the market, devising a new type of politics that may help to arbitrate the market's commanding role in the distribution of goods and services is certainly a valuable concern, as is public recognition of minorities as
consumers as a prerequisite for their partaking in these processes. Yet
we should never be blinded to the inequalities generated by marketing
discourse. Being attentive to consumption should not lead us to think
that the "consumer" will ever be the preeminent subject of future politics. We can never lose sight of the fact that consumers are not all conceived as equally rational and hence "empowered" within a politics that
prioritizes consumption; just as their needs are not considered worthy
of attention by the powers that be. The brand-loyal, traditional, minority consumers, we are told by marketers, can always be swayed by the
"right" ethnically loaded campaign that touches their hearts, making minorities the consumers who are the most docile, the most vulnerable, and
the least critical. This is why I am skeptically cautious about the abundance of reports and discussions about Latinas as a market. Yes, Latinas
are undoubtedly gaining visibility through such discussions, but only as
a market, never as a people, and "markets" are vulnerable; they must be
docile; they cannot afford to scare capital away.

Certainly ethnic consumers find value in campaigns that revalue their
"cultures," and I do not propose that they be represented as harmoniously
blended to middle-class Americana. In light of the continued marginalization of these groups from the dominant public space of debate in the
mainstream media, however, we are summoned to inquire into what the
spaces supposedly devoted to ethnic representativity communicate about
them to themselves and to society. In the general-market media, Asian
Americans are presented mostly as tokens, in business relationships not
in social settings, following the stereotype of the workaholic but anti-
social Asian (Taylor and Stern 1997)—the smart, yet calculating, anti-
social, and inscrutable Ling on *Ally McBeal* quickly comes to mind
here—while blacks and Latinas become more and more invisible in main-

stream media. Native Americans, on the other hand, are not even mentioned as the TV landscape remains a "white, white world" (Braxton 1999). In the meantime, ethnic marketing continues to promote culturally specific campaigns exhorting pride in the cultural difference that society sees as an impediment to upward mobility, a mark of foreignness, and hence a lack of social or political entitlement. We do not know how a third-generation Chinese American, who speaks no Chinese and has never been in China, reacts to a direct-marketing mailing in Chinese, or what a Filipina with a Hispanic last name, taken to be a Hispanic, thinks when she gets mailings in Spanish. I found it interesting that within months of my relocation in New York City, in a high-density Latina neighborhood of Washington Heights, I began to receive free offers to subscribe to Latina/Hispanic magazines and calls from telemarketers pitching their sales in Spanish. Even my computer "discovered" that I was a Latina and began to prompt me in Spanish during Web searches. Never in sixteen years of living in the city had I been discovered as a Latina consumer—granted, I did not always have credit cards, nor did I subscribe to Hispanic magazines—but my immediate reaction was one of feelings of surveillance. For indeed, more than ever, "ethnics" are part of listserves, catalogues, and databanks that increasingly remind them that they are different. This status, never a choice, is less and less so to the ethnic-subject-turned-consumer.

One last trait of all three ethnic markets is the similar ethos that is commonly associated with the minority consumer. Consider, for instance, what I was told by an African American advertising executive about multicultural marketing or how best to reach the ethnic consumer:

> We think that the way to approach all ethnic markets is to look into their hearts, not necessarily their heads, but look into their hearts in terms of who they are, and what they are all about, and what they feel about the company and the product. Yes, you have to talk about why they should buy the brand and fundamental product qualities but you have to talk to the human component also. . . . There are some similarities, and the key thread that runs through the multicultural group is that we all tend to be very sensitive people. Very sensitive people, so you have to approach them more from the emotional perspective than from a fact perspective. You should do things because of your family, you should do this because it's protective of the land, you should do this because it's going to make you feel more like a man, this macho thing. It's that kind of emotional piece of communication that is more unique among minority marketing than it is in majority marketing.

"Majority" marketing, he went on to say, was more cut and dried, more humorous, more irreverent, able to poke fun at itself, something you don't do among ethnic groups, who don't like the idea of being poked fun at, at least not publicly. These assessments should be familiar from my earlier discussion about Hispanic marketers' emphasis on speaking to people's hearts, and the sensitive nature of the ethnic consumer, who does not demand information so much as words spoken to the heart. Recall the dichotomy of the moral, spiritual Latina and the materialistic, rational Anglo that provided the backbone of both old and contemporary discourses of U.S. Latinidad. Once we realize the widespread dissemination of similar ideas among ethnic marketers, however, the arbitrariness of these ideas becomes more than apparent. In this context, the tropes of sensitivity, family values, and emotion surface for what they are: not so much valid descriptions of any single population but a culturalist rebuttal to the negative traits associated with marginal populations, as well as a projection of dominant society's longing for docile, unthreatening consumers. These preferred subjects work hard, have values and traditions that American society can be proud of, but remain unthreateningly in their place, at a distance, with their "culture," making them a visible and unquestionable reference to the existence of a white, nonraced world. Meanwhile, ethnic marketing continues to be politicized as the last bastion of representation for minority populations, highly charged and imbued with issues of rights and cultural visibility. Its discipline and containment of ethnic subjects remain concealed by the construction of the "good" ethnic consumer, as well as issues of rights and political entitlements. After all, "minorities" are obtaining the optimal, all-American right, that of being interpellated as consumers.

Notes

INTRODUCTION

1. As noted by Bean and Tienda (1987), prior to the 1970s census, what are now called "Hispanics" had been enumerated by the U.S. census since 1850 but by different categories, such as foreign birth, language, surname, or heritage. This lack of standardization in the categories by which Spanish-heritage peoples were distinguished hindered assessments of the growth and actual number of Hispanic populations until the 1970s, when "Spanish heritage" was standardized as a composite concept, and people's self-definition prioritized as a criterion for belonging to this ethnic category. This does not mean, however, that populations of Spanish descent had not imagined themselves in terms of a common ethnic category prior to the 1970s, as I note in the next chapter—just that it was only after this date that "Hispanic" was conceived of as a nationwide category.

2. To avoid the cumbersome "Latina/o" and "Latinos/as," I will alternately use the terms "Latinos" and "Latinas," "Latino" and "Latina," as gender-neutral terms, unless otherwise specified in the discussion.

3. For the media's role in the constitution of Latinos as a common identity, see Flores and Yúdice 1993; Peñaloza 1997; Rodríguez 1997; and Subervi-Vélez et al. 1994.

4. For a discussion of how Latina women, in different guises that vary according to wider political and economic trends and dominant racial climates in greater U.S. society, have often been conceived as "spitfires" or else as passive and dependent, while men are repeatedly characterized as villains, thieves, buffoons, or hot lovers, see Kanellos 1998; Subervi-Vélez et al.1994; Wilson and Gutiérrez 1995; Rodríguez 1997. A brief overview of Latino stereotypes in advertising is provided by Nuiry 1996a. For a discussion about how Latinos'

involvement in the media has challenged some of these stereotypes as well as dominant categories concerning gender, race, and sexuality prevailing among Latino/as themselves, see Noriega 2000; Noriega and López 1996; and Vázquez 1991.

5. While Peñaloza's analysis is generally positive towards this industry, she also notes that the Latino-oriented marketing industry simultaneously contributes to making Latinos even more invisible as advertisers increasingly target them through "minority" media, furthering their exclusion from the mainstream media (1997).

6. A recent analysis of Latino stereotypes in advertising, critical of mainstream media's portrayal of Latinos, leaves untouched the Hispanic advertising industry. Arguing that "images of Hispanics vary from good to garish, depending on such things as whether the ads appear in Spanish- or English-language media and whether Hispanic talent is in front of and behind the camera" (Nuiry 1996a: 26), the article intimates the widespread view that stereotyping can be lessened if not avoided when Hispanics are involved in all stages of production.

7. This work is growing rapidly in numbers and scope. In particular, anthropologists have paid attention to alternative, noncommercial, and state-owned media, emphasizing their potential as a means of struggle and self-making by indigenous groups and nation-states seeking to establish particular national identities, and revealing the disparate social fields and networks, be they local, national, or transnational networks, in which the products of these media are produced and consumed (Ginsburg 1991; Turner 1992; Rofel 1994; Spitulnik 1993; Mankekar 1999). For a review of recent trends and ethnographic approaches to the media, see Ginsburg et al. 2001.

8. The United States is the number one global advertising market; the projected 1999 total for ad spending was $117.0 billion (Koranteng 1999).

9. Later we will see marketers and some Latino cultural activists advancing this view by equating the growth of this sector with the "coming of age" of all Latinos. Though their arguments are not couched in terms of target marketing, similar dynamics guide debates about the decentralization and dispersion of the media, be it commercial or public, as contributing to a rise in the spheres of public debate (see Robbins 1993; Calhoun 1992, 1993; Urla 1995; and Dornfeld 1998).

10. Some of the trends that are increasing advertising's control of public forums include a greater ubiquity of advertising, the growth of database marketing, and cross-promotions with a great number of social institutions from entertainment venues to schools (McAllister 1996).

11. A growing literature addressing the politics of pleasure in popular culture is indicative of this trend (Dent 1992; Kondo 1997; Modleski 1982).

12. We thus avoid the technological determinism that has often accompanied analysis of the role of the media in the construction of cultural identities. This outlook, which sees a direct relationship between people's subjectivities and the media as the dominant force shaping and affecting people's subjectivities, has been a primary reference for theories of cultural imperialism and media determinism that have been amply challenged for not taking into account people's multiple appropriation of media texts (Waisbord 1998; Tomlinson 1991).

13. This shift is directly related to funding pressures that prioritize programs serving Latinos as a totality. This is evidenced in the transformation of many Puerto Rican Studies Departments to Latino Studies, and in the shift of mission by formerly Puerto Rican institutions such as El Museo del Barrio in New York City, which I discuss elsewhere in greater detail (Dávila 1999a, 1999b).

14. I am not arguing that commercial sponsors are not involved in funding Latino political, artistic, or nonprofit organizations. For instance, La Raza, one of the primary Hispanic political organizations nationwide, is heavily supported by Philip Morris, among other corporate sponsors. My point is that advertising is the one sector involved in image-making that is directly, not occasionally, supported by means of grants by corporate sponsors.

15. I am following here the distinctions drawn by Naficy in his 1993 discussion of Iranian television. As he states, unlike Iranian exile television, Spanish media in the United States have been largely transnational products serving the purposes of identity maintenance and assimilation into the host society.

16. Of course, there is also a trend toward mass customizing ads for both the U.S. and the Latin American market as a result of global trends in advertising (Zbar 1998a), and although I will comment on this trend, its likely effect on Hispanic marketing remains largely to be seen.

17. This difference makes Hispanic agencies additionally interesting in terms of the role they play in the creation of pan–Latin American advertising as "globalizers" of Latin American nationalities in the United States, as opposed to the role played by Latin American agencies, which have historically limited their efforts to producing national campaigns for their respective national constituencies. Indeed, Hispanic agencies are increasingly hired to develop or customize ads for both the U.S. and the Latin American markets—for example, for Payless, Western Union, Continental Airlines, and Avon. Siboney advertising, for instance, which handles Payless for the United States and the Caribbean, developed distinct ads to sell sandals in Puerto Rico and boots in the U.S. market. The ad for the Puerto Rican market used Puerto Rican models with local accents and revolved around the Three Kings celebration, whereas the ad for the U.S. market was similar to that developed for the general market.

18. I refer here to the literal not political translation of "Hispano" to "Hispanic." As Sandoval-Sánchez (1999) has noted, in Spanish hispano conveys a claim to heritage from Spain and a sense of commonality without necessarily implying the minority and racialized status implied by "Hispanic."

19. On this issue see Klor de Alva's (1997) discussion of cultural nationalism among Chicanos and Puerto Ricans, and Oboler's (1995) discussion of changes in the terminology of "Hispanic."

20. For an analysis of Latinization as a top-down process of commodification, see Olalquiaga 1992. My consideration of this process as one of struggle and contestation draws on the work of Aparicio and Chávez-Silverman 1997, Flores and Yúdice 1993, and Sandoval-Sánchez 1999, who provide more fluid assessments of these dynamics.

21. For the cultural construction of whiteness as non-ethnically marked, the utmost sign of normativity and universality, see Roediger 1999 and Dyer 1997.

Although, with Hartigan (1999), I recognize that whiteness is not a homogenous construct and that it needs to be historically and ethnographically situated, I still find it useful to use "Anglo" to mean whites and non-ethnics, in order to emphasize the widespread equation of whiteness with normativity in the U.S. advertising industry.

22. Gupta and Ferguson's (1997) critique is not only directed at the present ethnographic moment. Their analysis demystifies the canonical conventions of the Malinowskian archetype of "ethnographic fieldwork" to reveal that the "field" was always a social construction whose pure existence was always challenged by global processes. They also show how such archetypical ethnographic fieldwork reproduces inequalities in the practice of anthropology and in the evaluation of knowledge in ways that discriminate against fieldwork done by so-called native anthropologists, or studies that look up not down to power, or studies done by women, who face greater impediments in traveling alone to "exotic places."

23. Here I draw from Bourdieu's analysis of intellectuals: whether linked to the state or operating as free entrepreneurs, he sees them as "dominated fractions of the dominant class" since their field of operation is constrained to claims to knowledge and legitimacy—in this case, ethnic legitimacy—in speaking for and hence dominating the making of Hispanic ads, though not the structures and institutions that produce them (Bourdieu 1993).

24. In Los Angeles, San Francisco, and Chicago (the first, fourth, and fifth largest Hispanic markets, respectively), Mexicans make up 76 percent, 75 percent, and 78 percent of the total Hispanic population, while Cubans in Miami (the third market) still outnumber other groups at 59 percent of all Hispanics (Strategy Research Corporation 1998).

25. The sixteen agencies include nine in New York City and seven outside the city. The New York agencies include The Bravo Group; Castor Advertising Corp.; Conill Advertising; FOVA, Inc.; Siboney Advertising; JMCP Publicidad; Vidal Reynardus and Moya (split in 2000); Vanguard Communications; and Uniworld. I visited these agencies repeatedly during my research and I interviewed several of their staff, primarily creative and accounts staff and/or their founding members. I had less direct involvement with seven other Hispanic agencies outside N.Y.C. (mainly met and interviewed their directors or other key staff at national conventions, analyzed their promotional materials, and discussed their ads through phone interviews). These include Zubi Advertising (FL); Mendoza-Dillon and Associates (CA); Cartel Creativo (San Antonio); Bromley Aguilar and Associates (San Antonio); Lápiz (Chicago); San Jose and Associates (Chicago); and La Agencia de Orci (CA). Besides these sixteen agencies, I also analyzed and discussed the reels of del Rivero Messiano (FL); Acento Advertising (CA); and Robles Communication (NY). Contacts with Hispanic marketers were also established through national conventions, including the meetings of the Association of Hispanic Advertising Agencies in New York, San Antonio, and Chicago; the ethnic marketing conventions sponsored by the Direct Marketing Association; the International Summit on Multicultural Marketing, and advertising "Up-Front" presentations for Spanish TV networks.

CHAPTER 1

1. Many of these early founders have since retired or moved out of New York City, yet most periodically visit, and are still active in different segments of the advertising and marketing industry in the city.

2. This is also the case for the rise of advertising for Spanish-speaking populations throughout the United States. Already *El Misisipi,* the first newspaper published for Spanish-speaking populations within the confines of United States—a Louisiana-based trade and commercial publication—prints most of its advertising in Spanish (Subervi-Vélez et al.1994). Similarly, in New York City, *La Prensa,* founded in 1913, featured advertising for a variety of products, such as pianos and clothing, as well as for a range of local services. As noted by Robert Park (1970) in *The Immigrant Press and Its Control,* the Spanish presses of New Mexico, Texas, and New England had little national advertising. Mostly they advertised for local department stores, business, and romantic and religious groups. In New York City, a phonograph and record store on Sixth Avenue advertised records in twenty-three different languages (Park 1970: 133–34).Early issues of *La Prensa* include advertising for services (e.g., shopping assistance, translations), and ads for subscriptions to magazines such as the *Revista Universal,* which claimed to be the official organ of the Hispanic population.

3. Previously, advertising was done either by the newspaper or publication itself or else by the clients themselves, rather than by a specialized agency in charge of developing an image for specific products. For a discussion of the origins of New York's advertising industry, see Fred Danzig, "New York City: A Century in the Spotlight," *Advertising Age,* January 27, 1997, C2–C7.

4. Here I am distinguishing TV networks that provided continuous broadcasting to Hispanic populations, aware that already in the 1940s a variety of radio stations had brokered time in English-language channels for Hispanic Television. In New York City, prior to channel 47, there were Hispanic-oriented programs such as the weekly *El Show Hispano* on channel 13. Part-time Spanish programming was also available in cities with a large concentration of Hispanic populations, such as Los Angeles, Houston, Miami, and Phoenix (Subervi-Vélez et al. 1997).

5. These included Reynold Anselmo, Julian Kaufman, and Edward Noble, who, as American citizens, allowed Azcárraga to circumvent the FCC's limit on issuing broadcast licenses to non-U.S. citizens; they were already connected with Azcárraga's media operations, having been involved in the production of Mexican movies, broadcasting, and advertising. Under this arrangement Azcárraga owned only 20 percent of the license holding company while maintaining direct interest in SIN/SICC through his business partners. Until the FCC forced its sale in the 1980s, Azcárraga controlled 20 percent of SICC, the corporation holding broadcast licenses, and 75 percent of SIN, the network and business arm that provides programming and represents the network for advertising sales (Gutiérrez 1979).

6. According to a study by *Hispanic Business,* out of the $1.4 billion spent in Spanish-language advertising in 1997, $780 million (55 percent) went to national network and local television (Zbar 1998b).

7. For an overview of the FCC's court-ordered sale of SIN in 1986, see Sinclair 1990; for a historical overview of the development of SIN as an export market for Mexican programming, see Gutiérrez1979, and see Rodríguez 1996 for SIN's reconfiguring as Univision.

8. Recall that for these earlier Cuban immigrants, New York, not Miami, served as the preferred entry point to the United States. As Louis Pérez (1999) notes, New York was the embodiment of the "high life," the "metropolis of modernity," the site where Cuban elites had forged business, economic, and cultural connections, as well as the home of artists and political activists as early as the nineteenth century, to the point that going north was equated mostly with New York. Moreover, New York City played a central role in the "acculturation" of Cubans working in U.S. firms into U.S. corporate culture as the site of training seminars and programs to which many of them were sent. The Cuban presence in Miami, in contrast, developed slowly in the 1920s and did not peak until after the 1940s.

9. See, for instance, Leiss et al. 1997 on the current globalization and segmentation of the advertising industry, which they trace from the turn of the century up to the 1950s, when advertising agencies began to open overseas agencies, such as those in Cuba, to meet the transnational needs of particular clients.

10. For these issues, see the discussion in Louis Pérez 1999 of the intricate economic connections between the United States and Cuba since the nineteenth century. As he notes, U.S. advertising methods arrived early in Cuba with the establishment of major U.S. agencies during the early 1900s. Cubans were also immersed in U.S. marketing strategies. Many of the personnel in Cuban-owned and operated advertising agencies received training in the United States. Cubans were also familiar with brands, marketing, and U.S. corporate culture through employment as sales representatives and agents of U.S. companies.

11. This story is part of Campbell Soup's Oral History and Documentation Project compiled by the National Museum of American History, which interviewed the Conills on April 27, 1989. Overall, there are few details about the development of Conill advertising itself or about the development of Hispanic marketing in this interview, which revolved mostly around Campbell's Soup. The interviewer repeatedly narrowed the conversation to Campbell, making allusions to a second interview, which never took place, where the couple could speak about the Hispanic market. Nonetheless, despite the interview's limited scope, the transnational connections behind the development of Conill are still highly evident. (Collection 367, Box 8.)

12. Cristina Saralegui's autobiography gives further evidence of the relationships between the development of the U.S. Hispanic market and the sale of Latin America as a common market. As she describes, the success of *Vanidades,* still one of the most popular magazines in the U.S. Hispanic market and throughout Latin America, was directly tied to the sale of advertising at a set price in the United States to be distributed in all the different editions of the magazines circulating in all Latin American countries, all connected as a network by the magazine publishers in the United States (Saralegui 1998). While now a popular U.S. magazine, it started as a U.S.-made product for the Latin American market.

13. Alicia Conill, for instance, worked at Williams Este, an English adver-

tising agency, prior to working at Conill with her husband. At Williams Este she developed Puerto Rico's Winston campaign in the mid-1970s and represented other American companies throughout Latin America.

14. "Orcis Make Chicago Next Destination," *Advertising Age* ("Multicultural Marketplace," November 15, 1999, p. 41).

15. All extracts with no source cited are from interviews conducted during fieldwork.

16. This section, as well as the rest of the book after this chapter, uses pseudonyms were necessary for staff employees in the industry.

17. Caliente (105.9 FM) was launched in 1998 with a salsa and merengue format equal to that of its main rival La Mega (97.9 FM). Unable to compete, it has since renamed itself Latino Mix and adopted a new programming mix of pop and rock *en español,* along with its dominant fare of salsa and merengue.

18. On this issue, readers may consult Haslip-Viera and Baver (1996), Sánchez-Korroll (1983), and the memoirs of Bernardo Vega, edited by Cesar Iglesias (Vega 1977). All these sources attest to New York City's emerging pan-Hispanic population since the late 1900s and to the convergence of different Latino subnationalities in common causes and organizations of the times.

19. A longer discussion of the 1980 census and of its changes in the enumeration of Hispanics is included in Tienda and Ortíz (1986).

20. It is not surprising that Castor Fernández, founder of one of the most profitable enterprises in the 1970s, the still-active Castor Advertising, had already written in the late 1960s an M.A. thesis on Spanish advertising and the Hispanic market. This exemplifies the efforts by the early entrepreneurs to validate and legitimize the Hispanic market.

21. Thus, until the 1970s, when the *Standard Directory of Advertising* inaugurated its list according to specialized markets, there were only four agencies listed as focusing on Hispanics. All were located in New York and, with a few exceptions, were run by Cuban immigrants. The number of Hispanic agencies grew rapidly in the late 1970s and peaked in the 1980s with the development of advertising agencies in Miami, Los Angeles, and Chicago. By June 1980, there were twenty agencies listed, the June 1997 edition listed seventy-nine, and the January 2001 edition listed more than 100 Hispanic agencies spread throughout the United States (National Register Publishing 1980, 1997, 2001).

22. I am reminded here of Kobena Mercer's (1994) discussion of the "burden of representation," which notes that minorities are perceived as one and interchangeable, although here it would be more appropriate to think about the "profits" not burdens of representation.

23. An interesting point here is that the 1960s saw not only the growth of Hispanic advertising but also of the first generation of Latino film-makers and video artists becoming involved in their representation in media and television. Lillian Jiménez's assertion that for this generation, "picking up the camera was equivalent to 'picking up the gun,' " reminds us of the politicized context affecting the involvement of Latinos in their self-representation (Jiménez 1996: 22).

24. See also Wilson and Gutiérrez 1995: 127–32 for a discussion of the growing public interest in Latino culture since mid-1965 evidenced in news articles and trade magazines.

25. Hispanic Heritage Month had its origins in the early 1960s when President Lyndon Johnson designated the second week of September as Hispanic Heritage Week. It was extended to a month by Congress in 1988 and observed nationally from September 15 to October 15.

26. Some companies started targeting their efforts to ethnic consumers much earlier. Robert Weems notes that in the 1940s, Pepsi-Cola had already established a "Negro-Sales Department," headed by an African American, to court African American consumers (Weems 1998). It was only after the 1970s, however, that concerted efforts were made to reach minority consumers, involving the creation of departments and the incorporation of ethnic marketing as part of a company's organization. Breweries were among the first to target Hispanics as part of a new focus on ethnic and special-interest groups in the early 1980s (McDowell 1981). Other companies opening Hispanic or ethnic marketing divisions from the late 1970s onwards include Coca-Cola, Procter & Gamble, Anheuser-Busch, and retailers such as Sears and J. C. Penney (Khermouch 1996). For more information on American corporations' patterns of investments in the U.S. Hispanic market, see the reports issued by the Hispanic Policy Development Project (1987).

27. SAMS was bought by DeGarbo; Conill Advertising was bought by Saatchi and Saatchi; Bravo was instituted as a Hispanic shop for Young and Rubicam; Siboney U.S.A. was integrated with True North Communications; and Font and Vaamonte became part of Grey Advertising. Outside New York City, Bromley, Aguilar became 49 percent owned by the MacManus Group, and Mendoza-Dillon and Associates was bought by the WPP Group.

28. According to a study by Broadcast Investment Analysts in 1998, there were seven hundred fewer minority-owned radio stations since the passing of the Telecommunications Act in 1996 (Merli 1998). Similarly, out of more than twelve hundred TV stations in the United States, it is estimated that as of 1995 minorities owned only thirty-seven. Media ownership by minorities has been particularly affected by the eradication of the tax certificate policy, which gave tax breaks to broadcast and cable owners who sold to minority buyers (Marble 1997).

29. Many of these issues were discussed by Neil Comber, who initiated Hispanic marketing at Procter & Gamble, in a presentation on the "mundolization" of marketing at the AHAA semi-annual conference in San Antonio, February 25–28, 1999. He also explained the relative advantages to a transnational agency of hiring a Hispanic shop from the corporate clients' perspective.

CHAPTER 2

1. On this point, see Juan Flores's (1997) discussion of the demographic and analytical approaches to Latinos developed in the commercial and social science literature and how they affect conceptions of the Latino community. He makes a distinction between these approaches, which favor the quantification and hence manipulation of Latinos according to static or imposed categories, and a more fluid cultural imaginary composed of history, memory, and experience, which is thus not as quantifiable.

2. There are even reference books on "multicultural experts" available now that list ad agencies, research firms, and individual experts in multicultural mar-

kets. One example is the *Source Book of Multicultural Experts,* published by New York–based Multicultural Marketing Resources, Inc. (a multicultural marketing company tapping into this market by publishing news and information about upcoming conferences on ethnic and Hispanic marketing).

3. The Anglo/Latin dichotomy has long been at the center of nationalist ideologies in Latin America, as evidenced in the writings of Mexican José Vasconcelos, Uruguayan José E. Rodo, Cuban José Martí (Ramos 1989). These dynamics are primarily evocative of nationalist discourses in colonial contexts which have similarly established dichotomies between culture and technology and spiritualism and materialism (Chatterjee 1993). For the reformulation of these ideas by Hispanic marketers and advertisers, see Valdés and Seoane (1995), and Roslow and Therrien Decker (1998).

4. Some of these include the reports by Miami-based Strategy Research, such as its annual *Blue Book* and the *Star TV Ratings Reports.* These and other reports have been criticized for inflating statistics, generalizing about Hispanic populations on the basis of surveys conducted in high-density Hispanic urban neighborhoods, and failing to account fully for the acculturation of Hispanics (see, for instance, Soruco and Meyer 1993; Balkan 1982).

5. I am not implying here that qualitative marketing research would make a dramatic change in this situation. While consumers have been increasingly incorporated into the making of ads though research, problems in the application of ethnographic methods in marketing research and in the interpretation of this data make it far from representative of consumers' views (Stern 1998). A case in point is the screening of Hispanic consumers for focus group situations in ways that preselect the recently arrived, Spanish-dominant consumer—the one most likely to present the attitudes associated in the industry with the model Hispanic consumer.

6. These figures come mostly from the MDI/Yankelovich *Hispanic Monitor,* but readers will find them also corroborated in the reports by Strategy Research Corporation and other research reports.

7. In fact, concerns about a changing market have been debated in Hispanic marketing trade publications since the 1980s, although these issues have attained renewed importance because of the proliferation of research (Savage 1982; Gage 1983).

8. See Timothy Burke's discussion of advertising in Zimbabwe (1996) and of how knowledge of the processes of marketing research led to a general skepticism about marketing research and its use among advertising practitioners.

9. For a discussion of problems of context, perception, and interpretation in marketing research, see Leiss et al. 1997 and Ang 1996.

10. For a discussion of income disparities between English-dominant and Spanish-dominant Latinos, see Dávila and Mora 2000. Their study emphatically shows that English skills are directly correlated to income growth, even in regions where the minority language (Spanish) is dominant.

11. On this point, see Austin (1994) and Chin (2001), who discuss the pathologization of consumption among African Americans and their rendering as uncritical, compulsive shoppers.

12. This situation echoes Vilma Santiago-Irizarry's (1996) discussion of how

language was treated in therapeutic settings in the context of multicultural health policies. Just as Latinos were prescribed culturally sensitive or language-driven therapy as the default treatment, language purity is deemed the optimal medium through which to reach the Hispanic consumer.

13. See Bell 1995 for a discussion of these strategies by Sosa, Bromley, Aguilar, Noble and Associates of San Antonio.

14. These are the kinds of issues behind current debates about the accuracy of Nielsen's Hispanic ratings (Wartzman and Flint 2000). See also Soruco and Meyer (1993) for criticisms of sampling methods according to geography and surname—for instance, they note that in many areas of the country, Hispanics often do not have Hispanic surnames and are not counted or surveyed as such. Granted, the preselection of audiences for focus group purposes is not unique to the case at hand. Esther Hamburger's study of the use of focus groups by audience researchers at Brazil's Globo, for instance, perceptively revealed how the entire Brazilian audience is spoken for on the basis of a limited universe of viewers: urban, middle-class women selected only from Rio de Janeiro and São Paulo (Hamburger 2000).

15. Conference: Direct Marketing to Multicultural Markets, March 18–19, 1999, at the New York Helsmley Hotel.

16. These issues have been discussed in relation to multiculturalism by Cruz 1996; Segal and Handler 1995; Turner 1994; and Williams 1993. I also discuss them in greater detail in Dávila 1999a. Briefly, this research has noted that the process of identity creation forged by multiculturalism and nationalism reproduces an essentialized view of cultural identities, whereby these are seen and presented as single, concrete, and identifiable entities with a unique history and cultural property that corroborate their existence and connect them with a distinct past and territory.

17. An interesting study that dispels some of the generalizations about Hispanics' media habits was recently produced by the Tomás Rivera Policy Institute (1998). It attests to the bilingual nature of Latino TV viewership, contradicting the Spanish-centered viewing habits claimed by Hispanic marketers. It also evidences many similarities in Anglo and Latino viewing habits, as well as differences in the TV viewing habits of Spanish- and English-dominant Latinos, contradicting the representation of Latinos as one undifferentiated construct.

CHAPTER 3

1. Whether Latinas constitute a racial or ethnic group is a contentious issue. When describing "Hispanic" and "Latina" as racial categories I seek to call attention to the unavailability of race as a central variable affecting the incorporation and subordination of Latinas in the U.S. context. While some subgroups are certainly more likely to be racialized, all have to contend with the lingering effects that race plays in defining contemporary Latinidad. For discussion of these issues, see Alcoff 2000 and Gracia and De Greiff 2000.

2. Until the late 1960s, most advertising (approximately 84 percent) aired on Spanish-language TV consisted of local spots for local products and advertisers (Wilkinson 1995). Thus, whereas it was common for marketing presenta-

tions in the New York market to appeal to the growing number of Hispanics as a totality, this was done to justify and sell a local strategy that was ultimately meant only for the local Puerto Rican market.

3. This section is based on Goya's historical ad reel containing ads from 1960 to 1980. The reel is kept by Goya Food Products Corporate Headquarters in New Jersey.

4. These were all listed as clients of SAMS in a presentation to Colgate Palmolive in 1979. They are also corroborated by the Standard Directory of Advertising list of clients in 1969.

5. The development of Radio Unica in 1998 and of other national Spanish-language radio networks in the United States is likely to transform this trend.

6. See "Top 50 Advertisers Cultivating the Hispanic Market," in *Advertising Age*, August 24, 1998.

7. The discussion in this section was based on analysis of the agency reels of the following agencies: Conill, Siboney, FOVA, Bravo, Vidal, Reynardus, and Moya in New York, and from Mendoza and Dillon (California), Acento (California), Bromley and Associates (San Antonio), Dieste (Dallas), Del Rivero Mesiano (Miami), and AdAmericas (California). The historical material (ads shot in the early and late 1970s) was drawn from Univision's historical advertising reel, produced as part of the network's anniversary, and Bravo's historical reel. Univision's historical reel spans the period from the early 1970s to the 1980s. This reel included eighty-four ads, of which thirty-two showed or directly evoked the family. The most common image was that of the mother caring for her children.

8. While Castor Advertising managed Budweiser's nationwide campaign, the concept of "Rebudluciona las reglas" (turn around, or revolutionize, the rules) was developed jointly by Budweiser's ethnic marketing department and in the West for Bud Light by Sosa, Bramble, Aguilar, Noble and Associates. While also showing Hispanics interacting with Anglos, Sosa's campaign had a different focus. Two male Anglos are shown admiring Hispanic values, discovering how rich and valuable is their culture, realizing how much fun it is to be Hispanic, and aspiring to Hispanic values.

9. See Saralegui (1998) for a description of Cristina's fight to have her Cuban accent validated in the networks and Negrón Cruz (1998) for an interview with Raymond Arrieta, who describes how he finally learned to speak with "caution" on the airwaves.

10. This subtitle is based on Chatterjee's (1993) book, also titled *The Nation and Its Fragments,* to emphasize the nationalist dynamics reproduced by this industry as it seeks to tap into differences among Hispanics.

11. Total advertising expenditures in the Hispanic market are not available prior to 1982, when Hispanic business began to compile its annual list of the leading national Hispanic market advertisers. Nonetheless, while there was enough attention to the market in the 1980s to warrant the compilation of a list of national advertisers, these budgets were markedly low compared to those for the "general" market. In 1982, for instance, the leading U.S. advertiser, Procter & Gamble, spent $3.4 million advertising to Hispanics compared to the $671.8 million it spent for the general market. What is certain is that advertising rev-

enues did increase sharply throughout the 1980s; total expenditures doubled from 1982 to 1985 from $166 million to $333 million (Jacobson 1985: 14).

CHAPTER 4

1. On the issue of authorship, see Dornfeld's (1998) study of the production of public television. He shows that producers of public television, whose class background is similar to that of their target audience, act as surrogate audiences to assure the greater representativity of the audience, although this audience is not defined as encompassing the funders, but the totality of the United States, their imagined audience.

2. This incident refers to the exit of thousands of Cubans who gathered at Mariel Harbor in 1980. *Marielitos,* named after the Mariel Harbor boat lifts, were primarily working-class, darker, mulatto, and more racially representative of contemporary Cuba than the earlier upper-class exiles. In a political move, Castro also discharged many convicts in these boat lifts, which further tainted the white, upscale image of Miami Cubans.

3. As Frances Aparicio (1998) reminds us, the politics of feminine aesthetics, or the self-eroticizing of Latinas through dress and makeup, is a highly contested issue that cannot be reduced to simple explanations of women being subsumed into the patriarchal order or reappropriating their bodies and their looks in order to resist that same order. She does note, however, that the meanings of makeup and dress among Latinos differ from those in the Anglo feminist paradigm, which generally condemns female concerns over fashion and looks as signs of patriarchal impositions. We cannot necessarily assume, however, that there is congruence between body and subjectivity, or that behind the veil of the made-up and fashion-conscious Latina lies a person who is not touched by patriarchal demands on her behavior and demeanor.

4. Recall here that clients generally see Hispanic marketing not as a business strategy but as a sign of political correctness and are therefore likely to doubt the business edge of the industry and of its professionals. A revealing exposé of this dynamic is provided by Denise Leo, founder of Mosaic America, a multicultural marketing firm, in an editorial in *Advertising Age* (Leo 1999).

5. This situation is not unique to Hispanic marketers; it has been documented as a common method national advertisers have historically used when dealing with minority agencies. Rather than the more lucrative media-planning and buying roles in a given account, they are hired solely to do "creative" executions, which reduces the advertising revenues of minority shops (Turow 1997: 82).

6. Aside from their impact on sales, ads are increasingly judged on their putative artistic merit, conferring great prestige on their creators and agencies, as shown by the popularity of competitions and awards such as the Clios.

CHAPTER 5

1. This chapter appeared in a shorter form in *Television and New Media* 1 (February 2000): 75–94.

2. Some examples include the new publications *Latina, Latin Girl,* and *Urban Latino.*

3. Obviously, although Sony's involvement was interpreted as a sign of an "American" takeover, Sony is a Japanese not American company, and as such a minority partner, given U.S. regulations over foreign ownership of TV networks. Furthermore, concerns that the takeover by American corporations of Spanish networks would lead to their "assimilation" are certainly not new. Similar concerns were voiced when Univision was bought by Hallmark in 1986, although its subsequent reacquisition by its former owners, along with its present management and the few substantive programmatic changes made by Hallmark, which maintained its programming connections to Mexico's Televisa, exempted it from the type of criticism triggered by Sony's purchase of Telemundo. Prior to the current sale, Telemundo, for its part, was always in the hands of U.S. corporate holders, having been initially founded in 1986 by Reliance Capital Corp., controlled by Saul Steinberg, a Wall Street financier. The debate over whether Telemundo would become assimilated stemmed mostly from the entry of a powerful programming company into the Spanish TV networks and rumors about the development of bilingual programs (Esparza 1998).

4. This is particularly evident in bilingual or English-dominant media such as the magazines *Latina* and *Urban Latino.*

5. Both of the networks conducted "Up-Front" presentations for prospective advertisers for the first time in 1998, pointing to their renewed efforts to market themselves and define their "uniqueness" in this new context. This section is largely based on videos and observations of these presentations, analysis of their media kits, and interviews with people involved in their programming.

6. Miami's importance as a production center is being fueled not only by productions specifically targeted to the U.S. and Latin American markets by the Spanish networks, but also by cable channel production for Latin America's pay-TV networks, such as MTV, HBO, Nickelodeon, the Weather Channel, Gems, and Discovery Networks.

7. For a discussion of Miami's role in the trans–Latin Americanization of the soap opera industry, see Matos 1999; and Yúdice 1999.

8. These issues are also addressed by participants in my focus group sessions. Readers may also consult the following articles critiquing such inequalities: La Franco 1998; and Stewart 1998.

9. I recognize that there have been some exceptions to this trend. The ground-breaking *Dos Mujeres y un Destino,* featuring Erik Estrada, is a good example here, as is also *La Mujer de mi Vida,* featuring a young women who moves to Miami. I would nonetheless argue that when linkages between the United States and Latin America are developed, they almost invariably fail to problematize the tensions and problems of such connections. Scenes may be filmed in Miami but Hispanicized to an extent that leaves little or no room for recognizing the problems or experiences of U.S. Hispanics as minorities in the United States. Similarly, references to a transnational U.S.-Latin American world are most often done, not from the perspective of immigrants but from that of the rich and cosmopolitan characters. These are the "floating populations" who take shopping trips to New York, go to doctors in Houston, or vacation in Miami, but

whose trips never compromise their sense of place and national identity. I owe these soap opera insights to Tomás López-Pumarejo.

10. A good example of this trend is the "denationalization" of soap operas by decreasing historical and regional references to particular countries in order to make them more salable exports. Other strategies include filming soap operas in international Latino contexts like Miami, or drawing from generalizable themes like the "urban/rural" divide that is common to many Latin American countries (López 1995).

11. I am aware that the customization of Latin American soap operas for wider viewerships is a complex issue. Daniel Matos (1999) has noted that though producers of soap operas are increasingly concerned with reaching global audiences, the marketability of these products is directly tied to their success in particular localized/national markets. Hiring imported talent of widespread appeal, diminishing regional language mannerisms, and sacrificing local references may decrease rather than increase the potential marketability of soap operas if these globalizing tactics fail to attract a local audience.

12. See for instance a letter sent by Manuel Arce Trias to the editor of *El Nuevo Día* (Arce Trias 1998).

13. This ad was one of the winners of the *Advertising Age* Hispanic Creative Advertising Award in the Grocery Product category.

14. See Cristina Saralegui's account of the initial public reception of her show in Mexico (Saralegui 1998). The backlash against non-Mexican actors in Mexican soap operas was displayed in a show by Cristina on May 13, 1998, in which Mexican actors criticized these new actors for lacking acting skills and for their "faulty" Spanish.

15. Historically, Spanish has not only functioned in this way but has also served as an attenuating barrier against the already high flow of U.S. cultural products and programming into the Hispanic market (McAnany and Wilkinson 1996). That is, in contrast to exports to Canada, U.S. media exports to Latin America are translated, and this provides additional room for the indigenization of these products through language.

16. Thus, my intellectual Latino friends and myself use Spanglish playfully and as a vibrant linguistic resource, but such use never signals linguistic deficiencies. Class and linguistic ability in both English and Spanish render the use of Spanglish safe in ways that are not common among Latinos.

17. These dynamics are not unique to the case at hand. Writers have long noted that language ideologies construct language to be emblematic of particular peoples and of their national distinctiveness. Based on dominant, Western-based, nationalist premises, language that is creolized, mixed, or the product of code-switching is therefore seen as signaling the decay of its speakers and their culture. Not surprisingly, activists concerned with minority languages end up reproducing the same essentialized politics that reproduce distinctions and hierarchies in language use in the process of resisting their own marginalization (Woolard 1998).

18. The Institute of Dominican Studies at City College in New York City has reacted against media portrayal of Dominicans as drug lords or as a gang-

ridden population, particularly in the *New York Times* (CUNY Dominican Studies Institute, Press Release issued on June 8, 1998).

19. Keynote speech by Peter Tortoricci at the DMA Hispanic Direct Marketing Conference at the Marriott East, New York City, March 10, 1999.

20. Press release, "Telemundo's New Crime Series 'Angeles' Showcases Latina Power," released by Telemundo on January 4, 1999. The show featured Patricia Manterola, Mexico's best actress of the year in 1996, Argentinean Sandra Vidal, and Magali Caicedo from Colombia. The show was filmed at Baja Norte Studies in Tijuana, Baja California. Press release written by Gabriel Reyes and Steven Chapman.

21. Episode 106, "Chicago Rendezvous," 1998.

22. See Cashmore (1997) and Rodríguez (1997) respectively for discussions of the buffoon stereotype as applied to blacks and Latinos.

23. I am not denying that Latinos are racialized, but asserting that it is language that mainstream society associates most directly with their outsider status.

CHAPTER 6

1. While a number of studies exist about the consumption of different products, these have not been broken down in terms of Hispanics, hindering the ability of advertisers to prove the success of any given campaign. Advertisers in the Hispanic market rarely invest in the evaluative studies that they invest in for the general market to prove whether a campaign is really working.

2. Focus groups are relatively economical and fast, as opposed to other qualitative research methods that are adopted in the industry at large, such as house visits or ethnographies of product use.

3. Most focus groups are held with Spanish-dominants, requiring facilitators who are native speakers of Spanish. The ratio of Spanish-dominant to English-dominant focus groups held by marketing research companies ranged from 70:30 percent to 80:20 percent.

4. On this issue see Caroline Pauwels's (1999) critique of audience research and of the distorted all-or-nothing choices that are presented as "choices" to the consumer. Her critique warns against neoliberal conceptions of the citizen as having greater say and representation in the market as a consumer.

5. I moderated all of the groups except the one with Mexican informants. This group was recruited and moderated by assistant Frank Nuñez, according to the same questionnaire guidelines.

6. One key requirement for successful focus group discussion is that participants sense more sociocultural similarities than differences so that they feel comfortable sharing their ideas in a group situation. While most of my focus groups included one or two members of different nationalities or different class or occupational backgrounds, they also shared important similarities in language preference and in their self-identification as Latinos-Hispanics.

7. Although there is evidence of Mexican immigration into New York City since the mid-1940s, not until the mid- to late 1980s, particularly after the Immigration Reform and Control Act of 1986, did it grow steadily to reach its present peak (Smith 1996).

8. Jackson Heights' main Latino groups consist of 30.3 percent Dominican, 19.9 percent Colombian, and 10.9 percent Ecuadorian; that of the Upper West Side is 39.6 percent Puerto Rican, 18.1 percent Dominican, and 11.2 percent Mexican, and that of Astoria is 30.4 percent Puerto Rican, 10.6 percent Mexican, and 9.9 percent Colombian (Hanson-Sánchez 1996).

9. This rate was built into my grant to double the rate for focus group participants in marketing research, which is approximately $30.00 (1998 rate).

10. *Mirada de Mujer* was produced by Azteca TV, a Televisa rival in Mexico. Unlike Televisa's soap operas, which have grown increasingly vague and diluted in terms of historical context and place, Azteca's soap operas have incorporated daily news and showcased Mexico's political life. During its run, *Mirada de Mujer* beat Televisa by becoming the number one soap opera in Mexico (Business Mexico 1998).

11. The involvement of other Latino subgroups in the hip-hop movement is evident in the editorial and founding staff of the hip-hop magazines *Urban Latino* and *Stress,* which, according to their founding members, includes Chileans, Cubans, Ecuadorians, and Nicaraguans, along with Puerto Ricans and Dominicans

12. This association has multiple implications, among them the erasure of Latinos as contributors to the development of hip-hop and the denial of the Latinidad of Puerto Ricans and Dominicans, who are active in hip-hop culture (Rivera 2001).

CHAPTER 7

1. Distinctions are made between these categories by marketers, who use "black" to refer to the bulk of consumers who are black, regardless of their background and nationality, and "African-American" to designate U.S.-born black populations. These distinctions, however, are most often blurred and used indistinguishably in the literature, as are "Hispanic" and "Latino."

2. Consider for instance, Ikea's print ad campaigns depicting gay couples buying furniture as a sign of their commitment, or American Express Financial Advisor's ad featuring a lesbian couple in an ad whose tagline is, "When you're ready to plan a future together, who can you trust to understand the financial challenges that gay men and lesbians face?" See "Reaching the Gay Consumer," Future Dialogue #98, prepared for Young & Rubicam's Brand Futures Group, November 9, 1999 (Web access: www.brandfutures.com/Brand/index.asp).

3. As of this writing, the major black agencies have been courted by mainstream agencies, but none have sold. Boutique black agencies, however, have been established by large mainstream agencies in association with black creatives. These include Leo Burnett's Vigilante, DDB Needham's Spike DDB, and True North's Steadman, Graham, and Partners.

4. Poignantly, this view erases Native Americans, the only real indigenous minority in the U.S., who are totally invisible in marketing discourse.

5. The issue of whether African-American speech may exhibit traits of a dialect or of a different language than English and may not be intelligible to a wider public, as in the ebonics controversy, is never mentioned by marketers.

6. On these different philosophies, contrast the statements of Byron Lewis, founder of Uniworld (Adweek 1998) with those of Tom Burrell, founder of Burrell Communication Group in Chicago (Jensen 1999).

7. Presentation by Dr. Kathryn Alexander, president of Kathryn Alexander Enterprises, Inc., during the Invitation Summit on Multicultural Markets, January 18, 1999.

8. While Asian Americans, blacks, and Hispanics are all described by marketers as the "fastest growing," Asian Americans are indeed the fastest growing minority, although they are only the third most numerous minority population, with an average of 11 million, versus 30 and 35 million of Hispanics and blacks respectively.

9. On the different histories, migration patterns, and social and class composition of Southeast Asian immigrants, see Ong 1999.

References

Abu-Lughod, Lila.
　1993.　　Editorial Comment: On Screening Politics in a World of Nations.
　　　　　Public Culture 5 (3): 493–513.
　1999.　　The Interpretation of Culture(s) after Television. In *The Fate of
　　　　　Culture: Geertz and Beyond,* ed. Sherry Ortner, 110–135. Berke-
　　　　　ley: University of California Press.
Adweek (anonymous).
　1998.　　Byron Lewis: Hiphop Rules, Yet Black Agencies Still Struggle. *Ad-
　　　　　week.* November 9, 163. Twentieth anniversary issue.
Alaniz, Maria, and Chris Wilkes.
　1995.　　Reinterpreting Latino Culture in the Commodity Form: The Case
　　　　　of Alcohol Advertising in the Mexican American Community.
　　　　　Hispanic Journal of Behavioral Sciences 17 (4): 430–45.
Alcoff, Linda.
　2000.　　Is Latina/o Identity a Racial Identity? In *Hispanics/Latinos in the
　　　　　United States: Ethnicity, Race, and Rights,* ed. Jorge Gracia and
　　　　　Pablo De Greiff, 23–24. London: Routledge.
Alden, Dana, Wayne Hoyer, and Chal Lee.
　1993.　　Identifying Global and Culture-Specific Dimensions of Humor in
　　　　　Advertising: A Multinational Analysis. *Journal of Marketing*
　　　　　(April): 64–75.
Alejandro, Roberto.
　1993.　　*Hermeneutics, Citizenship, and the Public Sphere.* Albany: State
　　　　　University of New York Press.
Anderson, Benjamin.
　1983.　　*Imagined Communities: Reflections on the Origins and Spread
　　　　　of Nationalism.* London: Verso.

Ang, Ien.
1986.   Watching Dallas: Soap Opera and the Melodramatic Imagination. London: Methuen.
1996.   Living Room Wars: Rethinking Media Audiences for a Postmodern World. London: Routledge.
Aparicio, Frances.
1998.   Listening to Salsa: Gender, Latin Popular Music, and Puerto Rican Cultures. Hanover, NH: University Press of New England.
Aparicio, Frances, and Susana Chávez-Silverman.
1997.   Tropicalizations: Transcultural Representations of Latinidad. Hanover, NH: University Press of New England.
Aponte, Alex.
1998.   Miami the Media Heavy. Hispanic Business, July–August, 50–56.
Appadurai, Arjun.
1996.   Disjuncture and Difference in the Global Cultural Economy. In Modernity at Large: Cultural Dimensions of Globalization. Minneapolis: University of Minnesota Press, 27–47.
Arce Trias, Manuel.
1998.   Censura a Cristina Saralegui. El Nuevo Día, October 14, 101.
Astroff, Roberta.
1997.   Capital's Cultural Study: Marketing Popular Ethnography of U.S. Latino Culture. In Buy This Book: Studies in Advertising and Consumption, ed. Mica Nava, Andres Blake, Ian MacRury, and Barry Richards. London: Routledge.
Atanay, Reginaldo.
1998.   Porque Cristina no lleva a Henry Cisneros y a Linda? El Diario, March 27, 20.
Austin, Regina.
1994.   "A Nation of Thieves": Consumption, Commerce, and the Black Public Sphere. Public Culture 7 (1): 225–48.
Avila, Alex.
1997.   Trading Punches, Spanish-Language Television Pounds the Competition in the Fight of Hispanic Advertising Dollars. Hispanic, January–February, 39–44.
Balkan, Carlos.
1982.   The Crisis in Hispanic Marketing. Hispanic Business, December, 24–32.
Barbero, Jesús Martín.
1987.   De los Medios a las Mediaciones. Barcelona: Gustavo Gil.
Basch, Linda, Nina Glick-Schiller, and Cristina Szanton Blanc.
1994.   Nations Unbound: Transnational Projects, Postcolonial Predicaments, and Deterritorialized Nation-States. Longhourne, PA: Gordon and Breach.
Bean, Frank D., and Marta Tienda.
1987.   The Hispanic Population of the United States. For the National Committee for Research on the 1980 Census. New York : Russell Sage Foundation.

Bell, Brenda.
　1995.　Ads. Ads. Ads. Buy. Buy. Buy. Bueno. Bueno. Bueno. *Los Angeles Times Magazine,* September 17, 28–46.
Belton, Beth.
　1998.　Black Buying Power Soaring. *USA Today,* July 30, 1B.
Bernard, Russell.
　1994.　*Research Methods in Anthropology: Qualitative and Quantitative Approaches.* Thousand Oaks, CA: Sage.
Bolles, Lynn.
　1992.　Sand, Sea, and the Forbidden. *Transforming Anthropology* 3 (1): 30–34.
Bourdieu, Pierre.
　1993.　*The Field of Cultural Production.* New York: Columbia University Press.
Bourgois, Philippe.
　1995.　*In Search of Respect: Selling Crack in el Barrio.* New York: Cambridge University Press.
Boyd, Malia.
　1994.　Asian Dawn. *Incentive Marketing,* June, 37–40.
Braxton, Greg.
　1999.　A White, White World on TV's Fall Schedule. *Los Angeles Times,* May 28, 1.
Brendin, Marian.
　1996.　Transforming Images: Communication Technologies and Cultural Identity in Nishnawbe-Aski. In *Cross Cultural Consumption,* ed. David Howes, 138–60. London and New York: Routledge.
Brewer, Geoffrey.
　1993.　Spike Speaks and African American Consumers Listen. *Incentive Marketing,* February, 26–34.
Bright, Brenda.
　1995.　*Looking High and Low: Art and Cultural Identity.* Tucson, AZ: University of Arizona Press.
Broadcasting and Cable.
　1998.　Minority Ownership: A Not Much Progress Report. *Broadcasting and Cable,* July 20, 7.
Brody, Barbara.
　1998.　New Women's Titles Provide Glossy Options. *Advertising Age.* August 24, S24.
Burgi, Michael.
　1994.　Univision's New Vision. *Mediaweek,* February 21, 11.
Burke, Timothy.
　1996.　*Lifebuoy Men, Lux Women: Commodification, Consumption, and Cleanliness in Modern Zimbabwe.* Durham, NC: Duke University Press.
Business Mexico.
　1998.　Ratings War. *Business Mexico,* June 10: 10.

Calhoun, Craig.
1992.   *Habermas and the Public Sphere.* Cambridge, MA: MIT Press.
1993.   Civil Society and the Public Sphere. *Public Culture* 5: 267–80.
Campanelli, Melissa.
1995.   Asian Studies. *Sales and Marketing Management,* March, 51.
Carmichael, Matt.
2000.   McDonald's Ad Comes Across as Half-Baked. *Advertising Age,* February, 46.
Cashmore, Ellis.
1997.   *The Black Culture Industry.* London: Routledge.
Chatterjee, Partha.
1986.   *Nationalist Thought and the Colonial World: A Derivative Discourse?* London: Zed Books.
1993.   *The Nation and Its Fragments: Colonial and Postcolonial Histories.* Princeton, NJ: Princeton University Press.
Chin, Elizabeth.
2001.   *Purchasing Power: Black Kids and American Consumer Culture.* Minneapolis: University of Minnesota Press.
Cobas, José, and Jorge Duany.
1997.   *Cubans in Puerto Rico: Ethnic Economy and Cultural Identity.* Gainesville, FL: University of Florida Press.
Coombe, Rosemary.
1998.   *The Cultural Life of Intellectual Properties: Authorship, Appropriation, and the Law.* Durham, NC: Duke University Press.
Cruz, Jon.
1996.   From Farce to Tragedy: Reflections on the Reification of Race at Century's End. In *Mapping Multiculturalism,* ed. Avery F. Gordon and Christopher Newfield, 10–29. Minneapolis: University of Minnesota Press.
1999.   *Culture on the Margins: The Black Spiritual and the Rise of American Cultural Interpretation.* Princeton, NJ: Princeton University Press.
CUNY Dominican Studies Institute.
1998.   Institute Head Reacts to Portrayal of Dominicans in *New York Times* Articles. Press release issued on June 8.
Dávila, Alberto, and Marie Mora.
2000.   English Skills, Earnings, and the Occupational Sorting of Mexican Americans along the U.S. Mexico Border. *International Migration Review* 34 (1): 33-157.
Dávila, Arlene M.
1997.   *Sponsored Identities: Cultural Politics in Puerto Rico.* Philadelphia: Temple University Press.
1999a.   Culture in the Battleground: From Nationalist to Pan-Latino Projects. *Museum Anthropology* 23 (3): 2–42.
1999b.   Latinizing Culture: Art, Museums, and the Politics of U.S. Multicultural Encompassment. *Cultural Anthropology* 14 (2): 180–202.

Dent, Gina.
1992.   Black Pleasure, Black Joy: An Introduction. In *Black Popular Culture*. Seattle: Bay Press.
Dias, J.
1999.   Más Pudor, Please. *Latina Magazine,* January, 14.
Discount Merchandiser.
1998.   Under One Rainbow: African American Preferences Are Driving Children's Fashion. *Discount Merchandiser,* October, 70–73.
Dornfeld, Barry.
1998.   *Producing Public Television.* Princeton, NJ: Princeton University Press.
Duany, Jorge.
1990.   *Los Dominicanos en Puerto Rico: Migración en la Semiperiferia.* Rio Piedras, Puerto Rico: Ediciones Huracán.
Duany, Jorge, Luisa Hernández Angueira, and Cesar A. Rey.
1995.   El Barrio Gandul: Economia subterranea y migración indocumentada in Puerto Rico. Puerto Rico: Universidad del Sagrado Corazón.
Dyer, Richard.
1993.   *The Matter of Images.* London: Routledge.
1997.   *White.* London: Routledge.
El Diario.
1998.   Se quejan de cadenas hispanas de televisión. *El Diario/La Prensa,* March 2, 20.
Englis, Basil.
1994.   *Global and Multinational Advertising.* New Brunswick, NJ: Rutgers University Press.
Esparza, Elia.
1997.   Tragic Comedies: How Chronic Network Stereotypes Doom Latino Sitcoms. *Hispanic,* March, 48–54.
1998.   Must Sí TV. *Hispanic,* May, 20–28.
Espíritu, Yen Le.
1992.   *Asian American Panethnicity: Bridging Institutions and Identities.* Philadelphia: Temple University Press.
Ewen, Stuart.
1988.   *All Consuming Images: The Politics of Style in Contemporary Culture.* Basic Books: Harper Collins.
Ewen, Stuart, and Elizabeth Ewen.
1992.   *Channels of Desire: Mass Images and the Shaping of American Consciousness.* Minneapolis: University of Minnesota Press.
Fernández Retamar, Roberto.
1979.   *Calibán y otros ensayos: Nuestra America y el mundo.* Ciudad de La Habana, Cuba: Editorial Arte y Literatura.
Firat, Fuat, and Nikhilesh Dholakia.
1998.   *Consuming People: From Political Economy to Theaters of Consumption.* London: Routledge.

Fisher, Christy.
    1996.   Black, Hip, and Primed (to Shop). *American Demographics*, September, 52–58.
Fiske, John.
    1996.   *Media Matters: Race and Gender in U.S. Politics.* Minneapolis: University of Minnesota Press.
Fitzgerald, Thomas.
    1992.   Media, Ethnicity, and Identity. In *Culture and Power: A Media, Culture, and Society Reader,* ed. Paddy Scannel, Philip Schlesinger, and Colin Sparks, 112–36. London: Sage.
Flores, Juan.
    1996.   Puerto Rocks: New York Ricans Stake Their Claim. In *Dropping Science: Critical Essays on Rap Music and Hip Hop Culture,* ed. William Eric Perkings, 85–105. Philadelphia: Temple University Press.
    1997.   The Latino Imaginary: Dimensions of Community and Identity. In *Tropicalizations: Transcultural Representations of Latinidad,* ed. Frances Aparicio and Chavez-Silverman, 183–93. Hanover, NH: University Press of New England.
    2000.   *From Bomba to Hip Hop: Puerto Rican Culture and Latino Identity.* New York: Columbia University Press.
Flores, Juan, and George Yúdice.
    1993.   Living Borders/Buscando America: Languages of Latino Self-Formation. In *Divided Borders.* Houston: Arte Público Press.
Foster, Robert.
    1999.   The Commercial Construction of "New Nations." In *Journal of Material Culture* 4 (3): 263–82.
Fowles, Jib.
    1996.   *Advertising and Popular Culture.* London: Sage.
Fox, Geoffrey.
    1996.   *The Hispanic Nation.* New York: Carol Publishing Group.
Francisco, Steven.
    1999.   Latinos Underground: An Inquiry into the Representation and Representations of Latinos in New York City Subway Train Advertisements. Paper presented in Clara Rodríguez's "Latino in the Media" seminar at Columbia University, New York, NY, April 28.
Frank, Thomas.
    1997.   *The Conquest of Cool: Business Culture, Counterculture, and the Rise of Hip Consumerism.* Chicago: University of Chicago Press.
Friedman, Jonathan.
    1994.   *Consumption and Identity.* Chur, Switzerland: Harwood Academic Publishers.
Fusco, Coco.
    1990.   The Latin "Boom" in Hollywood. CENTRO Bulletin 2 (8): 48–55.
    1995.   *English Is Broken Here: Notes on Cultural Fusion in the Americas.* New York City: New Press.

Gage, Theodore.
    1983.   Second-Tier Marketing to English-Speaking Hispanics. *Hispanic Business*, December, 22–26.
García-Canclini, Nestor.
    1995.   Consumidores y Ciudadanos: Conflictos Multiculturales de la Globalización. México, DF: Grijalbo.
Garnham, Nicholas.
    1993.   The Mass Media, Cultural Identity, and the Public Sphere in the Modern World. *Public Culture* 5 (2): 251–66.
Gilman, Sander.
    1996.   *Smart Jews: The Construction of the Image of Jewish Superior Intelligence.* Lincoln: University of Nebraska Press.
Ginsburg, Faye.
    1991.   Indigenous Media: Faustian Contract or Global Village? *Cultural Anthropology* 6 (1): 92–112.
    1999.   Indigenous Production / Ethnography of Media. In *A Companion to Film Theory*, ed. Bob Stam and Toby Miller. Walden, MA: Blackwell.
Ginsburg, Faye, Lila Abu-Lughod and Brian Larking, eds.
    2001.   *The Social Practice of Media: Anthropology in the Age of Electronic Reproduction.* Berkeley and Los Angeles: University of California Press.
Gitlin, Saul.
    1999.   The Asian American Market: An Untapped Opportunity for America's Marketers. In *The Source Book of Multicultural Experts, 1999–2000.* New York: Multicultural Marketing Resources, 13–16.
González, Lisa.
    1999.   The Hollywood Outsider. *Urban Latino*, November / December, 89.
Gordon, Amy, and Christopher Newfield, eds.
    1996.   *Mapping Multiculturalism.* Minneapolis: University of Minnesota Press.
Gracia, Jorge, and Pablo De Greiff.
    2000.   *Hispanics / Latinos in the United States: Ethnicity, Race, and Rights.* London: Routledge.
Gray, Herman.
    1995.   *Watching Race: Television and the Struggle for Blackness.* Minneapolis: University of Minnesota Press.
Gray, Valerie Lynn.
    1998.   Shopping for Equality. *Black Enterprise*, July, 60–68.
Guernica, Antonio.
    1982.   *Reaching the Hispanic Market Effectively: The Media, the Market, the Methods.* New York: McGraw-Hill.
Gupta, Akhil, and James Ferguson.
    1997.   *Anthropological Locations: Boundaries and Grounds of a Field Science.* Berkeley: University of California Press.

Gutiérrez, Felix.
1979.   Mexico's Television Network in the United States: The Case of Spanish International Network. In *Proceedings of the Sixth Annual Telecommunications Policy Research Conference*, ed. Herbert Dordick. Lexington, MA: Lexington Books.

Hall, Stuart.
1973.   *Encoding and Decoding in the Media Discourse.* Stenciled Paper 7, Birmingham: Center for Contemporary Cultural Studies.
1981.   Notes on Deconstructing the Popular. In *People's History and Socialist Theory,* ed. R. Samuel. London: Routledge.
1991a   Old and New Identities, Old and New Ethnicities. In *Culture, Globalization, and the World System,* ed. A. King. Albany: State University of New York Press.
1991b   The Local and the Global: Globalization and Ethnicity. In *Culture, Globalization and the World System,* ed. A. King. Albany: State University of New York Press.
1997.   *Representation: Cultural Representations and Signifying Practices.* London: Sage, in Association with the Open University.

Halter, Marilyn.
2000.   *Shopping for Identity: The Marketing of Ethnicity.* New York: Schocken Books.

Hamburger, Esther.
2000.   *Politics and Intimacy in Brazilian Telenovelas.* Rio de Janeiro: Federal University of Rio de Janeiro Press.

Handler, Richard.
1988.   *Nationalism and the Politics of Culture in Quebec.* Madison, WI: University of Wisconsin Press.

Hang Shin, Eui, and Kyung-Sup Chang.
1998.   Peripheralization of Immigrant Professionals: Korean Physicians in the United States. In *Asians in America: The Peoples of East, Southeast, and South Asia in American Life and Culture,* ed. Franklin Ng. New York and London: Garland.

Hanson-Sánchez, Christopher.
1996.   *New York City Latino Neighborhoods Data Book.* New York: Institute of Puerto Rican Policy.

Hartigan, John Jr.
1999.   *Racial Situations: Class Predicaments of Whiteness in Detroit.* Princeton, NJ: Princeton University Press.

Haslip-Viera, Gabriel, and Sherrie Baver, eds.
1996.   *Latinos in New York: Communities in Transition.* South Bend, IN: University of Notre Dame Press.

Hill, Jane H.
1999.   Mock Spanish: A Site for the Indexical Reproduction of Racism in American English. Language and Culture Symposium (University of Chicago) (http: //www.cs.uchicago.edu/l-c/archives/subs/hill-jane/)

Hispanic.
    1999.   Facts and Figures. *Hispanic*, July / August, 17.
Hispanic Market Weekly.
    1998.   Oops. *Hispanic Market Weekly,* May 18, 8.
Hispanic Policy Development Project.
    1987.   *Windows of Opportunity: How Business Invests in U.S. Hispanic
                 Markets.* 2 vols. Washington, DC: Hispanic Policy Development
                 Project.
Honig, Bonnie.
    1999.   How Foreignness "Solves" Democracy's Problems. *Social Text*
                 56: 1–27.
Howes, David.
    1996.   *Cross-Cultural Consumption: Global Markets, Local Realities.*
                 London and New York: Routledge.
Jacobson, Harold.
    1985.   Trends in Hispanic Market Advertising Expenditures. *Hispanic
                 Business.* December 1985, 14.
Jacobson, Michael, and Laurie Mazur.
    1995.   *Marketing Madness: A Survival Guide for a Consumer Society.*
                 Boulder, CO: Westview.
Jensen, Trevor.
    1999.   Burrell's Brave New World. *Adweek,* June 7, 2.
Jiménez, Lillian.
    1996.   Moving from the Margin to the Center: Puerto Rican Cinema in
                 New York. In *The Ethnic Eye: Latino Media Arts,* ed. Chon Nor-
                 iega and Ana M. Lopez. Minneapolis: University of Minnesota
                 Press.
Johnson, John J.
    1980.   *Latin America in Caricature.* Austin: University of Texas Press.
Jones-Correa, Michael.
    1998.   *Between Two Nations: The Political Predicament of Latinos in
                 New York City.* Ithaca, NY: Cornell University Press.
Kanellos, Nicolas.
    1998.   *Thirty Million Strong: Reclaiming the Hispanic Image in Amer-
                 ican Culture.* Golden, CO: Fulcrum Publishing.
Kern-Foxworth, Marilyn.
    1994.   *Aunt Jemima, Uncle Ben, and Rastus: Blacks in Advertising, Yes-
                 terday, Today, and Tomorrow.* Westport, CT: Greenwood Press.
Khermouch, Gerry.
    1996.   Why Major Marketers Are Latin Lovers. *Brandweek.* August 5, 32.
Klor de Alva, Jorge.
    1997.   The Invention of Ethnic Origins and the Negotiation of Latino
                 Identity, 1969–1981. In *Challenging Fronteras: Structuring
                 Latina and Latino Lives in the United States,* ed. Mary Romero,
                 Pierrette Hondagneu-Sotelo, and Vilma Ortíz, 55–80. London:
                 Routledge.

Kondo, Dorinne.
  1997.   *About Face: Performing Race in Fashion and Theater.* London:
             Routledge.
Koranteng, Juliana.
  1999.   Top Global Ad Markets. Special report. *Ad Age International,*
             May, 35–37.
Krueger, Richard.
  1994.   *Focus Group: A Practical Guide for Applied Research.* Thousand
             Oaks, CA: Sage.
La Franco, Robert.
  1998.   All in la Familia. *Forbes,* March 23, 82.
Laó, Agustín.
  2001.   Niuyol: Urban Regime, Latinos Social Movements, Ideologies
             of Latinidad. In *Mambo Montage: The Latinization of New
             York,* ed. Agustín Laó and Arlene Dávila. New York: Columbia
             University Press.
Larmer, Brook.
  1999.   Latino America. *Newsweek,* July 12, 50–58.
Lazere, E., ed.
  1987.   *American Media and Mass Culture: Left Perspectives.* Berkeley:
             University of California Press.
Lears, Jackson.
  1994.   *Fables of Abundance: A Cultural History of Advertising in Amer-
             ica.* New York: Basic Books.
Lee, Sharon.
  1994.   Poverty and the U.S. Asian Population. *Social Science Quarterly*
             75 (3): 541–59.
Leiss, William, Stephen Kline, and Sut Jhally.
  1997.   *Social Communication in Advertising: Persons, Products and Im-
             ages of Well-Being.* London: Routledge.
Leo, Denise.
  1999.   After Gobbling Minority Shops, Indigestion Next? *Advertising
             Age,* September 27, 54.
Límon, Jose.
  2000.   "*Yo quiero Taco Bell*": Strategic Essentialism and the Limits of
             Hybridity. Paper presented at the 99th meeting of the American
             Anthropological Association, San Francisco.
Lipsitz, George.
  1994.   *Dangerous Crossroads: Popular Music, Postmodernism, and the
             Poetics of Place.* London: New York.
López, Ana.
  1995.   Our Welcomed Guests: Telenovelas in Latin America. In *To Be
             Continued: Soap Operas Around the World,* ed. Robert Allan,
             256–75. London: Routledge.
López, Ricardo.
  1998.   Hispanic Buying Power. *Quirk's Marketing Research Review,*
             April, 22–27.

Los Angeles Times.
  1999.   Advertising and Marketing: Census Preview Spurs Move for Ethnic Consumers. *Los Angeles Times,* January, 21, 6.
Lowe, Lisa.
  1996.   *Immigrant Acts: On Asian American Cultural Politics.* Durham, NC: Duke University Press.
Lury Adam.
  1994.   Advertising: Moving Beyond the Stereotypes. In *The Authority of the Consumer,* ed. Russell Keat, Nicholas Abercrombie, and Nigel Whitley. London: Routledge.
Lury, Celia, and Alan Warde.
  1997.   Investments in the Imaginary Consumer: Conjectures Regarding Power, Knowledge and Advertising. In *Buy This Book: Studies in Advertising and Consumption,* ed. Mica Nava, Andrew Blake, Ian McRury, and Barry Richards. London: Routledge.
Lutz, Catherine, and Jane Collins.
  1993.   *Reading National Geographic.* Chicago: University of Chicago Press.
Mankekar, Purnima.
  1993.   National Texts and Gendered Lives: An Ethnography of Television Viewers in a North Indian City. *American Ethnologist* 20 (3): 543–63.
  1999.   *Screening Culture, Viewing Politics: An Ethnography of Television, Womanhood, and Nation in Postcolonial India.* Durham, NC: Duke University Press.
Marble, Manning.
  1997.   A Minority Presence. *Los Angeles Sentinel* 63 (14): A6.
Marcus, George.
  1998.   *Ethnography Through Think and Thin.* Princeton, NJ: Princeton University Press.
Marcus, George, and Fred Myers.
  1996.   *The Traffic in Culture: Refiguring Art in Anthropology.* Berkeley: University of California Press.
Matos, Daniel.
  1999.   Telenovelas: Transnacionalización de la industria y transformaciones del género. In *Las Industrias Culturales en la Integración Latinoamericana,* ed. Nestor García-Canclini and Carlos Moneta. Buenos Aires: Eudeba.
Mattelart, Armand, and Michele Mattelart.
  1992.   *Rethinking Media Theory.* Minneapolis: University of Minnesota Press.
Mazzarella, William.
  2000.   Shoveling Smoke: Advertising and the Cultural Politics of Globalization in India. Ph.D. diss. University of California–Berkeley.
McAllister, Matthew.
  1996.   *The Commercialization of American Culture: New Advertising, Control, and Democracy.* London: Sage.

McAnany, Emile, and Kenton Wilkinson.
1996.   *Mass Media and Free Trade.* Austin: University of Texas Press.
McCracken, Grant.
1990.   *Culture and Consumption: New Approaches to the Symbolic Character of Consumer Goods and Activities.* Bloomington: Indiana University Press.
McDowell, Robert.
1981.   Beer's Main Title Bout: It's Miller vs. Budweiser. *Marketing Times.* November / December, 35.
McKenzie-Kelly, Margaret.
1998.   Highlighting the Strengths of African American Families: The Family Center's Approach. *Journal of Family and Consumer Sciences* 90 (1): 8–10.
McLaughlin, Rachel.
1999.   African Americans. *Target Marketing,* March 22, 100–101.
MDI/Yankelovich.
1994.   *Hispanic Monitor.* Yankelovich Partners.
Mejia, Victor.
1998.   Sony Introduces Telemundo's New Management. *Hispanic Magazine,* October, 16.
Mendosa, Rick.
1989.   Accounts, Billings, and Top Dogs. *Hispanic Business,* December, 32–36.
Mercer, Kobena.
1994.   *Welcome to the Jungle: New Positions in Black Cultural Studies.* New York: Routledge.
Merli, John.
1998.   BIA Study Tracks Decrease of Ownership Diversity. *Broadcasting and Cable,* June 8, 40.
Miller, Daniel.
1995.   Consumption and Commodities. *Annual Review of Anthropology* 24: 141–61.
1997.   *Capitalism: An Ethnographic Approach.* London: Berg.
Miller, Toby.
1998.   *Technologies of Truth: Cultural Citizenship and the Popular Media.* Minneapolis: University of Minnesota Press.
1999.   Television and Citizenship: A New International Division of Cultural Labor? In *Communication, Citizenship, and Social Policy: Rethinking the Limits of the Welfare State,* ed. Andrew Calabrese and Jean-Claude Burgelman, 279–92. New York: Rowman & Littlefield.
Minority Markets Alert.
1997.   Urban Influence Is Blurring the Lines Between Ethnic Markets and Mainstream. *Minority Markets Alert* 9 (9): 1.
Modleski, T.
1982.   *Loving with a Vengeance: Mass-Produced Fantasies for Women.* London: Methuen.

Moeran, Brian.
1996.   *A Japanese Advertising Agency: An Anthropology of Media and Markets.* Honolulu: University of Hawaii Press.

Morton, Linda.
1997.   Targeting Minority Publics. *Public Relations Quarterly* 42 (2): 23–28.

Mukerji, Chandra, and Michael Schudson.
1991.   *Rethinking Popular Culture.* Los Angeles: University of California Press.

Mummert, Hallie.
1995.   Reaching Ethnic Markets. *Target Marketing,* November, 14–16.

Naficy, Hamid.
1993.   *The Making of Exile Culture.* Minneapolis: University of Minnesota Press.

National Register Publishing.
1964.   *Standard Directory of Advertising.* Wilmette, IL: National Register.
1980.   *Standard Directory of Advertising.* Wilmette, IL: National Register.
1997.   *Standard Directory of Advertising.* Wilmette, IL: National Register.
2001.   *Standard Directory of Advertising.* Wilmette, IL: National Register.

Nederveen Pieterse, Jan.
1992.   *White on Black: Images of Africa and Blacks in Western Popular Culture.* New Haven, CT: Yale University Press.

Negrón Cruz, Wanda.
1998.   Un Profesional Serio Entre Risas. *Cristina* 8 (11): 56–57.

Nelson, Candace, and Marta Tienda.
1997.   The Structuring of Hispanic Ethnicity: Historical and Contemporary Perspectives. In *Challenging Fronteras: Structuring Latina and Latino Lives in the U.S.,* ed. Mary Romero, Pierrette Hondagneu-Sotelo, and Vilma Ortíz, 7–30. London: Routledge.

Noriega, Chon.
2000.   *Shot in America: Television, the State, and the Rise of Chicano Cinema.* Minneapolis: University of Minnesota Press.

Noriega, Chon, and Ana M. López, eds.
1996.   *The Ethnic Eye: Latino Media Arts.* Minneapolis: University of Minnesota Press.

Notar, Beth.
1994.   Of Labor and Liberation: Images of Women in Current Chinese Television Advertising. *Visual Anthropology Review* 10 (2): 29–44.

Nuiry, Octavio.
1996a.   Ban the Bandito. *Hispanic Magazine,* July, 26–31.
1996b.   Magazine Mania: Whose Media Is This, Anyway? *Hispanic,* December, 53–58.

O'Barr, William.
   1989.   The Airbrushing of Culture: An Insider Looks at Global Adver-
              tising. *Public Culture* 2 (1): 1–20 (Interview with Marcio M.
              Moreira).
   1994.   *Culture and the Ad: Exploring Otherness in the World of Ad-
              vertising.* Boulder, CO: Westview.
Oboler, Suzanne.
   1995.   *Ethnic Labels, Latino Lives: Identity and the Politics of (Re)Pre-
              sentation in the United States.* Minneapolis: University of Min-
              nesota Press.
Olalquiaga, Celeste.
   1992.   *Megalopolis: Contemporary Cultural Sensibilities.* Minneapolis:
              University of Minnesota Press.
Olay, Liliana.
   1998.   Azcárraga Jean Lanza Hoy desde Cancún "Alianza Latinoamer-
              icana." *Diario P & D Net,* July 17 (http: //www.produ.com).
Ong, Aihwa.
   1999.   Cultural Citizenship as Subject Making: Immigrants Negotiate
              Racial and Cultural Boundaries in the United States. In *Race,
              Identity, and Citizenship,* ed. Rodolfo Torres, Louis Miron, and
              Jonathan Xavier Inda. New York: Blackwell.
Padilla, Félix M.
   1985.   *Latino Ethnic Consciousness: The Case of Mexican Americans
              and Puerto Ricans in Chicago.* South Bend, IN: University of
              Notre Dame Press.
Park, Robert Ezra.
   1970.   *The Immigrant Press and Its Control.* Westport, CT: Greenwood
              Press.
Pauwels, Caroline.
   1999.   From Citizenship to Consumer Sovereignty: The Paradigm Shift
              in European Audiovisual Policy. In *Communication, Citizenship,
              and Social Policy: Rethinking the Limits of the Welfare State,* ed.
              Andrew Calabrese and Jean-Claude Burgelman, 65–76. New
              York: Rowman & Littlefield.
Peñaloza, Lisa.
   1994.   Atravesando Fronteras/Border Crossings: A Critical Ethno-
              graphic Exploration of the Consumer Acculturation of Mexican
              Immigrants. *The Journal of Consumer Research* 21 (June): 32–35.
   1997.   Ya Viene Aztlán! Latinos in U.S. Advertising. In *The Media in
              Black and White,* ed. Dennis Everette and Edward Pease, 113–20.
              New Brunswick, NJ: Transaction Publishers.
Pérez, Louis.
   1999.   *On Becoming Cuban: Identity, Nationality, and Culture.* Chapel
              Hill: University of North Carolina Press.
Pérez, Richie.
   1990.   From Assimilation to Annihilation: Puerto Rican Images in U.S.
              Films. *CENTRO* Bulletin 2 (8): 8–27.

Petersen, Lisa Marie.
 1992. Ethnic Cable: Advertisers Look to Asian Immigrants. *Mediaweek*, November 30, 2.
Poole, Sheila.
 1999. Black Buying Power Rises to $393 Billion. *Atlanta Constitution*, February 18, FO1.
Portes, Alejandro, and Alex Stepick.
 1993. *City on the Edge: The Transformation of Miami*. Berkeley: University of California Press.
Price, Monroe.
 1995. *Television, The Public Sphere, and National Identity*. Oxford: Clarendon Press.
Quiroga, Jorge.
 1995. *Hispanic Voices: Is the Press Listening?* Cambridge, MA: Joan Shorenstein Center, John F. Kennedy School of Government, Harvard University.
Ramos, Julio.
 1989. *Desencuentros con la Modernidad*. Mexico City: Ediciones Huracán.
Riggens, Harold.
 1992. *Ethnic Minority Media: An International Perspective*. Thousand Oaks, CA: Sage.
Riley, Jennifer.
 2000. AHAA Creating a Bridge Between Corporate America and the Hispanic Media. *Hispanic Magazine*, June, 2000, 40–46.
Rivera, Raquel.
 2001. Hip-Hop: Puerto Ricans and Ethno-Racial Identities in New York. In *Mambo Montage: The Latinization of New York*, ed. Agustín Laó and Arlene Dávila. New York: Columbia University Press.
Robbins, Bruce.
 1993. *The Phantom Public Sphere*. Minneapolis: University of Minnesota Press.
Rodríguez, America.
 1996. Objectivity and Ethnicity in the Production of the *Noticiero Univision*. *Critical Studies in Mass Communication* 13: 59–81.
 1999. *Making Latino News, Race, Language, Class*. Thousand Oaks, CA: Sage
Rodríguez, Clara.
 1997. *Latin Looks: Images of Latinas and Latinos in the U.S. Media*. Boulder, CO: Westview Press.
Roediger, David.
 1999. *The Wages of Whiteness: Race and the Making of the American Working Class*. New York: Verso.
Rofel, Lisa.
 1994. Yearnings: Televisual Love and Melodramatic Politics in Contemporary China. *American Ethnologist* 21 (4): 700–722.

Rohter, Larry.
   2000.   Brazil Builds Bigger and Better Telenovelas. *New York Times,*
              August 27, P. 21
Root, Deborah.
   1996.   *Cannibal Culture: Art, Appropriation, and the Commodification
              of Difference.* Boulder, CO: Westview Press.
Rosaldo, Renato.
   1989.   *Culture and Truth: The Remaking of Social Analysis.* Boston: Bea-
              con Press.
Rosaldo, Renato, and William V. Flores.
   1997.   *Latino Cultural Citizenship: Claiming Identity, Space and Rights.*
              Ed. Rina Benmayor and William Flores. Boston, MA: Beacon
              Press.
Roslow, Peter, and Janel Therrien Decker.
   1998.   *A Guide to Building Market Dominance: Case Histories in His-
              panic Marketing.* Roslow Research Group, Inc.
Rossman, Marlene.
   1994.   *Multicultural Marketing: Selling to a Diverse America.* New
              York: AMACON (division of the American Management Asso-
              ciation).
Rowe, Kathleen.
   1995.   *The Unruly Woman: Gender and the Genres of Laughter.* Austin:
              University of Texas Press.
Salem Manganaro, Elise.
   1996.   When Foreign Sells: Exotica in American TV Ads of the Eighties
              and Nineties. In *Advertising and Culture: Theoretical Perspec-
              tives,* ed. Mary Cross, 11–27. Westport, CT: Praeger.
Sánchez-Korroll, Virginia.
   1983.   *From Colonia to Community: The History of Puerto Ricans in
              New York City.* Westport, CT: Greenwood Press.
Sandoval-Sánchez, Alberto.
   1999.   *José, Can You See? Latinos On and Off Broadway.* Madison: Uni-
              versity of Wisconsin Press.
Santiago-Irizarry, Vilma.
   1996.   Culture as Cure. *Cultural Anthropology* 11 (1): 3–24.
   2001.   Deceptive solidity: Public Signs, Civic Inclusion, and Language
              Rights. In *Mambo Montage: The Latinization of New York,* ed.
              Agustín Laó and Arlene Dávila. New York: Columbia University
              Press.
Santoro, Elaine.
   1996.   East Meets West: Uncovering the Asian Market in America. *Di-
              rect Marketing* 96 (October): 34–39.
Saralegui, Cristina.
   1998.   *Cristina: Confidencias de Una Rubia.* New York: Warner Books.
Savage, David.
   1982.   Is the Market Going English? *Hispanic Business,* December,
              20–21.

Scholle, David.
1990. Resistance: Pinning Down a Wandering Concept in Cultural Studies Discourse. *Journal of Urban and Cultural Studies* 1 (1): 87–105.

Schwirtz, Mira.
1998. Ratings Racism: When No. 1 Is Not. *Mediaweek*, June 22, 14–15.

Segal, Daniel, and Richard Handler.
1995. U.S. Multiculturalism and the Concept of Culture. *Identities: Global Studies of Culture and Power* 1 (4): 391–408.

Sherry, John F.
1995. *Contemporary Marketing and Consumer Behavior: An Anthropological Sourcebook*. Thousand Oaks, CA: Sage.

Shohat, Ella, and Robert Stam.
1994. *Unthinking Eurocentrism: Multiculturalism and the Media*. London and New York: Routledge.

Silverstein, Michael.
1996. "Monoglot "Standard" in America: Standardization and Metaphors of Linguistic Hegemony. In *The Matrix of Language: Contemporary Linguistic Anthropology*, ed. Donald Brenneis and Ronald Macaulay, 284–306. Boulder, CO: Westview Press.

Silverstone, Roger.
1994. *Television and Everyday Life*. London: Routledge.

Silverstone, Roger, and Eric Hirsch.
1992. *Consuming Technologies: Media and Information in Domestic Spaces*. London: Routledge.

Sinclair, John.
1990. Spanish-Language Television in the United States: Televisa Surrenders Its Domain. *Studies in Latin America Popular Culture* 9: 39–63.

Sinclair, John, Elizabeth Jacka, and Stuart Cunningham.
1996. *New Patterns in Global Television*. London: Oxford University Press.

Smith, Robert.
1996. Mexicans in New York: Memberships and Incorporation in a New Immigrant Community. In *Latinos in New York: Communities in Transition,* ed. Gabriel Haslip-Viera and Sherrie L. Baver, 57–103. South Bend, IN: University of Notre Dame.

Soruco, Gonzalo, and Timothy P. Meyer.
1993. The Mobile Hispanic Market: New Challenges in the '90s. *Marketing Research* (winter): 7–11.

Sosa, Lionel.
1998. *The Americano Dream: How Latinos Can Achieve Success in Business and in Life*. New York: Dutton.

Spitulnik, Debra.
1993. Anthropology and Mass Media. *Annual Review of Anthropology* 22: 293–315.

Squire, Corinne.
1997. Who's White? Television Talk Shows and Representations of Whiteness. In *Off White: Readings on Race, Power, and Society,* ed. Michael Fine, Lois Weiss, Linda Powell, and L. Mun Wong, 242–50. London: Routledge.

Stallybrass, P., and Allon White.
1986. *The Politics and Poetics of Transgression.* Ithaca, NY: Cornell University Press

Steere, John.
1995. How Asian-Americans Make Purchase Decisions. *Marketing News,* March 13, 9.

Stern, Barbara.
1998. *Representing Consumers: Voices, Views and Visions.* London: Routledge.

Stewart, Jill.
1998. Tele-crapola: Meet the Guys Who Run the Univision TV Network, Which Serves Up Relentlessly Dumb, Vulgar Programming to L.A.'s Spanish Speakers. *New Times* (Los Angeles), April, 23.

Storey, John.
1993. *Cultural Theory and Popular Culture.* Athens: University of Georgia Press.

Strategy Research Corporation.
1998. *U.S. Hispanic Market Study.* Miami, FL: Strategy Research Corporation.

Subervi-Vélez, Federico (with Charles Ramírez Berg, Patricia Constantakis-Valdés, Chon Noriega, Diane Ríos, and Kenton Wilkinson).
1986. The Mass Media and Ethnic Assimilation and Pluralism: A Review and Research Proposal with Special Focus on Hispanics. *Communication Research* 13 (1): 71–96.
1994. Mass Communication and Hispanics. In *Hispanic Media: Handbook of Hispanic Cultures in the United States: Sociology,* ed. Félix Padilla. Houston, TX: Arte Público Press.

Subervi-Vélez, Federico, Charles Ramírez Berg, Patricia Constantakis-Valdés et al.
1997. Hispanic-Oriented Media. In *Latin Looks: Images of Latinas and Latinos in the U.S. Media.* Boulder, CO: Westview Press.

Sveberny-Mohammadi, Annabelle.
1991. The Global and the Local in International Communications. In *Mass Media and Society,* ed. Curran and Gurevitch, 118–38. London: Edward Arnold.

Takaki, Ronald.
1989. *Strangers from a Different Shore: A History of Asian Americans.* Boston: Little, Brown.
1993. *A Different Mirror: A History of Multicultural America.* Boston, MA: Little, Brown.

Taylor, Charles, and Barbara Stern.
1997. Asian Americans: Television Advertising and the "Model Minority" Stereotype. *Journal of Advertising* 26 (2): 47–61.

Teinowitz, Ira, and Mercedes M. Cardona.
1999.   Sharpton Sets Timetable for Minority Ad Changes. *Advertising Age*, January 25, 18.
Tienda, Marta, and Vilma Ortíz.
1986.   Hispanicity and the 1980 Census. *Social Science Quarterly* 67 (1): 3–20.
Tobekin, David.
1997.   Univision Versus Telemundo. *Broadcasting and Cable*, October 6, 34–42.
Tomás Rivera Policy Institute.
1998.   Talking Back to Television: Latinos Discuss How Television Portrays Them and the Quality of Programming Options. Research Report. Claremont, CA: Tomás Rivera Policy Institute.
Tomlinson, John.
1991.   *Cultural Imperialism*. Baltimore, MD: Johns Hopkins University Press.
Tong, Jennie.
1994.   Complexity of Asian American Market Causes Some to Stay Away. *Marketing News*, January 17, 6–9.
Treise, Debbie, and Elaine Wagner.
1999.   Learning to Create Ad Strategies for "Different" Target Audiences. *Journalism and Mass Communication Educator* 54 (1): 42–50.
Tuan, Mia.
1998.   *Forever Foreigners or Honorary Whites? The Asian Ethnic Experience Today.* New Brunswick, NJ: Rutgers University Press.
Turner, Terrence.
1992.   Defiant Images: The Kayapo Appropriation of Video. *Anthropology Today* 8 (6): 5–16.
1994.   Anthropology and Multiculturalism: What Is Anthropology That Multiculturalism Should Be Mindful Of? In *Multiculturalism: A Critical Reader*, ed. David Theo Goldberg, 406–25. Oxford: Blackwell.
Turow, Joseph.
1997.   *Breaking Up America: Advertisers and the New Media World.* Chicago: University of Chicago Press.
Urciuoli, Bonnie.
1998.   *Exposing Prejudice: Puerto Rican Experiences of Language, Race, and Class.* Boulder, CO: Westview Press.
1999.   Containing Language Differences: Advertising in Hispanic Magazines. In *Language and Social Identity*, ed. Richard Blot. Amsterdam: Gordon and Breach.
Urla, Jacqueline.
1995.   Outlaw Language: Creating Alternative Public Spheres in Basque Free Radio. *Pragmatics* 5 (2): 245–61.
U.S. Census Bureau.
1998.   *Poverty by Selected Characteristics.* www.census.gov/poverty/poverty98/pv98est.html.

Valdes, M. Isabel.
2000.   *Marketing to American Latinos: A Guide to the In-Culture Approach.* Ithaca, NY: Paramount Market Publishing.
Valdes, Isabel, and Marta Seoane.
1995.   *Hispanic Market Handbook: The Definite Source for Reaching This Lucrative Segment of American Consumers.* Detroit, MI: Gale Research, Inc.
Vasconcelos, José.
1958.   La Raza Cósmica. In *Obras Completas,* 2: 903–42. México, DF: Colección Laurel, Libreros Mexicanos Unidos.
Vázquez, Blanca.
1991.   Puerto Ricans and the Media: A Personal Statement. CENTRO Bulletin 3 (1): 4–15.
Vega, Bernardo.
1977.   *Memorias de Bernardo Vega: Contribución a la historia de la comunidad puertorriqueña en Nueva York.* Ed. Cesar Andreu Iglesias. Rio Piedras, Puerto Rico: Ediciones Huracán.
Von Bergen, Jane M.
1997.   Cultural Factors Make Asian-Americans Tough to Reach. *Buffalo News* (Financial Edition), March 30, B13.
Waisbord, Silvio.
1998.   When the Cart of Media Is Before the Horse of Identity: A Critique of Technology-Centered Views on Globalization. *Communication Research* 25 (4): 377–98.
Wartzman, Rick, and Joe Flint.
2000.   Nielsen Ratings Spark a Battle Over Just Who Speaks Spanish. *Wall Street Journal,* Feb. 25, B1.
Watrous, Peter.
1999.   A Country Ready to Listen. *New York Times,* June 27, Arts, 25.
Weems, Robert.
1998.   *Desegregating the Dollar: African American Consumerism in the Twentieth Century.* New York: New York University Press.
Weitz, Rose.
1998.   *The Politics of Women's Bodies: Sexuality, Appearance, and Behavior.* Oxford: Oxford University Press.
Wernick, Andrew.
1991.   *Promotional Culture: Advertising, Ideology and Symbolic Expression.* London: Sage.
Whisler, Kirk, and Octavio Nuiry.
1998.   *The National Hispanic Media Directory.* Carlsbad, CA: WPR Publishing.
Wilk, Richard.
1993.   "It's Destroying a Whole Generation": Television and Moral Discourse in Belize. *Visual Anthropology* 5: 229–44.
1994.   Consumer Goods as Dialogue about Development: Colonial Time and Television Time in Belize. In *Consumption and Iden-*

tity, ed. J. Friedman, 97–118. Chur, Switzerland: Harwood Academic Publishers.

Wilke Michael.
1998. Marketers Boost Spending on Spanish-Language Radio. *Advertising Age*, August 24, S22.

Wilkinson, Kenton.
1995. *Where Culture, Language, and Communication Converge: The Latin American Cultural-Linguistic Television Market*. Ph.D. diss. University of Texas at Austin.

Williams, Brackette.
1989. A Class Act: Anthropology and the Race to Nation among Ethnic Terrain. *Annual Review of Anthropology* 18: 401–44.
1993. The Impact of the Precepts of Nationalism on the Concept of Culture: Making Grasshoppers of Naked Apes. *Cultural Critique* 24: 143–93.
1996. *Women Out of Place: The Gender of Agency and the Race of Nationality*. London: Routledge.

Williamson, Judith.
1978. *Decoding Advertisements: Ideology and Meaning in Advertising*. London: Boyars.
1986. *Consuming Passions: The Dynamics of Popular Culture*. London: M. Boyars.

Wilson, Clint, and Felix Gutiérrez.
1995. *Race, Multiculturalism, and the Media: From Mass to Class Communication*. London: Sage.

Woolard, Kathryn A.
1998. Introduction: Language Ideology as a Field of Inquiry. In *Language Ideologies: Practice and Theory*, ed. Bambi Schieffelin, Kathryn A. Woolard, and Paul Kroskrity, 3–50. New York: Oxford University Press.

Yúdice, George.
1999. La Integración del Caribe y de America Latina a Partir de Miami. In *Las Industrias Culturales en la Integración Latinoamericana*, ed. Nestor García-Canclini and Carlos Moneta. Buenos Aires: Eudeba.
2001. From Hybridity to Policy: For a Purposeful Cultural Studies. Preface to Nestor García-Canclini's *Consumers and Citizens: Globalization and Multicultural Conflicts*. Minneapolis: University of Minnesota Press.

Zate, Maria.
1998a. The Big Picture. *Hispanic Business*, May, 26–30.
1998b. From Niche to Mainstream. *Hispanic Business*, December, 50–60.

Zbar, Jeffery.
1998a. Agency Execs Say Marketers Want In. *Advertising Age*, August 24, S16.

1998b.   Spanish-Language TV Upgrades Program Fare. *Advertising Age,*
            August 24, S18.
1998c.   Furman to Sell Marketers on Univision Audiences: TV Ad Sales
            Veteran's Goal Will Be to Woo Advertisers to Hispanic Net. *Ad-*
            vertising Age, May 25, 28.
Zentella, Ana Celia.
1997.   *Growing Up Bilingual.* New York: Blackwell.
Zukin, Sharon.
1995.   *The Cultures of Cities.* Cambridge, MA: Blackwell.

Index

advertising: market research methodology and, 12; as privileged discourse, 9–15; racial diversity issues in, 112–113; "referent system" and, 93; research challenges and, 19–20; stereotyping in, 14–15; synergy between campaigns and, 139. *See also* global advertising trends; marketing industry; stereotyping

Advertising Educational Foundation, 20

advertising executives. *See* corporate intellectuals

Advil ad, 105, 107

affluence: Asian Americans and, 228–229; authenticity and, 69, 232–233, 234; images of Hispanic consumer and, 68–69; politics of equality and, 235

African Americans, 50; as consumers, 222–223, 233; communication and, 225–226; congruence with mainstream culture and, 224–225; as diverse population, 218; ethnic marketing and, 217; language and, 220, 257n6; marketing to, 219–226

La Agencia de Orci, 32

Aguilar, Al, 53

AHAA. *See* Association of Hispanic Advertising Agencies

Albertini, Luis Díaz, 29

The American Dream (Sosa), 86, 172–173

"Americanization," 10

Anglo, as term, 17

Anglo clients. *See* corporate clients

Anglo/Latina dichotomy: ethnic pride and, 102–109; focus group and, 214–215; Hispanic media personalities and, 172–174; Latin America and, 111, 249n3; marketing decisions by Latinos and, 144; stereotyping and, 98–101, 102

Anheuser Busch campaign, 144

Asian Americans, 50; as diverse population, 218, 227–220, 230–232; marketing to, 226–232; media representation of, 238

Asian Indians, 227

assimilation, 229–230, 253n3

Association of Hispanic Advertising Agencies (AHAA), 53–54, 74, 112–113

AT&T ads, 95, 101, 103, 121

authenticity, discourse of, 4; advertising trends and, 7; affluence and, 69, 232–233, 234; appropriate ethnicity and, 235–237; Asian Americans and, 231–232; ethnic division of labor and, 37–38; Hispanic agencies and, 133–135, 148; ideal ethnic consumer and, 233–235; identity politics and, 146–147; language and, 178; self-perceptions of Hispanics and, 210–213; TV programming and, 178, 194; U.S.-born ethnics vs. recent immigrants, 82–83, 186–187, 233–234

Avon advertising strategy, 97–98

Text:	10/13 Sabon
Display:	Sabon
Compositor:	Integrated Composition Systems
Printer & binder:	Thomson-Shore, Inc.